RIDING

the

RAILS

Tourist Guide To America's Scenic Train Rides

By

William C. Herow

Published by:
Roundabout Publications
2767 S. Parker Rd., Suite 240
Aurora, Colorado 80014

Please Note

Every effort has been made to make this book as complete and as accurate as possible. However, there may be mistakes both typographical and in content. Therefore, this text should be used as a general guide to the scenic train rides covered. Although we regret any inconvenience caused by inaccurate information, the author and Roundabout Publications shall have neither liability nor responsibility to any person or entity with respect to any loss or damage caused, or alleged to be caused, directly or indirectly by the information contained in this book.

Library of Congress Catalog Card Number: 95-73314

ISBN: 1-885464-25-8

Publisher's Cataloging in Publication
(*Prepared by Quality Books Inc.*)

Herow, William C.
    Riding the rails : tourist guide to America's scenic train rides / William C. Herow.
    p. cm.
    Includes index.
    LCCN: 95-73314.
    ISBN: 1-885464-25-8

    1. Railroad travel—United States—Guidebooks. 2. Railroad—United States. I. Title.

E158.H47 1996
                           917.304'929
                           QBI96-20035

TABLE OF CONTENTS

Delaware

Florida

Illinois

Indiana

Iowa

Kansas

Kentucky

Maine

Maryland

Massachusetts

North Carolina

Ohio

Oklahoma

Oregon

Pennsylvania

Rhode Island

South Dakota

Tennessee

Texas

Utah

Vermont

Washington

West Virginia

Wisconsin

INTRODUCTION

Trains! Trains!

From the very youngest to the young at heart, all of us have a fascination with trains. Whether it's remembering a model train make its way around the track, dreaming of riding or operating a real train, or listening to the sounds of the whistle blow. Others may remember counting the cars as the train passed by at the railroad crossing, waiting for the gates to lift. And who didn't enjoy waving to the caboose, anxiously awaiting a reply?

Riding The Rails will help you re-experience, or experience for the first time, the excitement associated with rail travel. Found in the pages of this book are over 90 scenic train rides ranging from a short round trip ride to a two-day excursion with a stayover in Denali National Park.

To get the most from *Riding The Rails*, may we suggest you take a few minutes and read through this introduction. It will explain the different sections and icons used throughout this book.

The Rides

Two or three pages are devoted to describing each scenic train ride. At the start of each ride description you will find an area map showing the location within the state for that ride and the boarding area(s). Next to the area map is a route summary which shows you at a glance the town, operating season, total miles for a round trip ride, and the adult ticket price.

Next, each train ride description is divided into seven categories or headings. Listed below is a list of those headings and an explanation of the information provided.

The Ride: Includes a description of the scenery traveled through and highlights points of interest. Provides the total miles covered and the amount of time required for a round trip.

All Aboard: Lists the location and address for the boarding area(s).

Schedule: Provides information on train departure times and days of operation.

Fares: Includes ticket prices for adults and children and mentions any discounts available to seniors or family packages.

Ride Information: Provides the ride operation's address, phone and fax number. A free brochure is usually available from this source.

Local Information: The sources listed here will provide you with general travel information and points of interest for the local communities.

Notes: Provides helpful tips and information so you can better plan and enjoy the train ride.

To round out the description of each scenic train ride, a *Special Events And Excursions* chart is included. This chart will show you any other special events or train rides offered by the ride operation.

Traveler's Directory

At the end of some ride descriptions you will find references to the *Traveler's Directory*. This exclusive feature to *Riding The Rails* provides information on over 100 local businesses that have extended a special welcome to all train passengers. The icons, followed by reference numbers, will guide you to lodging, shopping, dining, attractions, and entertainment possibilities in that town.

The following icons are used to refer you to the main headings of the *Traveler's Directory:*

 Attractions / Recreation

 Entertainment

 Food / Beverage

 Lodging

 Shopping

For more information on the *Traveler's Directory*, see page 208.

Railroad Attractions

Starting on page 232 is a directory of over 150 railroad attractions across the country. The attractions include railroad museums and displays, dinner train rides, model train museums and displays plus more. For more information on this section, please see page 232.

United States Maps

On the pages following this introduction are three maps of the United States. Each map, Western, Eastern, and Northeastern, shows the location of each scenic train ride with a corresponding number for that ride in the alphabetical list, by state, of train rides. The page number for that ride description is also provided.

Please Note

The ride operations adhere to the schedules as closely as possible, but due to various reasons, schedules are subject change. Substitution of motive power and/or rolling stock is also possible as operating conditions demand. It is advisable to contact the ride operation for up to date information regarding ride schedules and conditions.

WESTERN UNITED STATES

Alaska

1. Alaska Railroad, 15
2. White Pass & Yukon Route, 18

Arizona

1. Grand Canyon Railway, 20
2. San Pedro & Southwestern Railroad, 22
3. Verde Canyon Railroad, 22

California

1. Blue Goose, 31
2. Roaring Camp & Big Trees Narrow-Gauge Railroad, 33
3. Skunk Train, 36
4. Yolo Shortline Railroad, 38

Colorado

1. Durango & Silverton Narrow-Gauge Railroad, 40
2. Georgetown Loop Railroad, 43
3. Leadville, Colorado & Southern Railroad, 45
4. Manitou & Pike's Peak Railway, 47

Kansas

1. Abilene & Smoky Valley Railroad, 70
2. Midland Railway, 72

Nebraska

1. Fremont & Elkhorn Valley Railroad, 104

Nevada

1. Nevada Northern Railway, 106
2. Virginia & Truckee Railroad, 108

New Mexico

1. Cumbres & Toltec Scenic Railroad, 117
2. Santa Fe Southern Railway, 120

Oklahoma

1. Hugo Heritage Railroad, 149

Oregon

1. Mt. Hood Railroad, 151
2. Sumpter Valley Railroad, 153

South Dakota

1. Black Hills Central Railroad, 174

Texas

1. Austin Steam Train, 178
2. Texas State Railroad, 180

Utah

1. Heber Valley Railroad, 182

Washington

1. Chehalis - Centralia Railroad, 186
2. Lake Whatcom Railway, 188
3. Lewis & Clark Railway, 190
4. Mount Rainier Scenic Railroad, 192
5. Puget Sound & Snoqualmie Valley Railroad, 194
6. Toppenish, Simcoe & Western Railroad, 196

Western United States

EASTERN UNITED STATES

Arkansas

1. Arkansas & Missouri Railroad, 26
2. Eureka Springs & North Arkansas Railway, 29

Florida

1. Florida Gulf Coast Railroad, 55
2. Seminole Gulf Railway, 57

Illinois

1. Monticello Railway Museum, 60

Indiana

1. Carthage, Knightstown & Shirley Railroad, 62
2. French Lick, West Baden & Southern Railway, 64
3. Whitewater Valley Railroad, 66

Iowa

1. Boone & Scenic Valley Railroad, 68

Kentucky

1. Big South Fork Scenic Railway, 74
2. Bluegrass Railroad Museum, 76
3. Kentucky Railway Museum, 78

Michigan

1. Adrian & Blissfield Railroad, 88
2. Coe Rail Scenic Train, 90
3. Coopersville & Marne Railway, 92
4. Little River Railroad, 94
5. Southern Michigan Railroad, 96

Missouri

1. Branson Scenic Railway, 98
2. Smoky Hill Railway, 100
3. St. Louis, Iron Mountain & Southern Railway, 102

North Carolina

1. Great Smoky Mountains Railway, 134

Ohio

1. Ashtabula, Carson & Jefferson Scenic Line, 137
2. Cuyahoga Valley Scenic Railroad, 139
3. Hocking Valley Scenic Railway, 141
4. Indiana & Ohio Scenic Railway, 143
5. Ohio Central Railroad, 145
6. Toledo, Lake Erie & Western Railway, 147

Tennessee

1. Tennessee Valley Railroad, 176

West Virginia

1. Cass Scenic Railroad, 198
2. Potomac Eagle, 201

Wisconsin

1. Mid-Continent Railway, 203
2. Osceola & St. Croix Valley Railway, 205

Eastern United States

NORTHEASTERN UNITED STATES

Connecticut

1. Valley Railroad, 49

Delaware

1. Queen Anne's Railroad, 51
2. Wilmington & Western Railroad, 53

Maine

1. Belfast & Moosehead Lake
   Railroad, 80
2. Maine Coast Railroad, 82

Maryland

1. Western Maryland Scenic
   Railroad, 84

Massachusetts

1. Cape Cod Scenic Railroad, 86

New Hampshire

1. Conway Scenic Railroad, 110
2. Mt. Washington Cog Railway, 113

New Jersey

1. Black River & Western Railroad, 115

New York

1. Adirondack Scenic Railroad, 122
2. Arcade & Attica Railroad, 124
3. Champagne Trail Excursion
   Train, 126

4. Delaware & Ulster Rail Ride, 128
5. New York & Lake Erie Railroad, 130
6. Tioga Scenic Railroad, 132

Pennsylvania

1. Bellefonte Historical Railroad, 155
2. Gettysburg Railroad, 157
3. Knox & Kane Railroad, 159
4. Middletown & Hummelstown
   Railroad, 161
5. New Hope & Ivyland Rail Road, 163
6. Oil Creek & Titusville Railroad, 165
7. Rail Tours, 167
8. Strasburg Rail Road, 169

Rhode Island

1. Old Colony & Newport Railway, 172

Vermont

1. Green Mountain Railroad, 184

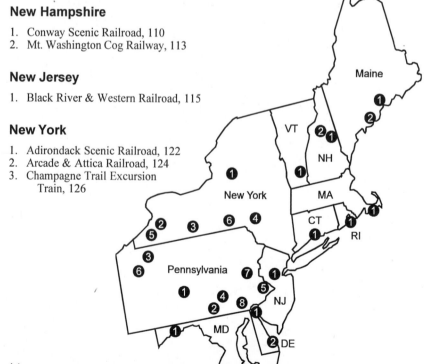

ALASKA RAILROAD

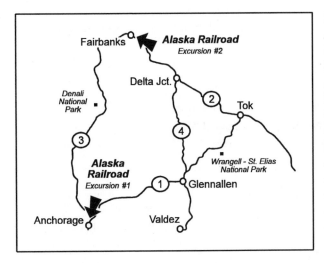

LOCATION
Anchorage and Fairbanks
SEASON
May - September
ROUND TRIP
Exc. #1, 467 Miles
Exc. #2, 245 Miles
FARES
Adult,
Excursion #1,
$219.00 - $269.00
Excursion #2,
$147.00 - $179.00

The Ride

There are several scenic train excursions offered from the Alaska Railroad, traveling primarily between Fairbanks and Anchorage. Please contact the train operation for a detailed brochure describing all of the excursions available.

Anchorage to Denali (Excursion #1):

This two day scenic train ride begins in Anchorage and travels north to the spectacular Denali National Park. Passengers arrive in the park by 4:00 p.m. and stay overnight. The train departs the park at 12:30 p.m. the following day and returns to Anchorage by 8:30 p.m. The entire round trip is approximately 467 miles.

Fairbanks to Denali (Excursion #2):

This excursion begins in Fairbanks and also travels to Denali National Park. Passengers will arrive in the park by 12:15 p.m. and depart at 4:15 p.m. the following day to return to Fairbanks by 8:30 p.m. The entire round trip is approximately 245 miles.

All Aboard

Excursion #1: Passengers board the train in Anchorage from the depot located at 411 West First Avenue.

Excursion #2: Passengers boarding the train in Fairbanks will depart from the depot located at 280 North Cushman.

Schedule

Both excursions operate on a daily basis from mid-May through mid-September. Peak season is from early June through early September. The train departs from Anchorage and Fairbanks at 8:30 a.m. for either excursion.

Fares

Excursion #1: The adult fare is $269.00 during the peak season and $216.00 during the "value season". Above fares are per person, double occupancy.

Excursion #2: The adult fare is $179.00 during the peak season and $147.00 during the "value season". Above fares are per person, double occupancy.

Ride Information

Alaska Railroad Corporation
Passenger Services
P.O. Box 107500
Anchorage, AK 99510
Phone: 800-544-0552

Local Information

Excursion #1:
Anchorage Chamber of Commerce
441 West 5th Avenue, #300
Anchorage, AK 99501
Phone: 907-272-2401
Fax: 907-272-4117

Excursion #2:
Greater Fairbanks Chamber of Commerce
709 Second Avenue
Fairbanks, AK 99701
Phone: 907-452-1105
Fax: 907-456-6968

Notes

Facilities are accessible to the physically challenged. Prices include overnight accommodations in Denali National Park. A gift shop is located on board the train. Many other excursions and package options are available including one way and round trips to or from Anchorage or Fairbanks as well as round trips from either Anchorage or Seward. A 12 hour round trip from Anchorage to Talkeetna offers some of the best views of Mt. McKinley. Additional lodging as an add-on is available in Anchorage, Seward, Denali National Park or Fairbanks.

SPECIAL EVENTS AND EXCURSIONS	
CHILDREN'S DAY	
DINING:	
BRUNCH	
LUNCH	✓
DINNER	✓
EASTER BUNNY	
FAIRS/FESTIVALS	
FALL FOLIAGE	
FATHER'S DAY	
GRANDPARENT'S DAY	
HALLOWEEN	
INDEPENDENCE DAY	
LABOR DAY	
MEMORIAL DAY	
MOONLIGHT	
MOTHER'S DAY	
MURDER MYSTERIES	
NEW YEAR	
SANTA CLAUS	
THANKSGIVING	
TRAIN ROBBERIES	
VALENTINE'S DAY	
VETERAN'S DAY	

Call for current information, schedule and fares on the above special events.

Anchorage

 013, 017

 103

Fairbanks

 062

Seward

 018

WHITE PASS & YUKON ROUTE

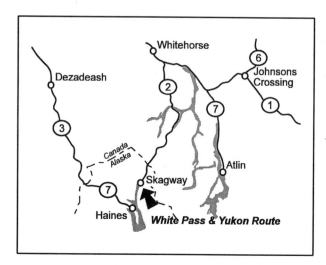

LOCATION
Skagway
SEASON
May thru Sept.
ROUND TRIP
41 miles
FARES
Adult, $75.00

The Ride

Considered the engineering marvel of its time, the White Pass & Yukon Route was built in 1898 and began operations in 1900. Supplies, miners, and gold were transported on this rugged mountain route between Skagway and the Yukon Territory. The route has been designated an International Historic Civil Engineering Landmark. The 41 mile round trip ride follows the original Klondike Gold Rush trail, climbing from sea level to over 2,800 feet to the summit of White Pass which is the border between British Columbia, Canada and Alaska. Allow three hours to complete the round trip.

All Aboard

The excursion train departs from the railroad depot in Skagway located at 2nd and Spring streets. Skagway is approximately 100 miles north of Juneau.

Schedule

Train departs twice daily from May 13 to September 20, 1996. The morning train leaves at 8:45 a.m. and returns to Skagway around 11:35 a.m. The afternoon train leaves at 1:15 p.m. and returns at 4:05 p.m.

Fares

The adult fare is $75.00 and $37.50 for children 12 and under. Infants ride free.

Ride Information

White Pass & Yukon Route
P.O. Box 435
Skagway, AK 99840
Phone: 800-343-7373 / 907-983-2217
Phone: 800-478-7373 (in northwest Canada)
Fax: 907-983-2734

Local Information

Skagway Visitors Bureau
P.O. Box 415
Skagway, AK 99840
Phone: 907-983-2854
Fax: 907-983-2151

Skagway Chamber of Commerce
P.O. Box 194
Skagway, AK 99840
Phone: 907-983-1898

SPECIAL EVENTS AND EXCURSIONS

CHILDREN'S DAY
DINING:
   BRUNCH
   LUNCH
   DINNER
EASTER BUNNY
FAIRS/FESTIVALS
FALL FOLIAGE
FATHER'S DAY
GRANDPARENT'S DAY
HALLOWEEN
INDEPENDENCE DAY
LABOR DAY
MEMORIAL DAY
MOONLIGHT
MOTHER'S DAY
MURDER MYSTERIES
NEW YEAR
SANTA CLAUS
THANKSGIVING
TRAIN ROBBERIES
VALENTINE'S DAY
VETERAN'S DAY

NONE

Call for current information, schedule and fares on the above special events.

Notes

Reservations are recommended 30 days in advance. Group rates and charters are available. Travelers to or from Whitehorse, Yukon can travel by bus between Whitehorse and Fraser, British Columbia and by train between Fraser and Skagway.

GRAND CANYON RAILWAY

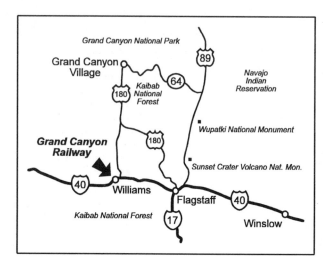

LOCATION
Williams
SEASON
Year-round
ROUND TRIP
130 miles
FARES
Adult,
$49.00 - $99.00

The Ride

The Grand Canyon Railway takes passengers to the south rim of the Grand Canyon aboard a vintage train. The ride offers views of northern Arizona's pine forests, plains, and canyons. The trip also includes live entertainment. While at the historic 1908 Williams Depot, cowboys entertain you with gunfights in their western show. The 130 mile round trip lasts approximately 4½ hours. Visitors stay at the Grand Canyon for about 3½ hours before returning to Williams. Passengers are advised to keep their eyes open for the lawless bandits who are famous for holding up the train and taking passengers hostage.

All Aboard

Passengers board the train at the Williams Depot located ½ mile south of I-40 (Exit 163) on Grand Canyon Boulevard in Williams. The depot is listed on the National Register of Historic Places.

Schedule

The train operates daily, except on December 24 and 25. The train leaves the depot at 9:30 a.m. and arrives at the Grand Canyon Depot at 11:45 a.m. Passengers depart the Grand Canyon Depot at 3:15 p.m. and return to Williams by 5:30 p.m.

Fares

Adult ticket prices for Coach Class are $49.00, children ages 3 to 16 are $19.00. Visitors can upgrade to Club Class by adding $12.00 per person. Chief Class tickets are an additional $50.00 per person from the Coach Class price.

Ride Information

Grand Canyon Railway
123 N. San Francisco - Suite 210
Flagstaff, AZ 86001
Phone: 800-843-8724
Fax: 520-773-1610

Local Information

Williams/Grand Canyon C of C
200 W. Railroad Ave.
Williams, AZ 86046
Phone: 520-635-4061
Fax: 520-635-1417

Notes

One-way fares, group rates, and charters are available. Access to the train for the physically challenged is available but limited. The Williams Depot complex offers live entertainment, an historic hotel, museum and gift shop. The depot complex includes the original Fray Marcos Hotel, which in its heyday was among the most prominent Harvey Houses in the nation. A new 89 room Fray Marcos hotel has been opened next to the depot featuring turn of the century elegance with modern amenities. Visitors are also treated to scores of historic artifacts and photographs on display in the Grand Canyon Railway museum. Admission to the museum is free.

SPECIAL EVENTS AND EXCURSIONS	
CHILDREN'S DAY	
DINING:	
BRUNCH	
LUNCH	
DINNER	
EASTER BUNNY	
FAIRS/FESTIVALS	
FALL FOLIAGE	
FATHER'S DAY	✓
GRANDPARENT'S DAY	
HALLOWEEN	✓
INDEPENDENCE DAY	✓
LABOR DAY	✓
MEMORIAL DAY	✓
MOONLIGHT	
MOTHER'S DAY	✓
MURDER MYSTERIES	
NEW YEAR	✓
SANTA CLAUS	
THANKSGIVING	✓
TRAIN ROBBERIES	✓
VALENTINE'S DAY	
VETERAN'S DAY	

Call for current information, schedule and fares on the above special events.

 054

 115

 131, 139, 142, 152

SAN PEDRO & SOUTHWESTERN RR

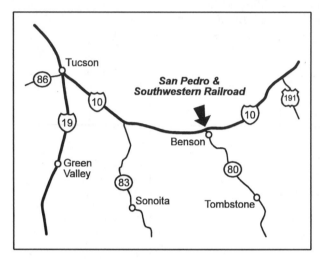

LOCATION
Benson
SEASON
Year-round
ROUND TRIP
50 Miles
FARES
Adult, $24.00

The Ride

Travelers depart Benson on San Pedro & Southwestern's *Gray Hawk* Excursion Train for a spectacular 50 mile round trip journey through the pristine San Pedro Riparian National Conservation Area. Here, lush cottonwoods and mesquite thrive among various species of birds, mammals, and reptiles. Travel through an area speckled with the remains of once powerful silver mills. Pass the ruins of Contention City and the historic ghost town of Fairbank. Expert narration of western and railroad history and folklore throughout trip. Train includes both open-air and climate-controlled enclosed coaches, observation and bar cars. Stop at Fairbank on return to Benson for western entertainment and optional barbecue. Allow about 4 hours to complete the entire round trip.

All Aboard

The train boards from the depot in Benson located at 796 East Country Club Drive. Benson is approximately 40 miles east of Tucson.

Schedule

Trains operate year-round on Thursdays, Fridays, Saturdays, and Sundays. Times vary with season. Please call for departure times.

Fares

Adults, $24.00, students (K-12), $15.00, and seniors ages 60 and over, $21.00. Children under school age ride free. Family plan available for $72.00 (includes 2 adults and up to 4 children).

Ride Information

San Pedro & Southwestern Railroad
P.O. Box 1420
Benson, AZ 85602
Phone: 520-586-2266
Fax: 520-586-2999

Local Information

Benson-San Pedro Valley
Chamber of Commerce
P.O. Box 226
Benson, AZ 85602
Phone: 520-586-2842

Notes

SPECIAL EVENTS AND EXCURSIONS	
CHILDREN'S DAY	
DINING:	
BRUNCH	
LUNCH	
DINNER	
EASTER BUNNY	✓
FAIRS/FESTIVALS	✓
FALL FOLIAGE	✓
FATHER'S DAY	
GRANDPARENT'S DAY	
HALLOWEEN	✓
INDEPENDENCE DAY	✓
LABOR DAY	
MEMORIAL DAY	
MOONLIGHT	✓
MOTHER'S DAY	✓
MURDER MYSTERIES	
NEW YEAR	
SANTA CLAUS	✓
THANKSGIVING	
TRAIN ROBBERIES	✓
VALENTINE'S DAY	
VETERAN'S DAY	

Call for current information, schedule and fares on the above special events.

Reservations are recommended. Charters and group rates are available. Please contact for complete details. Benson is the gateway to Cochise County, Arizona, a prime tourist destination. Tombstone is 25 minutes from the depot, and the historic mining town of Bisbee is just an hour away. Depot has a complete gift shop and is open from 7:00 a.m. to 6:00 p.m. daily.

VERDE CANYON RAILROAD

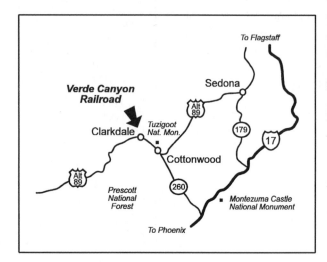

LOCATION
Clarkdale
SEASON
Year-round
ROUND TRIP
38 miles
FARES
Adult, $34.95

The Ride

This 38 mile scenic train ride travels through the Verde River Canyon area of the Prescott National Forest. Passengers experience a ride to Arizona's other Grand Canyon, accessible only by rail, alongside steep canyon walls, through a 680-foot tunnel, and near ancient Indian cliff dwellings. Open-air viewing cars are accessible from either first class or coach cars. Allow approximately four hours to complete the round trip.

All Aboard

Passengers board the train at the railroad station located at 300 North Broadway in Clarkdale. Clarkdale is about 55 miles southwest of Flagstaff.

Schedule

The Verde Canyon Railroad operates year-round and departs at 11:00 a.m. Wednesday through Sunday. During the months of April, May, and October, the train operates daily except on Tuesday and departs at 11:00 a.m.

Fares

Adult tickets are $34.95, children 3 through 12 are $19.95, senior citizen (over 65) tickets are $30.95, and all first class tickets are $52.95 (includes hors d'oeuvres). Children under 3 ride free.

Ride Information

Verde Canyon Railroad
300 North Broadway
Clarkdale, AZ 86324
Phone: 800-293-7245 / 520-639-0010
Fax: 520-639-1653

Local Information

Clarkdale Chamber of Commerce
P.O. Box 161
Clarkdale, AZ 86324

Cottonwood/Verde Valley C of C
1010 South Main Street
Cottonwood, AZ 86326
Phone: 520-634-7593
Fax: 520-634-7594

SPECIAL EVENTS AND EXCURSIONS	
CHILDREN'S DAY	
DINING:	
BRUNCH	✓
LUNCH	✓
DINNER	✓
EASTER BUNNY	✓
FAIRS/FESTIVALS	
FALL FOLIAGE	✓
FATHER'S DAY	✓
GRANDPARENT'S DAY	
HALLOWEEN	
INDEPENDENCE DAY	
LABOR DAY	
MEMORIAL DAY	
MOONLIGHT	✓
MOTHER'S DAY	✓
MURDER MYSTERIES	
NEW YEAR	
SANTA CLAUS	✓
THANKSGIVING	
TRAIN ROBBERIES	
VALENTINE'S DAY	✓
VETERAN'S DAY	

Call for current information, schedule and fares on the above special events.

Notes

Advance reservations are required. No refunds are given on cancellations made within 48 hours of the train ride. Special group rates for 20 or more people are available. Charters are also available. A full service deli and souvenir shop are available on board. Other special events and excursions not listed in the chart include weddings, company parties, and western barbecues on request. A "room, ride and meal" package is also available from the Railroad Inn at Sedona, call 800-858-7245, 520-282-1533, or fax 520-282-2033 for more information.

ARKANSAS & MISSOURI RAILROAD

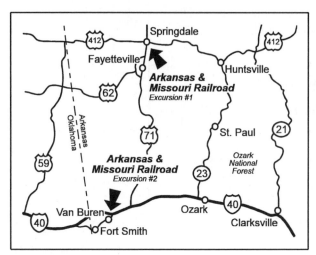

LOCATION
Springdale and Van Buren
SEASON
April - November
ROUND TRIP
Exc. #1, 134 miles
Exc. #2, 70 miles
FARES
Adult,
#1, $33.00 - $44.00
#2, $19.00 - $27.00

The Ride

Springdale to Van Buren (Excursion #1):
This 134 mile round trip departs Springdale and travels across the Ozark Mountains, over trestles and through the Winslow Tunnel. A complimentary breakfast buffet is provided as are snacks and soft drinks on the return trip to Springdale. A three hour layover provides travelers the opportunity to shop and dine in historic Van Buren. Allow approximately nine hours to complete the round trip.

Van Buren to Winslow (Excursion #2):
This 70 mile round trip leaves Van Buren and travels across the Ozark Mountains and through the Winslow Tunnel. Complimentary snacks and soft drinks are served by hostesses. There is no layover in Winslow. The round trip takes about three hours to complete.

All Aboard

Springdale to Van Buren (Excursion #1) boards at the Springdale Depot located at 306 East Emma.

Van Buren to Winslow (Excursion #2) boards in Van Buren at the Old Frisco Depot located at 813 Main Street.

Schedule

Excursion #1: Train boards at 7:45 a.m., departs 8:00 a.m. and returns to Springdale at about 5:00 p.m. Train rides operate on Wednesdays, most Fridays, Saturdays, and some Sundays from April through mid-November. Rides on Tuesday are added in October.

Excursion #2: Train boards 11:00 a.m., leaves at 11:15 a.m. and returns to Van Buren at approximately 2:15 p.m. Rides are operated on Wednesdays, most Fridays, Saturdays, and some Sundays from April through mid-November.

Fares

Excursion #1: Wednesday and Friday, $33.00; Saturday and Sunday, $38.00. In October: Tuesday, Wednesday, Friday, $38.00; Saturday and Sunday, $44.00. All seats same price, taxes are included in price.

Excursion #2: Wednesday and Friday, $19.00; Saturday and Sunday, $21.00. In October: Wednesday and Friday, $25.00; Saturday and Sunday, $27.00. All seats are the same price, taxes included in price.

Notes

Reservations are accepted Monday through Friday from 8:00 a.m. to 5:00 p.m. MasterCard, Visa, and Discover credit cards are accepted. Payments must be made 48 hours in advance, cancellations within 24 hours of trip. All ticket purchases are to be made at the depot in Springdale. Gift certificates are available. Restrooms are located on the coaches. Group rates and charters are available. Smoking and alcoholic beverages are not permitted.

Ride Information

Arkansas & Missouri Railroad Co.
306 East Emma St.
Springdale, AR 72764
Phone: 800-687-8600

Local Information

Excursion #1:

Springdale Chamber of Commerce
P.O. Box 166
Springdale, AR 72765
Phone: 501-751-4694
Fax: 501-751-4699

Fayetteville Chamber of Commerce
P.O. Box 4216
Fayetteville, AR 72702
Phone: 501-521-1710
Fax: 501-521-1791

Excursion #2:

Van Buren Chamber of Commerce
P.O. Box 652
Van Buren, AR 72956
Phone: 501-474-2761
Fax: 501-474-5084

Fort Smith Chamber of Commerce
P.O. Box 1668
Forth Smith, AR 72902
Phone: 501-783-6118
Fax: 501-783-6110

SPECIAL EVENTS AND EXCURSIONS

CHILDREN'S DAY	
DINING:	
BRUNCH	✓
LUNCH	
DINNER	
EASTER BUNNY	
FAIRS/FESTIVALS	✓
FALL FOLIAGE	✓
FATHER'S DAY	
GRANDPARENT'S DAY	
HALLOWEEN	
INDEPENDENCE DAY	
LABOR DAY	
MEMORIAL DAY	
MOONLIGHT	
MOTHER'S DAY	
MURDER MYSTERIES	
NEW YEAR	
SANTA CLAUS	
THANKSGIVING	
TRAIN ROBBERIES	
VALENTINE'S DAY	
VETERAN'S DAY	

Call for current information, schedule and fares on the above special events.

Springdale		*Van Buren*	
	001		025
	026		032
	034, 060		149
	106		
	137		

EUREKA SPRINGS & N. ARKANSAS

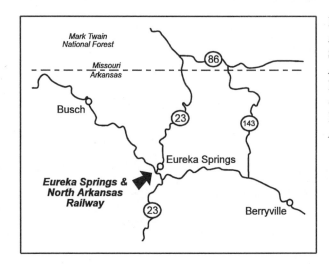

LOCATION
Eureka Springs
SEASON
April - October
ROUND TRIP
4 Miles
FARES
Adult, $8.00

The Ride

Passengers aboard the Eureka Springs & North Arkansas Railway follow along a winding creek through the wooded valleys of northern Arkansas' Ozark Mountain countryside. The entire 4 mile round trip takes about 45 minutes to complete.

All Aboard

Passengers board the train at the historic depot located at 299 North Main Street at the northern end of the Eureka Springs city limits. Trolley rides from downtown Eureka Springs to the depot are also available. Eureka Springs is about 10 miles south of the Missouri border in the northwest corner of Arkansas.

Schedule

The excursion train operates daily except on Sunday from April through October. The train departs Eureka Springs at 10:00 and 11:10 a.m., 12:20, 2:50, and 4:00 p.m.

Fares

Adult ticket prices are $8.00, children ages 4 through 11 are $4.00. Children under 4 ride free.

Ride Information

Eureka Springs & North Arkansas Railway Co.
P.O. Box 310
Eureka Springs, AR 72632
Phone: 501-253-9623 / 501-253-9677

Local Information

Eureka Springs Chamber of Commerce
P.O. Box 551
Eureka Springs, AR 72632
Phone: 501-253-8737

Notes

Group rates for 20 or more available. Chartered trains are also available. Facilities are accessible to the physically challenged. Trains operate rain or shine. The Eureka Springs & North Arkansas Railway also offers lunch and dinner excursions. The lunch train runs from May through October and the dinner train operates April through November. Please call or write for current schedule, menu information, and fares.

SPECIAL EVENTS AND EXCURSIONS	
CHILDREN'S DAY	
DINING:	
BRUNCH	
LUNCH	✓
DINNER	✓
EASTER BUNNY	
FAIRS/FESTIVALS	
FALL FOLIAGE	
FATHER'S DAY	
GRANDPARENT'S DAY	
HALLOWEEN	
INDEPENDENCE DAY	✓
LABOR DAY	✓
MEMORIAL DAY	✓
MOONLIGHT	
MOTHER'S DAY	
MURDER MYSTERIES	
NEW YEAR	
SANTA CLAUS	
THANKSGIVING	
TRAIN ROBBERIES	
VALENTINE'S DAY	
VETERAN'S DAY	

Call for current information, schedule and fares on the above special events.

 037

 064, 067, 071, 124

 145

Blue Goose

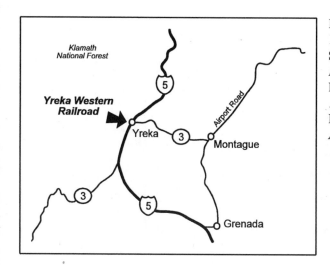

LOCATION
Yreka
SEASON
May - October
ROUND TRIP
16 Miles
FARES
Adult, $9.00

The Ride

Passengers aboard the Blue Goose steam train travel from Yreka to the historic town of Montague. The train, a 101 year old historic short line railroad, crosses the Shasta River, offers views of 14,162-foot Mount Shasta, and enters cattle ranches that were established in the 1850's. There is a one hour layover in Montague, providing opportunities for shopping, taking a wagon ride, or visiting the 1887 Depot Museum. The entire round trip is 16 miles and lasts for approximately 3 hours.

All Aboard

Passengers board the train at the Yreka Western Railroad Depot located at 300 East Miner Street, just east of the Central Yreka exit from I-5.

Schedule

All departures are 10:00 a.m. The Blue Goose operates Memorial Day weekend and the first two weekends in June. From mid-June to Labor Day, the train runs Wednesday through Sunday and on weekends from September through October.

Fares

Adult ticket prices are $9.00, children ages 3 through 12 are $4.50.

Ride Information

Yreka Western Railroad Company
P.O. Box 660
Yreka, CA 96097
Phone: 916-842-4146

Local Information

Yreka Chamber of Commerce
117 West Main Street
Yreka, CA 96097
Phone: 916-842-1649

Notes

Reservations are recommended. Charters and group rates are available. Please contact for details. Yreka's historic district offers many attractive Victorian homes that are on the National Register of Historic Places. The Yreka Depot offers a 1000-foot model railroad display and railroad memorabilia. Depot opens one hour before departure.

SPECIAL EVENTS AND EXCURSIONS

CHILDREN'S DAY
DINING:
    BRUNCH
    LUNCH
    DINNER
EASTER BUNNY
FAIRS/FESTIVALS
FALL FOLIAGE
FATHER'S DAY
GRANDPARENT'S DAY
HALLOWEEN
INDEPENDENCE DAY
LABOR DAY   ✓
MEMORIAL DAY   ✓
MOONLIGHT
MOTHER'S DAY
MURDER MYSTERIES   ✓
NEW YEAR
SANTA CLAUS
THANKSGIVING
TRAIN ROBBERIES
VALENTINE'S DAY
VETERAN'S DAY

Call for current information, schedule and fares on the above special events.

ROARING CAMP & BIG TREES

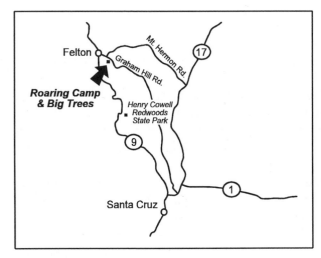

LOCATION
Felton
SEASON
Year-round
ROUND TRIP
Exc. #1, 6 Miles
Exc. #2, 14 Miles
FARES
Adult,
Exc. #1, $13.00
Exc. #2, $15.00

The Ride

Roaring Camp & Big Trees Narrow-Gauge Railroad (Excursion #1):
This scenic train ride is powered by an antique steam locomotive that takes passengers in open-air cars through redwood forests, climbs an 8½% grade before reaching the summit of Bear Mountain and then returns to Roaring Camp Depot. The 6 mile round trip lasts approximately 1¼ hours.

Santa Cruz, Big Trees & Pacific Railway (Excursion #2):
This 14 mile, 2 hour round trip takes passengers through the Henry Cowell Redwoods State Park, into the San Lorenzo River Canyon, and stops at the Beach and Boardwalk in Santa Cruz before returning to the Roaring Camp Depot. Trains are scheduled for continuous round trips or passengers can layover in Roaring Camp or Santa Cruz One—way trips are also available.

All Aboard

Excursion #1: Passengers board at the Roaring Camp Depot located on Graham Hill Road in Felton.

Excursion #2: There are two locations in which passengers may board, one being at the Roaring Camp Depot located on Graham Hill Road in Felton, and the second at the Beach and Boardwalk in Santa Cruz.

Schedule

Excursion #1:

January 1 - March 31: Saturday, Sunday, and holidays 12:00 noon, 1:30, and 3:00 p.m.

April 1 - June 9: Saturday, Sunday, and holidays 12:00 noon, 1:30, and 3:00 p.m.; Monday through Friday, 11:00 a.m.

June 10 - September 4: Saturday, Sunday, and holidays 11:00 a.m., 12:15, 1:30, 2:45, and 4:00 p.m.; Monday through Friday, 11:00 a.m., 12:15, 1:30, and 2:45 p.m.

September 5 - October 1: Saturday, Sunday, and holidays 11:00 a.m., 12:15, 1:30, 2:45, and 4:00 p.m.; Monday through Friday, 11:00 a.m.

October 2 - November 30: Saturday, Sunday, and holidays 12:00 noon, 1:30, and 2:45 p.m.; Monday through Friday, 11:00 a.m.

December 1 - December 31: Saturday, Sunday, and holidays 12:00 noon, 1:30, and 2:45 p.m.; no trains on Christmas Day.

Excursion #2:

May 18 - June 7: Saturday, Sunday, and holidays departing from Roaring Camp at 10:30 a.m. and 2:30 p.m.; departing from Santa Cruz at 12:30 and 4:30 p.m.

June 8 - September 2: Train departs daily at 10:30 a.m. and 2:30 p.m. from Roaring Camp and at 12:30 and 4:30 p.m. from Santa Cruz.

September 3 - October 27: Saturday, Sunday, and holidays departing from Roaring Camp at 10:30 a.m. and 2:30 p.m.; departing from Santa Cruz at 12:30 and 4:30 p.m.

Fares

Excursion #1: Adults $13.00, children ages 3 through 12 $9.50, children under 3 ride free.

Excursion #2: Adults $15.00, children ages 3 through 12 $11.00, children under 3 ride free.

Ride Information

Excursion #1:
Roaring Camp & Big Trees Narrow-Gauge RR
P.O. Box G-1
Felton, CA 95018
Phone: 408-335-4484
Fax: 408-335-3509

Excursion #2:
Santa Cruz, Big Trees & Pacific Railway Co.
P.O. Box G-1
Felton, CA 95018
Phone: 408-335-4484 / 408-335-4400
Fax: 408-335-3509

Local Information

Excursions #1 and #2:
San Lorenzo Valley Chamber of Commerce
P.O. Box 67
Felton, CA 95018
Phone: 408-335-2764
Fax: 408-335-0222

Excursion #2:
Santa Cruz Area Chamber of Commerce
P.O. Box 921
Santa Cruz, CA 95061
Phone: 408-423-1111
Fax: 408-423-1847

SPECIAL EVENTS AND EXCURSIONS	
CHILDREN'S DAY	
DINING:	
BRUNCH	✓
LUNCH	✓
DINNER	✓
EASTER BUNNY	✓
FAIRS/FESTIVALS	
FALL FOLIAGE	
FATHER'S DAY	✓
GRANDPARENT'S DAY	
HALLOWEEN	✓
INDEPENDENCE DAY	✓
LABOR DAY	✓
MEMORIAL DAY	✓
MOONLIGHT	✓
MOTHER'S DAY	✓
MURDER MYSTERIES	
NEW YEAR	
SANTA CLAUS	✓
THANKSGIVING	✓
TRAIN ROBBERIES	✓
VALENTINE'S DAY	
VETERAN'S DAY	

Call for current information, schedule and fares on the above special events.

Notes

Advance reservations are not required, however, it is recommended that passengers arrive at least ½ hour before train departs to purchase tickets. Special train runs may be scheduled for groups of 25 or more; reservations are required. A chuckwagon barbecue is offered from 12:00 noon to 3:00 p.m. on Saturdays and Sundays from May through October; discounted prices when barbecue tickets purchased at same time as train ride tickets.

SKUNK TRAIN

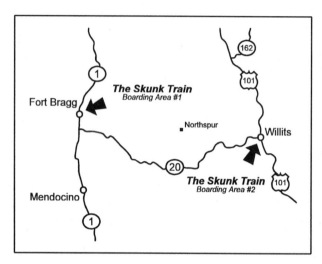

LOCATION
Fort Bragg and Willits
SEASON
Year-round
ROUND TRIP
80 Miles
FARES
Adult, $26.00

The Ride

Travelers of the Skunk Train pass through northern California's redwood forests and mountains. For well over 100 years, rail cars carrying logs, loggers, freight, and passengers have traveled this scenic route through the towering redwoods and mountain meadows while offering breathtaking views of the Noyo River. There are several rides available from a complete 80 mile round trip from either Fort Bragg or Willits to a 40 mile round trip ride to Northspur, the halfway point along the line, and then return to either Fort Bragg or Willits. Whether passengers begin there trip in Fort Bragg or Willits, they will pass through at least one of the railroad's two mountain tunnels and several of its bridges and trestles. Travelers can enjoy open-air observation cars during summer months and some spring and fall days.

All Aboard

Passengers may board the train at the Fort Bragg Depot located at the intersection of Highway 1 (Main Street) and Laurel Street or the Willits Depot at 299 E. Commerce Street.

Schedule

The train operates daily all year long except on Thanksgiving, Christmas

Day, and New Year's Day. From June 10 to September 9, the train leaves Fort Bragg at 9:20 a.m. and 1:40 p.m.; from Willits at 9:00 a.m. and 1:25 p.m. From January 1 to June 9 and September 10 through December 31, the train departs Fort Bragg at 9:20 a.m., 10:00 a.m., and 2:00 p.m.; from Willits at 1:20 p.m.

Fares

Full day trips for adults, $26.00; for children ages 5 to 11, $12.00. Half way or one way trips for adults are $21.00 and for children, $10.00. Children under 5 and not occupying a seat ride free.

Ride Information

California Western Railroad
P.O. Box 907
Fort Bragg, CA 95437
Phone: 707-964-6371

Local Information

Fort Bragg-Mendocino Coast C of C
P.O. Box 1141
Fort Bragg, CA 95437
Phone: 800-726-2780 / 707-961-6300
Fax: 707-964-2056

Willits Chamber of Commerce
239 South Main Street
Willits, CA 95490
Phone: 707-459-7910 *Fax:* 707-459-7914

SPECIAL EVENTS AND EXCURSIONS	
CHILDREN'S DAY	
DINING:	
BRUNCH	
LUNCH	
DINNER	
EASTER BUNNY	
FAIRS/FESTIVALS	
FALL FOLIAGE	
FATHER'S DAY	✓
GRANDPARENT'S DAY	
HALLOWEEN	
INDEPENDENCE DAY	
LABOR DAY	
MEMORIAL DAY	
MOONLIGHT	
MOTHER'S DAY	✓
MURDER MYSTERIES	
NEW YEAR	
SANTA CLAUS	✓
THANKSGIVING	
TRAIN ROBBERIES	
VALENTINE'S DAY	✓
VETERAN'S DAY	

Call for current information, schedule and fares on the above special events.

Notes

Passengers may disembark in Northspur to enjoy a light snack at the refreshment stand before continuing their trip. Reservations are recommended. Discounts are available for groups of 35 or more. Charters also available.

Fort Bragg			*Willits*	
🍴 053, 056	🛏 075, 088, 099		🛏 104	

Yolo Shortline Railroad

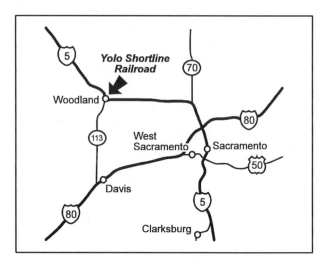

Location
Woodland
Season
May - October
Round Trip
28 Miles
Fares
Adult,
$11.00 - $13.00

The Ride

The Yolo Shortline Railroad offers a 28 mile round trip between Woodland and West Sacramento. The route of the train passes through scenic farmland of the Sacramento Valley and travels alongside the Sacramento River. The train crosses an 8,000-foot long trestle. Passengers can choose to ride in an open observation car or coach. The entire round trip takes about 2 hours and 20 minutes to complete. One-way trips are also available. One Saturday a month a special train run departs from West Sacramento and travels to Clarksburg. Passengers taking the trip to Clarksburg enjoy live music and should note that the train is subject to train robberies by the Sierra Outlaws.

All Aboard

Passengers board the train in Woodland at the depot located at the intersection of East Main and Thomas Streets. Woodland is located about 20 miles northwest of Sacramento. The special trips to Clarksburg depart from West Sacramento at Jefferson Blvd. and South River Road.

Schedule

The Yolo Shortline Railroad operates train rides on Saturdays, Sundays and selected holiday weekends beginning May 11 through mid-October. The train departs at 10:00 a.m. and 2:00 p.m. The Clarksburg train departs at 1:30 p.m. Please call for reservations and schedule.

Fares

The adult ticket prices are $11.00 for the diesel-powered excursion and $13.00 for steam-powered excursions. Seniors over 65 receive a $2.00 discount. Children ticket prices are $6.00 for the diesel-powered excursions and $8.00 for steam-powered rides.

Ride Information

Yolo Shortline Railroad Company
P.O. Box 724
West Sacramento, CA 95691
Phone: 916-372-9777
Fax: 916-372-3545

Local Information

Woodland Area Chamber of Commerce
520 Main Street
Woodland, CA 95695
Phone: 916-662-7327
Fax: 916-662-4086

SPECIAL EVENTS AND EXCURSIONS

CHILDREN'S DAY	
DINING:	
BRUNCH	
LUNCH	
DINNER	
EASTER BUNNY	
FAIRS/FESTIVALS	✓
FALL FOLIAGE	
FATHER'S DAY	✓
GRANDPARENT'S DAY	
HALLOWEEN	
INDEPENDENCE DAY	✓
LABOR DAY	✓
MEMORIAL DAY	✓
MOONLIGHT	
MOTHER'S DAY	✓
MURDER MYSTERIES	
NEW YEAR	
SANTA CLAUS	✓
THANKSGIVING	
TRAIN ROBBERIES	✓
VALENTINE'S DAY	
VETERAN'S DAY	

Call for current information, schedule and fares on the above special events.

Notes

Souvenirs and refreshments are sold on board the train. Chartered trips available. Other excursions available for private groups. Please note that steam-powered trains do not operate every Saturday or Sunday. No excursion trains from Woodland on the days of the special Clarksburg trips.

🍴 057

DURANGO & SILVERTON

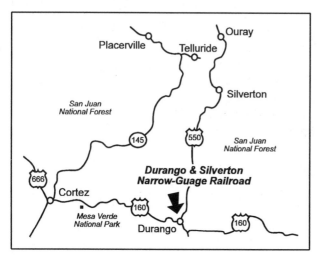

LOCATION
Durango
SEASON
Year-round
ROUND TRIP
90 Miles
FARES
Adult, $42.70

The Ride

This coal-fired, steam operated authentic narrow-gauge train, *The Silverton*, takes passengers on a 90 mile round trip through the beautiful Animas Canyon of the southern Rockies. Enjoy the spectacular Rocky Mountain scenery as you travel from Durango through the San Juan National Forest to the historic mining town of Silverton. There is a 2¼ hour layover in Silverton, providing plenty of time to shop or dine. One-way trips are also available. The shorter *Cascade Canyon Train* offers a 52 mile round trip ride to the wilderness area of Cascade Canyon and back to Durango. The Durango & Silverton also offers a *Winter Train* ride from Durango to Cascade Canyon and back.

All Aboard

Trains depart from Durango at the depot located at 479 Main Avenue. Durango is located in the Southwest corner of Colorado about 20 miles north of the New Mexico border. Call the Silverton Depot at 970-387-5416 for information on one-way departures from Silverton.

Schedule

Several trains depart Durango at various times of the year. The *San Juan Express* runs daily from late June through mid-August and departs at 7:30 a.m. *The Silverton* runs daily from late April through October. The train departs at 8:30 a.m. late April through mid-October. From mid-May through October, a second train departs at 9:15 a.m. A third train departs at 10:10 a.m. from early June through mid-August and early September to early October. The *Cascade Canyon Train* operates from early July through mid-August, Monday through Friday only, and departs at 4:45 p.m. From late November through late April the *Winter Train* departs Durango at 10:00 a.m.

Fares

Round trip fares to or from Silverton: Adults $42.70, children ages 5 through 11 $21.45; tickets for a ride in the parlor car are $73.40 and $67.85 for the caboose tickets. Round trip fares to Cascade Canyon: Adults $36.15, children ages 5 through 11 $18.05. Ticket price for riding in the parlor car is $60.40 and $55.80 for the caboose.

Ride Information

Durango & Silverton Narrow-Gauge Railroad
479 Main Avenue
Durango, CO 81301
Phone: 970-247-2733

Local Information

Durango Area Chamber Resort Association
P.O. Box 2587
Durango, CO 81302
Phone: 800-463-8726 / 970-247-0312
Fax: 970-385-7884

Silverton Chamber of Commerce
P.O. Box 565
Silverton, CO 81433
Phone: 970-387-5654

Notes

Due to the popularity of this scenic train ride, the Durango & Silverton strongly recommends that advance reservations be made at least 4 to 6 weeks prior to the trip. If reservations can not be made, there are tickets available from cancellations and/or no shows. Contact the ticket office in Durango at 970-247-2733 for more information. Refreshments and snacks are available on all trains. Alcoholic beverages are available on the Parlor Car and the Cascade Canyon Train. Overnight layovers in Silverton are available except for Parlor Car ticket holders. Private cars are available for charter. One-way reservations from Durango to Silverton are available and may be booked in advance. One-way service from Silverton to Durango is also available; tickets are sold at the Silverton Depot on a first come, first served basis and cannot be reserved. A mile-by-mile guide of the trip entitled "Cinders and Smoke" is available on the train and in the depot gift shop. Inquire about "photo specials" on the Fall Foliage runs.

SPECIAL EVENTS AND EXCURSIONS

CHILDREN'S DAY
DINING:
    BRUNCH
    LUNCH
    DINNER
EASTER BUNNY
FAIRS/FESTIVALS
FALL FOLIAGE   ✓
FATHER'S DAY
GRANDPARENT'S DAY
HALLOWEEN
INDEPENDENCE DAY
LABOR DAY
MEMORIAL DAY
MOONLIGHT
MOTHER'S DAY
MURDER MYSTERIES
NEW YEAR
SANTA CLAUS
THANKSGIVING
TRAIN ROBBERIES
VALENTINE'S DAY
VETERAN'S DAY

Call for current information, schedule and fares on the above special events.

Durango

 065, 066, 070, 085, 095, 098, 107, 113, 114, 116, 120, 122

Silverton

 093

GEORGETOWN LOOP RAILROAD

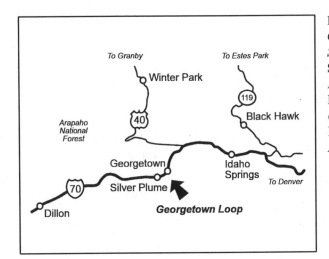

LOCATION
Georgetown and Silver Plume
SEASON
May - October
ROUND TRIP
6½ Miles
FARES
Adult, $11.95

The Ride

Passengers aboard the steam-powered Georgetown Loop Railroad ride in open-air cars as they travel through the scenic Rocky Mountains. Passengers cross the nearly 100-foot high Devils Gate High Bridge, an engineering feat of the 1880's. The 6½ mile round trip takes about 70 minutes to complete. Passengers can extend their trip with a 1 hour and 20 minute walking tour of the Lebanon Silver Mine. An additional fee is charged for the guided tour and reservations are recommended.

All Aboard

Passengers may board in either Georgetown or Silver Plume. The Devil's Gate boarding area in Georgetown (exit #228 off I-70) is located 1 mile west of the Old Georgetown Station at 1106 Rose Street, where tickets can be purchased. The Silver Plume Depot is located off Interstate 70 at exit #226.

Schedule

The train operates daily from late May through mid-October. Departure times from Devil's Gate are 10:00 and 11:20 a.m., 12:40, 2:00, and 3:20 p.m. The train departs Silver Plume at 9:20 and 10:40 a.m., 12:00 noon, 1:20, 2:40, and 4:00 p.m. During the month of September, the train departs

Devil's Gate on weekdays at 11:20 a.m., 12:40 and 2:00 p.m. and from Silver Plume at 10:40 a.m., 12:00 noon, 1:20 and 2:40 p.m. The full schedule applies on weekends through the end of the season.

Fares

The round trip ticket price for adults is $11.95 and for children ages 3 to 15, $7.50. Children under 3 ride free when not occupying a seat. Tours of the Lebanon Silver Mine are available for an additional charge and are only available through Labor Day.

Ride Information

Georgetown Loop Railroad, Inc.
c/o Old Georgetown Station
P.O. Box 217
Georgetown, CO 80444
Phone: 800-691-4386 / 303-569-2403
Fax: 303-569-2894

Local Information

Georgetown Chamber of Commerce
P.O. Box 444
Georgetown, CO 80444
Phone: 303-569-2888

SPECIAL EVENTS AND EXCURSIONS

CHILDREN'S DAY
DINING:
    BRUNCH
    LUNCH
    DINNER
EASTER BUNNY
FAIRS/FESTIVALS
FALL FOLIAGE ✓
FATHER'S DAY
GRANDPARENT'S DAY
HALLOWEEN
INDEPENDENCE DAY
LABOR DAY ✓
MEMORIAL DAY ✓
MOONLIGHT
MOTHER'S DAY
MURDER MYSTERIES
NEW YEAR
SANTA CLAUS
THANKSGIVING
TRAIN ROBBERIES
VALENTINE'S DAY
VETERAN'S DAY

Call for current information, schedule and fares on the above special events.

Notes

Reservations are accepted for Silver Plume departures only. The mine tour is not offered on the last departure of the day from both Silver Plume and Georgetown. Facilities are accessible to the handicapped. Group rates and charters are available. The Depot Express Cafe and Baggage Cart Gifts are located in the Old Georgetown Station. Passengers can also book downhill mountain bike guided tours at the Old Georgetown Station. One-way trips are available at regular fare. Meal service is available on the Tahoe Car for an additional fee and departs from Silver Plume only.

Georgetown

 009   043   079, 084   150

LEADVILLE, COLORADO & SOUTHERN

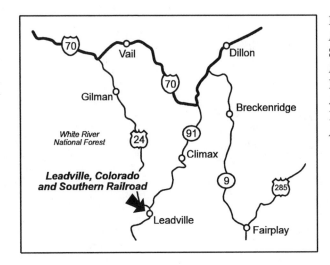

LOCATION
Leadville
SEASON
May - September
ROUND TRIP
23 Miles
FARES
Adult, $22.50

The Ride

You'll enjoy Colorado's high country and the colorful history in one of Colorado's richest mining districts on this scenic railroad trip. From Leadville, the highest incorporated city in the U.S.A., this 23 mile scenic train ride follows the headwaters of the Arkansas River offering views of Fremont Pass and Mt. Elbert, Colorado's highest peak. The train climbs to 11,120 feet, making this the highest railroad line in the United States. Allow 2½ hours for the round trip.

All Aboard

Passengers board the train at Leadville's century-old depot located at 326 East 7th Street.

Schedule

The Leadville, Colorado & Southern Railroad operates daily from late May through September. The train departs at 1:00 p.m. from May 25 through June 16. From June 17 through September 2, the train departs twice daily at

10:00 a.m. and 2:00 p.m. From September 3 through September 29, the train departs at 1:00 p.m. only.

Fares

Adult tickets are $22.50, children ages 4 through 12 are $9.75, children 3 and under ride for free.

Ride Information

Leadville, Colorado & Southern Railroad Co.
P.O. Box 916
Leadville, CO 80461
Phone: 719-486-3936

Local Information

Greater Leadville Area Chamber of Commerce
P.O. Box 861
Leadville, CO 80461
Phone: 800-933-3901 / 719-486-3900

Notes

Group rates are available. Facilities are accessible to the physically challenged. A gift shop is located at the depot.

SPECIAL EVENTS AND EXCURSIONS

CHILDREN'S DAY
DINING:
    BRUNCH
    LUNCH
    DINNER
EASTER BUNNY
FAIRS/FESTIVALS
FALL FOLIAGE
FATHER'S DAY
GRANDPARENT'S DAY
HALLOWEEN
INDEPENDENCE DAY
LABOR DAY   ✓
MEMORIAL DAY   ✓
MOONLIGHT
MOTHER'S DAY
MURDER MYSTERIES
NEW YEAR
SANTA CLAUS
THANKSGIVING
TRAIN ROBBERIES
VALENTINE'S DAY
VETERAN'S DAY

Call for current information, schedule and fares on the above special events.

 015, 019

 023

 073

 140, 141

MANITOU & PIKE'S PEAK RAILWAY

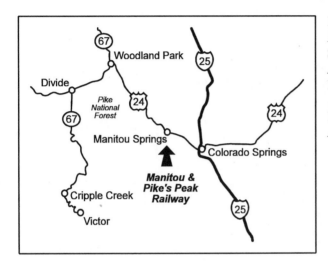

LOCATION
Manitou Springs
SEASON
April - October
ROUND TRIP
18 Miles
FARES
Adult, $21.00

The Ride

Passengers aboard the world's highest cog railway begin their journey in Manitou Springs and make their way through a steep canyon and dense pine forests before reaching the summit of 14,110-feet high Pike's Peak. The train travels approximately 8 miles per hour, giving ample time for sightseeing and picture taking. From the summit, passengers are treated to far reaching views of the Sangre de Cristo Mountains and mile upon mile of snow-capped mountains making up the great Continental Divide. The 18 mile round trip lasts approximately 3 hours and 10 minutes. Passengers are given about 30 to 40 minutes at the summit where a gift shop and snack bar are located.

All Aboard

Passengers board the cog railway at the depot in Manitou Springs located at 515 Ruxton Avenue. Manitou Springs is 6 miles west of Colorado Springs.

Schedule

The Manitou & Pike's Peak Railway operates daily from late April through

October. Departure times are 8:00, 9:20, and 10:40 a.m., 12:00 noon, 1:20, 2:40, 4:00, and 5:20 p.m. depending on weather and the season. Call for complete details.

Fares

Round trip fares are $21.00 for adults and $9.50 for children ages 5 through 11. Children under 5 ride free when not occupying a seat.

Ride Information

Manitou & Pike's Peak Railway
P.O. Box 351
Manitou Springs, CO 80829
Phone: 719-685-5401
Fax: 719-685-9033

Local Information

Manitou Springs Chamber of Commerce
354 Manitou Avenue
Manitou Springs, CO 80829
Phone: 800-642-2567 / 719-685-5089
Fax: 719-685-1963

SPECIAL EVENTS AND EXCURSIONS

CHILDREN'S DAY
DINING:
    BRUNCH
    LUNCH
    DINNER
EASTER BUNNY
FAIRS/FESTIVALS
FALL FOLIAGE
FATHER'S DAY
GRANDPARENT'S DAY
HALLOWEEN
INDEPENDENCE DAY
LABOR DAY   ✓
MEMORIAL DAY   ✓
MOONLIGHT
MOTHER'S DAY
MURDER MYSTERIES
NEW YEAR
SANTA CLAUS
THANKSGIVING
TRAIN ROBBERIES
VALENTINE'S DAY
VETERAN'S DAY

Call for current information, schedule and fares on the above special events.

Notes

Group rates for 15 or more available. Charters are also available. One-way trips are very limited, tickets are sold on a space-available basis only. Reservations are not required, but are strongly recommended. Food service and a gift shop are located in the Manitou Springs depot. Food may be taken on board the trains. It is recommended that warm clothing be worn.

 029
 089

VALLEY RAILROAD

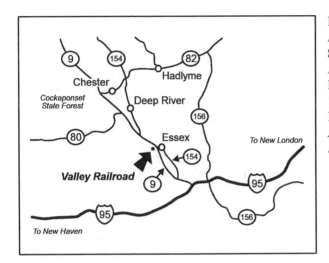

LOCATION
Essex
SEASON
May - October
ROUND TRIP
7 Miles
FARES
Adult,
$10.00 - $14.00

The Ride

The Valley Railroad takes you through the picturesque countryside along the Connecticut River through the scenic river valley. All of the excursions, except for the last one of the day, includes a riverboat cruise that departs from Deep River. The first train of the day, from early June through October, travels to the end of the line in Chester. The train ride and riverboat combination takes about 2½ hours to complete. The train ride only lasts for 1 hour.

All Aboard

Boarding for all scenic train excursions takes place at the Essex Freight Depot located ¼ mile west of State Highway 9 on County Road 154.

Schedule

The Valley Railroad operates daily from early June through Labor Day with departures times of 10:00 a.m., 12:00 noon, 1:30, 3:00, 4:30 and 6:00 p.m. From early May to early June, the train operates at 2:00 and 3:30 p.m.

Wednesday through Friday and on weekends with departures at 12:00 noon, 1:30, 3:00, and 4:30 p.m. During the months of September and October, the train operates Wednesday through Sunday and departs at 10:00 a.m., 12:00 noon, 1:30, 3:00, and 4:30 p.m.

Fares

The fare for the train ride and riverboat combination for adults is $14.00; train ride only $10.00. Ticket prices for children ages 3 to 11 are $7.00 for the train/boat ride and $5.00 for train ride only. Children under 3 ride free. Parlor car tickets available for an additional fee.

Ride Information

The Valley Railroad Company
P.O. Box 452
Essex, CT 06426
Phone: 800-377-3987 / 203-767-0103

Local Information

Chamber of Commerce of
    Southeastern Connecticut
105 Huntington Street
New London, CT 06320
Phone: 203-443-8332
Fax: 203-444-1529

Notes

The train, special cars, and riverboats are available for charter. Discounts available for groups of 25 or more. The Essex Freight Depot has been listed on the National Register of Historic Places.

SPECIAL EVENTS AND EXCURSIONS

CHILDREN'S DAY	
DINING:	
BRUNCH	✓
LUNCH	✓
DINNER	✓
EASTER BUNNY	✓
FAIRS/FESTIVALS	✓
FALL FOLIAGE	✓
FATHER'S DAY	
GRANDPARENT'S DAY	
HALLOWEEN	✓
INDEPENDENCE DAY	
LABOR DAY	✓
MEMORIAL DAY	✓
MOONLIGHT	
MOTHER'S DAY	✓
MURDER MYSTERIES	
NEW YEAR	
SANTA CLAUS	✓
THANKSGIVING	
TRAIN ROBBERIES	
VALENTINE'S DAY	
VETERAN'S DAY	

Call for current information, schedule and fares on the above special events.

QUEEN ANNE'S RAILROAD

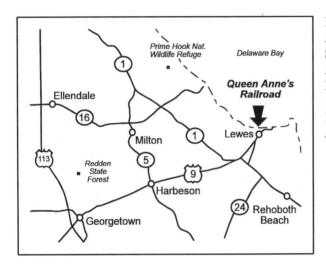

LOCATION
Lewes
SEASON
May - October
ROUND TRIP
16 Miles
FARES
Adult, $7.00

The Ride

The Queen Anne's Railroad offers a 1¾ hour excursion beginning in Lewes and traveling through southern Delaware's scenic countryside. Passengers may also choose to board the "Royal Zephyr" for a 2½ hour dinner scenic excursion. Both train rides travel a distance of 16 miles.

All Aboard

Passengers board the excursion and dinner train at the depot in Lewes located at 730 King's Highway. Lewes is located in southeastern Delaware on Delaware Bay.

Schedule

The Queen Anne's Railroad operates the excursion train on various days of the week from May through October. In May, the train operates every Wednesday and departs at 12:00 noon. During the month of June, the train operates every Wednesday and Saturday, departing at 1:00 p.m. The train operates on Tuesday, Wednesday, Thursday, and Saturday during the months of July and August and departs at 1:00 p.m. In September, the train departs at 1:00

p.m. every Saturday. In October the train runs on Sundays with a departure time of 1:30 p.m. Additional runs are added on select days in June, August, and September. Please contact Queen Anne's Railroad for the dinner train schedule.

Fares

The adult fare for the excursion train is $7.00 and $5.00 for children ages 3 through 12. Children under 3 ride for free when not occupying a seat. Fares for the dinner train vary, please call or write for complete details.

Ride Information

Queen Anne's Railroad
730 King's Highway
Lewes, DE 19958
Phone: 302-644-1720

Local Information

Lewes Chamber of Commerce
P.O. Box 1
Lewes, DE 19958
Phone: 302-645-8073
Fax: 302-645-8412

SPECIAL EVENTS AND EXCURSIONS	
CHILDREN'S DAY	
DINING:	
BRUNCH	✓
LUNCH	
DINNER	✓
EASTER BUNNY	✓
FAIRS/FESTIVALS	
FALL FOLIAGE	
FATHER'S DAY	✓
GRANDPARENT'S DAY	
HALLOWEEN	
INDEPENDENCE DAY	
LABOR DAY	✓
MEMORIAL DAY	
MOONLIGHT	
MOTHER'S DAY	✓
MURDER MYSTERIES	
NEW YEAR	
SANTA CLAUS	✓
THANKSGIVING	
TRAIN ROBBERIES	
VALENTINE'S DAY	
VETERAN'S DAY	

Call for current information, schedule and fares on the above special events.

Notes

Chartered trains available for special occasions. Refreshments available on most of the excursion trains. Appropriate dress and reservations are required for the dinner excursion.

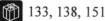 041, 048

133, 138, 151

WILMINGTON & WESTERN RR

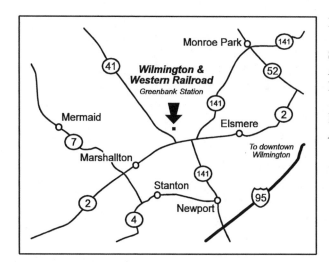

LOCATION
Wilmington
SEASON
May - November
ROUND TRIP
10 Miles
FARES
Adult, $7.00

The Ride

The Wilmington & Western Railroad offers several ride options at various times of the year. The most common route is a 10 mile round trip ride from the Greenbank Station to Mt. Cuba Picnic Grove. Passengers aboard this train travel a leisurely route through the beautiful Red Clay Valley of northern Delaware. The entire round trip takes approximately 1 hour to complete. Passengers can take a later train back in order to spend more time at the picnic area.

All Aboard

The train boards at the Greenbank Station located on Greenbank Road off of Newport Gap Pike (State Highway 41), just ¼ mile north of the Kirkwood Highway (State Highway 2).

Schedule

The Wilmington & Western Railroad operates various train rides from April through December. The train ride to Mt. Cuba Picnic Grove runs on most Sundays from May through November. Additional runs are added on most

Saturdays from June through August. Departure times for both Saturday and Sunday are 12:30, 2:00, and 3:30 p.m.

Fares

The ticket price for adults is $7.00 and for children ages 2 through 12, $4.00. Children under 2 ride for free. The fare for seniors aged 60 and over is $6.00

Ride Information

Wilmington & Western Railroad
P.O. Box 5787
Wilmington, DE 19808
Phone: 302-998-1930
Fax: 302-998-7408

Local Information

New Castle County Chamber of Commerce
P.O. Box 11247
Wilmington, DE 19850
Phone: 302-737-4343 / 302-378-6582
Fax: 302-737-8450

SPECIAL EVENTS AND EXCURSIONS	
CHILDREN'S DAY	✓
DINING:	
BRUNCH	
LUNCH	
DINNER	✓
EASTER BUNNY	✓
FAIRS/FESTIVALS	✓
FALL FOLIAGE	✓
FATHER'S DAY	✓
GRANDPARENT'S DAY	
HALLOWEEN	✓
INDEPENDENCE DAY	
LABOR DAY	
MEMORIAL DAY	✓
MOONLIGHT	
MOTHER'S DAY	✓
MURDER MYSTERIES	
NEW YEAR	
SANTA CLAUS	✓
THANKSGIVING	
TRAIN ROBBERIES	✓
VALENTINE'S DAY	
VETERAN'S DAY	

Call for current information, schedule and fares on the above special events.

Notes

Chartered trains are available. Open-air cars available during the warmer months. Discounts are offered to groups of 25 or more. Several other excursions are offered, please call or write for complete details. A gift shop, snack bar, and picnic area are located on the station premises.

FLORIDA GULF COAST RAILROAD

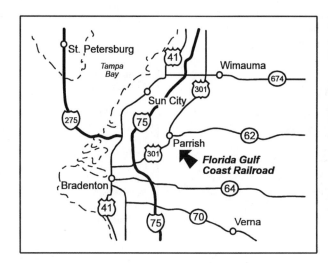

LOCATION
Parrish
SEASON
Year-round
ROUND TRIP
12 Miles
FARES
Adult, $8.00

The Ride

The Florida Gulf Coast Railroad Museum offers a 12 mile round trip excursion train ride beginning in Parrish. Passengers can ride in an open-window coach, caboose, or air conditioned lounge car on their journey through the scenic rural countryside of Manatee County. The round trip takes approximately 1 hour and 15 minutes to complete.

All Aboard

Passengers board the train in Parrish at the depot located behind the post office on 83rd Street East, just east of U.S. Highway 301. Parrish is located in southwestern Florida, about 25 miles north of Sarasota.

Schedule

The Florida Gulf Coast Railroad operates on weekends year-round. On Saturdays, the train departs at 11:00 a.m., 1:00 and 3:00 p.m. On Sundays, the train departs the depot at 1:00 and 3:00 p.m.

Fares

The adult fare is $8.00 and $5.00 for children.

Ride Information

Florida Gulf Coast Railroad Museum
P.O. Box 355
Parrish, FL 34219
Phone: 941-377-4016

Local Information

Manatee Chamber of Commerce
P.O. Box 321
Bradenton, FL 34206
Phone: 941-748-3411
Fax: 941-745-1877

Notes

The caboose, lounge car, or the entire train is available for charter. The Baggage Car Gift Shop is located in the depot. Train runs rain or shine.

SPECIAL EVENTS AND EXCURSIONS

CHILDREN'S DAY
DINING:
　BRUNCH
　LUNCH
　DINNER
EASTER BUNNY
FAIRS/FESTIVALS
FALL FOLIAGE
FATHER'S DAY
GRANDPARENT'S DAY
HALLOWEEN
INDEPENDENCE DAY
LABOR DAY
MEMORIAL DAY
MOONLIGHT
MOTHER'S DAY
MURDER MYSTERIES
NEW YEAR
SANTA CLAUS
THANKSGIVING
TRAIN ROBBERIES
VALENTINE'S DAY
VETERAN'S DAY

NONE

Call for current information, schedule and fares on the above special events.

SEMINOLE GULF RAILWAY

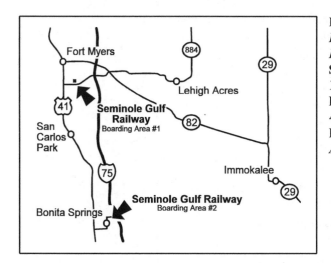

LOCATION
*Fort Myers and
Bonita Springs*
SEASON
Year-round
ROUND TRIP
40 Miles
FARES
Adult, $11.00

The Ride

The Seminole Gulf Railway offers several scenic excursion trips through historic southwest Florida. Brunch and five-course dinner trains are available in addition to the scenic excursion described here. This excursion train travels between Fort Myers and Old Bonita Springs. The round trip train ride is approximately 40 miles and lasts 2 hours. All passenger cars of the Seminole Gulf Railway are air-conditioned.

All Aboard

Passengers may board the train at two locations, from the Metro Mall Station in Fort Myers or the platform in Old Bonita Springs. The Metro Mall Station is located at 2805 Colonial Blvd. The platform in Old Bonita Springs is located in a park just west of Old 41 Road on Pennsylvania Ave., one-half mile north of Bonita Beach Road.

Schedule

The Seminole Gulf Railway operates year-round on Wednesdays and weekends. Departures from Fort Myers are 9:30 a.m. (except Sunday) and 12:00

noon. The train departs Old Bonita Springs at 10:30 a.m. on Wednesday and Saturday and at 1:00 p.m. on Sunday. The schedule is expanded from mid-February through early April and from mid-June through mid-August when the train operates Tuesday through Thursday, Saturday and Sunday. Departures from Fort Myers are 9:30 a.m. (except Sunday), 12:00 noon, and 2:30 p.m. The train will depart Old Bonita Springs at 10:30 a.m (except Sunday) and 1:00 p.m.

Fares

Adult ticket prices for the excursion train are $11.00, children $6.00. Please call or write for fares on the various dinner trains.

Ride Information

Seminole Gulf Railway
4110 Centerpointe Drive
Fort Myers, FL 33916
Phone: 800-SEM-GULF / 941-275-6060

Local Information

Chamber of Southwest Florida
1520 Royal Palm Sq. Blvd. - #210
Fort Myers, FL 33919
Phone: 941-278-4001 / 941-278-1231 (info.)
Fax: 941-278-3319

Greater Fort Myers Chamber of Commerce
P.O. Box 9289
Fort Myers, FL 33902
Phone: 800-366-3622 / 941-332-3624
Fax: 941-332-7276

SPECIAL EVENTS AND EXCURSIONS

CHILDREN'S DAY
DINING:
    BRUNCH   ✓
    LUNCH   ✓
    DINNER   ✓
EASTER BUNNY   ✓
FAIRS/FESTIVALS   ✓
FALL FOLIAGE
FATHER'S DAY   ✓
GRANDPARENT'S DAY
HALLOWEEN
INDEPENDENCE DAY
LABOR DAY
MEMORIAL DAY
MOONLIGHT
MOTHER'S DAY   ✓
MURDER MYSTERIES   ✓
NEW YEAR   ✓
SANTA CLAUS   ✓
THANKSGIVING   ✓
TRAIN ROBBERIES   ✓
VALENTINE'S DAY   ✓
VETERAN'S DAY

Call for current information, schedule and fares on the above special events.

Bonita Springs Area Chamber of Commerce
P.O. Box 1240
Bonita Springs, FL 33959
Phone: 941-992-2943
Fax: 941-992-5011

Notes

A snack bar and narration are provided on the excursion train. No reservations are required and group charters are available. Reservations and proper attire are required on the dinner excursion trains.

Bonita Beach

 105, 127

Bonita Springs

 006

 055

Fort Myers

 022

 030, 042

 123

Monticello Railway Museum

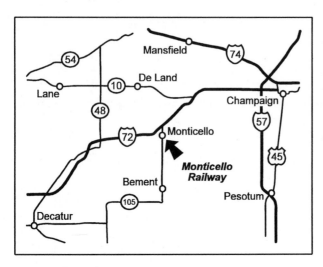

Location
Monticello
Season
May - October
Round Trip
4 Miles
Fares
Adult, $5.00

The Ride

The Monticello Railway Museum offers a 4 mile round trip ride between the museum and the 1899 Wabash Depot in downtown Monticello. The route of the train travels through east-central Illinois' woods and farmland. The conductor will answer your questions and bring to your attention points of interest along the route. The entire trip takes about 1 hour to complete. Passengers may layover at either depot and take a later train back to their origin of departure.

All Aboard

Passengers may board the train at either the Wabash Depot located in downtown Monticello or the restored Illinois Central Depot located at the museum. The museum is located on the frontage road at exit 166 off Interstate 72.

Schedule

The museum is open and operates the train ride on weekends and holidays from May through October. The train departs from the Illinois Central Depot at 1:00, 2:00, 3:00 and 4:00 p.m. Departures from the Wabash Depot are 1:30, 2:30 and 3:30 p.m.

Fares

The adult ticket price is $5.00 and for children ages 4 through 12, $3.00. Senior citizens aged 62 and over receive a $2.00 discount. Children under 3 ride free when not occupying a seat.

Ride Information

Monticello Railway Museum
P.O. Box 401
Monticello, IL 61856
Phone: 800-952-3396 / 217-762-9011

Local Information

Monticello Chamber of Commerce
P.O. Box 313
Monticello, IL 61856
Phone: 800-952-3396 / 217-762-7921
Fax: 217-762-9307

SPECIAL EVENTS AND EXCURSIONS	
CHILDREN'S DAY	
DINING:	
BRUNCH	
LUNCH	
DINNER	
EASTER BUNNY	
FAIRS/FESTIVALS	
FALL FOLIAGE	
FATHER'S DAY	✓
GRANDPARENT'S DAY	
HALLOWEEN	✓
INDEPENDENCE DAY	✓
LABOR DAY	✓
MEMORIAL DAY	✓
MOONLIGHT	
MOTHER'S DAY	✓
MURDER MYSTERIES	
NEW YEAR	
SANTA CLAUS	✓
THANKSGIVING	
TRAIN ROBBERIES	✓
VALENTINE'S DAY	
VETERAN'S DAY	

Call for current information, schedule and fares on the above special events.

Notes

A gift shop and snack bar are located at the museum's depot. Special fares and schedules may apply to the special events and excursions offered throughout the year. Facilities for the physically challenged are limited, please make your needs known to the Monticello Railway Museum.

CARTHAGE, KNIGHTSTOWN

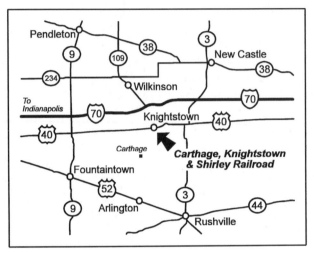

LOCATION
Knightstown
SEASON
May - October
ROUND TRIP
10 Miles
FARES
Adult, $6.00

The Ride

Passengers aboard the Carthage, Knightstown & Shirley Railroad begin their 10 mile round trip in Knightstown and travel south to Carthage. The route of the train passes under the old "Pennsy" railroad bridge and crosses the Big Blue River as it travels across the scenic Indiana countryside. The round trip ride takes about 1 hour to complete including a 20 minute stop in Carthage where passengers may enjoy ice cream or drinks while the train is prepared for the return trip. Passengers may also choose to stay longer in Carthage and return on a later train. One-way trips are also available.

All Aboard

Passengers board the train in Knightstown at the depot located at 112 West Carey Street. Knightstown is located in east-central Indiana, about 30 miles east of Indianapolis.

Schedule

The Carthage, Knightstown & Shirley Railroad operates Friday through Sunday from May through October. The train departs at 11:00 a.m. on Fri-

day, 11:00 a.m., 1:00 and 3:00 p.m. on Saturday and Sunday.

Fares

The adult round trip ticket price is $6.00. Chil-
dren ages 3 through 11 are $4.00. Children
under 3 ride for free.

Ride Information

Carthage, Knightstown & Shirley Railroad
112 W. Carey Street
Knightstown, IN 46148
Phone: 317-345-5561
           800-345-2704 (Indiana only)

Local Information

Knightstown Area Chamber of Commerce
P.O. Box 44
Knightstown, IN 46148
Phone: 317-345-2177

Rush County Chamber of Commerce
P.O. Box 156
Rushville, IN 46173
Phone: 317-932-2880
Fax: 317-932-4191

SPECIAL EVENTS AND EXCURSIONS	
CHILDREN'S DAY	
DINING:	
BRUNCH	
LUNCH	
DINNER	
EASTER BUNNY	
FAIRS/FESTIVALS	✓
FALL FOLIAGE	
FATHER'S DAY	✓
GRANDPARENT'S DAY	
HALLOWEEN	✓
INDEPENDENCE DAY	✓
LABOR DAY	✓
MEMORIAL DAY	✓
MOONLIGHT	
MOTHER'S DAY	✓
MURDER MYSTERIES	
NEW YEAR	
SANTA CLAUS	
THANKSGIVING	
TRAIN ROBBERIES	
VALENTINE'S DAY	
VETERAN'S DAY	

Call for current information, schedule and fares on the above special events.

Notes

Group discount offered for groups of 20 or more. Chartered trips available.
Reservations are recommended. A gift shop is located in the Knightstown
depot. Facilities are accessible to the handicapped.

143

FRENCH LICK, WEST BADEN

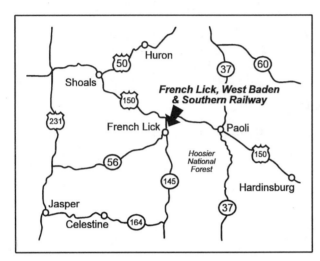

LOCATION
French Lick
SEASON
April - November
ROUND TRIP
20 Miles
FARES
Adult, $8.00

The Ride

The French Lick, West Baden & Southern Railway is operated by the Indiana Railway Museum. This 20 mile round trip scenic excursion travels through the wooded Hoosier National Forest and through the 2,200-foot long Burton tunnel, one of the longest railroad tunnels in the state. The entire round trip takes approximately 1¾ hours to complete. The museum also operates a trolly car between French Lick and West Baden.

All Aboard

All trains depart from the Monon Railroad Station located on State Highway 56 in French Lick. French Lick is located in south-central Indiana approximately 50 miles south of Bloomington.

Schedule

The scenic train operates on weekends from April through November and on Memorial Day, Independence Day, and Labor Day. The train departs at 10:00 a.m., 1:00 and 4:00 p.m. An additional run is added on Tuesdays during the summer months and departs at 1:00 p.m.

Fares

Adult ticket prices are $8.00 and children ages 3 through 11 are $4.00. Children under 3 ride for free. Discounts are given to senior citizens.

Ride Information

Indiana Railway Museum
P.O. Box 150
French Lick, IN 47432
Phone: 800-748-7246 / 812-936-2405

Local Information

French Lick-West Baden Chamber of Commerce
P.O. Box 347
French Lick, IN 47432
Phone: 812-936-2405

Notes

Group rates offered for school, private, and corporate excursions. Catering is available upon request. Refreshments, souvenirs, and railroad memorabilia are available in the station's gift shop. A snack bar is provided on all excursions.

SPECIAL EVENTS AND EXCURSIONS

CHILDREN'S DAY
DINING:
    BRUNCH
    LUNCH
    DINNER   ✓
EASTER BUNNY
FAIRS/FESTIVALS
FALL FOLIAGE
FATHER'S DAY
GRANDPARENT'S DAY
HALLOWEEN
INDEPENDENCE DAY   ✓
LABOR DAY   ✓
MEMORIAL DAY   ✓
MOONLIGHT
MOTHER'S DAY
MURDER MYSTERIES
NEW YEAR
SANTA CLAUS
THANKSGIVING
TRAIN ROBBERIES   ✓
VALENTINE'S DAY
VETERAN'S DAY

Call for current information, schedule and fares on the above special events.

WHITEWATER VALLEY RAILROAD

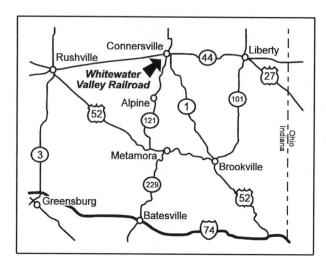

LOCATION
Connersville
SEASON
May - October
ROUND TRIP
32 Miles
FARES
Adult, $11.00

The Ride

This 32 mile round trip takes passengers from Connersville to the historic town of Metamora. One-way trips are also available from either location. The route travels alongside the towpath of the Whitewater Canal. The Laurel Feeder Dam and remnants of the old locks can be seen along the way. The ride includes a 2 hour layover in Metamora so passengers have the opportunity to visit the 100 plus shops in this 1800's town.

The Whitewater Valley Railroad also offers a "Train To Dinner" on the first and third Friday of each month, April through November. Passengers are taken to the town of Laurel where they stay 1½ hours at the Laurel Hotel Restaurant for dinner before returning to Connersville.

All Aboard

Passengers board the train at the depot in Connersville located at 300 S. Eastern Avenue.

Schedule

The Whitewater Valley Railroad operates weekends and holidays from the first Saturday in May to the last Sunday in October. The train departs at

12:01 p.m. and returns between 5:30 and 6:00 p.m. Additional train runs at 10:00 a.m. on Wednesday, Thursday, and Friday during the month of May and on Thursday and Friday during October. *Please note that the times given are Indiana Time, they are not on Daylight Savings Time.*

Fares

Adult ticket prices for a round trip are $11.00, children from 2 to 12 are $5.00. One-way tickets are available for $9.00 for adults and $4.00 for children. Children under 2 ride for free.

Ride Information

Whitewater Valley Railroad
P.O. Box 406
Connersville, IN 47331
Phone: 317-825-2054

Local Information

Connersville/Fayette County C of C
504 Central Avenue
Connersville, IN 47331
Phone: 317-825-2561
Fax: 317-825-4613

Brookville/Franklin County Chamber of Commerce
P.O. Box 211
Brookville, IN 47012
Phone: 317-647-3177

SPECIAL EVENTS AND EXCURSIONS	
CHILDREN'S DAY	
DINING:	
BRUNCH	
LUNCH	
DINNER	✓
EASTER BUNNY	
FAIRS/FESTIVALS	✓
FALL FOLIAGE	✓
FATHER'S DAY	
GRANDPARENT'S DAY	
HALLOWEEN	
INDEPENDENCE DAY	✓
LABOR DAY	✓
MEMORIAL DAY	✓
MOONLIGHT	
MOTHER'S DAY	
MURDER MYSTERIES	
NEW YEAR	
SANTA CLAUS	
THANKSGIVING	
TRAIN ROBBERIES	
VALENTINE'S DAY	
VETERAN'S DAY	

Call for current information, schedule and fares on the above special events.

Notes

Several special trips are offered throughout the operating season. Discounts are offered for groups of 30 or more. Reservations are required for groups. The train is also available for charter. A gift shop, museum, and soft drinks are available at the station. Call or write for information on the "Train To Dinner" schedule and fares.

 061   111

BOONE & SCENIC VALLEY RR

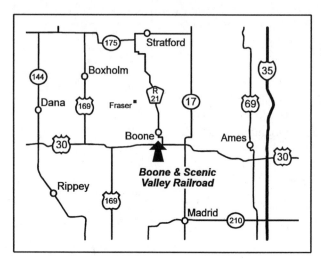

LOCATION
Boone
SEASON
May - October
ROUND TRIP
14 Miles
FARES
Adult,
$8.00 - $10.00

The Ride

The Boone & Scenic Valley Railroad travels through the Des Moines River Valley. The 14 mile round trip from Boone to Fraser takes passengers across a 156-foot high trestle and over another river bridge at the Des Moines "Y" camp. The trip takes about 1 hour and 45 minutes to complete. One-way trips are available. The Boone & Scenic Valley Railroad is also the home of "The Iowan" JS #8419, the first Chinese steam locomotive imported to this country and the only engine of its class in the United States. The Boone & Scenic Valley Railroad also offers a trolley ride from the depot to downtown Boone.

All Aboard

Passengers board the train at the depot in Boone located at 11th and Division streets. Boone is approximately 40 miles north of Des Moines.

Schedule

The Boone & Scenic Valley Railroad operates from Memorial Day weekend through October. A diesel locomotive powers the train Monday through

Friday and departs at 1:30 p.m. On weekends and holidays the train is pulled by a steam locomotive and departs at 11:00 a.m., 1:30 and 4:00 p.m. Trolley rides operate on Saturdays and Sundays.

Fares

Adult ticket prices during the week are $8.00; for children ages 5 through 12, $4.00. Weekend prices are $10.00 for adults and $4.00 for children 5 to 12. Children under 5 ride for free when not occupying a seat. The fare for the trolley ride is $2.00.

Ride Information

Boone & Scenic Valley Railroad
P.O. Box 603
Boone, IA 50036
Phone: 800-626-0319 (in Iowa)
          515-432-4249

Local Information

Boone Area Chamber of Commerce
806 7th Street
Boone, IA 50036
Phone: 515-432-3342
Fax: 515-432-3343

SPECIAL EVENTS AND EXCURSIONS	
CHILDREN'S DAY	
DINING:	
BRUNCH	
LUNCH	
DINNER	
EASTER BUNNY	
FAIRS/FESTIVALS	✓
FALL FOLIAGE	✓
FATHER'S DAY	
GRANDPARENT'S DAY	
HALLOWEEN	
INDEPENDENCE DAY	✓
LABOR DAY	✓
MEMORIAL DAY	✓
MOONLIGHT	
MOTHER'S DAY	
MURDER MYSTERIES	
NEW YEAR	
SANTA CLAUS	
THANKSGIVING	
TRAIN ROBBERIES	✓
VALENTINE'S DAY	
VETERAN'S DAY	

Call for current information, schedule and fares on the above special events.

Notes

Group rates and charters are available. A gift shop, snack bar, and the Iowa Railroad Museum are located at the depot. Extra trains run on July 4th, Labor Day, and Pufferbilly Days (the weekend after Labor Day). Boone is the home of the Kate Shelly High Bridge, the longest and highest double-track railroad bridge in the world.

008

ABILENE & SMOKY VALLEY RR

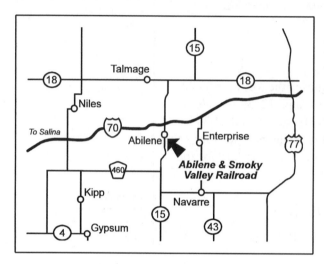

LOCATION
Abilene
SEASON
May - October
ROUND TRIP
10 Miles
FARES
Adult, $7.50

The Ride

The Abilene & Smoky Valley Railroad takes passengers on a 10 mile round trip through fertile Kansas farmland. The scenic train excursion starts in Abilene and travels to Enterprise. The train crosses the Smoky Hill River where in 1867 cowboys watered their longhorn cattle enroute to Abilene where the cattle were loaded onto trains. The round trip lasts approximately 1½ hours.

All Aboard

Passengers board the Abilene & Smoky Valley train at the station in Abilene located at 417 S. Buckeye (State Highway 15). Abilene is about 80 miles west of Topeka on I-70.

Schedule

The train operates daily, except Mondays unless a holiday, from Memorial Day through Labor Day. Departure times Tuesday through Friday are 10:00 a.m. and 2:00 p.m. Saturday departures are 10:00 a.m., 2:00 and 4:00 p.m. Departures on Sunday, 2:00 and 4:00 p.m. Special operations take place on weekends in May, September and October. Saturday departures are 10:00 a.m. and 2:00 p.m. On Sunday the train departs at 2:00 and 4:00 p.m.

Fares

Adults $7.50, children ages 3 through 11 are $5.50. Children 2 and under ride free.

Ride Information

Abilene & Smoky Valley Railroad
P.O. Box 744
Abilene, KS 67410
Phone: 913-263-1077 / 913-263-0118 (depot)

Local Information

Abilene Area Chamber of Commerce
P.O. Box 446
Abilene, KS 67410
Phone: 913-263-1770

Abilene Convention & Visitors Bureau
201 West 2nd St.
Abilene, KS 67410
Phone: 800-569-5915

SPECIAL EVENTS AND EXCURSIONS

CHILDREN'S DAY	
DINING:	
BRUNCH	
LUNCH	✓
DINNER	
EASTER BUNNY	
FAIRS/FESTIVALS	✓
FALL FOLIAGE	
FATHER'S DAY	
GRANDPARENT'S DAY	
HALLOWEEN	
INDEPENDENCE DAY	
LABOR DAY	✓
MEMORIAL DAY	✓
MOONLIGHT	
MOTHER'S DAY	
MURDER MYSTERIES	✓
NEW YEAR	
SANTA CLAUS	
THANKSGIVING	
TRAIN ROBBERIES	✓
VALENTINE'S DAY	
VETERAN'S DAY	

Call for current information, schedule and fares on the above special events.

Notes

Charters and discounts for groups of 30 or more are available as are rates for school groups. Special rates for private parties are also offered. Facilities are accessible to the physically challenged.

 010

 091, 096

MIDLAND RAILWAY

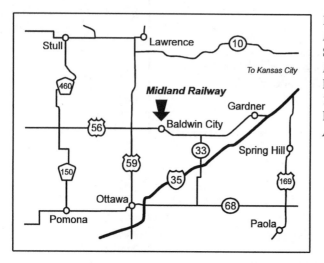

LOCATION
Baldwin City
SEASON
May - October
ROUND TRIP
7 Miles
FARES
Adult, $5.50

The Ride

Passengers aboard the Midland Railway begin their 7 mile journey in Baldwin City and travel to "Nowhere". The excursion train operates on track originally constructed in 1867. The train crosses a 250-foot wooden trestle as it travels through the scenic farmland and wooded areas of eastern Kansas. The entire round trip takes approximately 45 minutes to complete. Future plans call for extending the train ride to Norwood for a total round trip of 10 miles.

All Aboard

Passengers board the train at the depot in Baldwin City located at 1515 High Street, just west of the downtown area. Baldwin City is located about 45 miles southwest of Kansas City.

Schedule

The Midland Railway operates on weekends and holidays from the third weekend in May through the last weekend in October. The train departs at 11:30 a.m., 1:30 and 3:00 p.m.

Fares

The ticket price for adults is $5.50 and for children ages 4 through 12, $2.50. Children under 4 years ride for free.

Ride Information

Midland Railway
P.O. Box 412
Baldwin City, KS 66006
Phone: 913-594-6982 / 913-371-3410 (Kansas City area)

Local Information

Baldwin City Chamber of Commerce
P.O. Box 501
Baldwin City, KS 66006
Phone: 913-594-3200

Notes

Group discounts and all-day fares offered. Charters are also available. Reservations are not required. Trains run rain or shine. Other special events offered but not listed in the chart include Hobo Days and Railfan Days. School Days and senior citizen trips are offered in May and October.

SPECIAL EVENTS AND EXCURSIONS

CHILDREN'S DAY
DINING:
    BRUNCH
    LUNCH
    DINNER
EASTER BUNNY
FAIRS/FESTIVALS ✓
FALL FOLIAGE ✓
FATHER'S DAY
GRANDPARENT'S DAY ✓
HALLOWEEN ✓
INDEPENDENCE DAY ✓
LABOR DAY ✓
MEMORIAL DAY ✓
MOONLIGHT
MOTHER'S DAY
MURDER MYSTERIES
NEW YEAR
SANTA CLAUS
THANKSGIVING
TRAIN ROBBERIES
VALENTINE'S DAY
VETERAN'S DAY

Call for current information, schedule and fares on the above special events.

BIG SOUTH FORK SCENIC RAILWAY

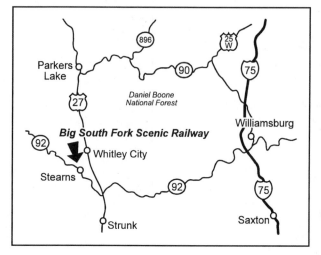

LOCATION
Stearns
SEASON
April - October
ROUND TRIP
14 Miles
FARES
Adult, $10.00

The Ride

Travelers aboard the Big South Fork Scenic Railway enjoy a ride in covered, open-air cars through the Big South Fork National River and Recreation Area. A 265-foot long tunnel takes you through the mountains in an area rich in coal mining history. The ride currently includes a 1½ hour stop at the Blue Heron Mine where a museum is located as well as a snack bar and gift shop. Scheduled to open in the summer of 1996 is the Barthell Platform, accessible only by the scenic train, where travelers will find a replica of a mining village. The village will include a boarding house, country store, church, boutiques, and a snack bar. The entire 14 mile round trip takes about 3 hours to complete.

All Aboard

The train depot is located in Stearns on State Highway 92, 1½ miles west of U.S. Highway 27.

Schedule

The Big South Fork Scenic Railway operates Wednesday through Sunday in April, May, and September. Departure time is 10:00 a.m. weekdays and 10:00 a.m. and 2:00 p.m. on weekends. The train runs daily in June, July, August, and October. Departure times remain the same.

Fares

Adult round trip ticket price is $10.00, children 3 to 12 $4.95. Children under 3 are free when not occupying a seat. Discounts available to senior citizens.

Ride Information

Big South Fork Scenic Railway
P.O. Box 368
Stearns, KY 42647
Phone: 800-462-5664 / 606-376-5330

Local Information

McCreary County Chamber of Commerce
P.O. Box 548
Whitley City, KY 42653
Phone: 606-376-5004

SPECIAL EVENTS AND EXCURSIONS

CHILDREN'S DAY	
DINING:	
BRUNCH	
LUNCH	✓
DINNER	✓
EASTER BUNNY	✓
FAIRS/FESTIVALS	✓
FALL FOLIAGE	✓
FATHER'S DAY	✓
GRANDPARENT'S DAY	
HALLOWEEN	✓
INDEPENDENCE DAY	✓
LABOR DAY	
MEMORIAL DAY	
MOONLIGHT	
MOTHER'S DAY	✓
MURDER MYSTERIES	
NEW YEAR	
SANTA CLAUS	
THANKSGIVING	
TRAIN ROBBERIES	
VALENTINE'S DAY	
VETERAN'S DAY	

Call for current information, schedule and fares on the above special events.

Notes

Train operates special excursions in July, August, September, and October. Group discounts and charter trips are available. Facilities are accessible to the handicapped.

Bluegrass Railroad Museum

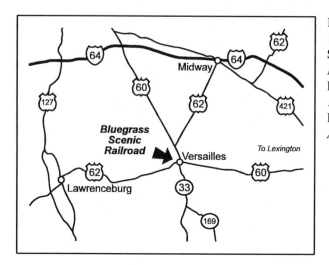

Location
Versailles
Season
May - October
Round Trip
11 Miles
Fares
Adult, $7.00

The Ride

The Bluegrass Scenic Railroad begins its journey in Versailles and takes passengers through the rolling hills and farmland of central Kentucky known as the "Bluegrass" region. The train stops midway along the 11 mile round trip and provides the opportunity for passengers to disembark and walk to the "Young's High Bridge", an historic trestle built in 1888 that is 1,658 feet long and stands 280 feet above the Kentucky River. The entire trip takes 90 minutes to complete.

All Aboard

The train departs from the museum located on Beasley Road in the Woodford County Park, 1½ miles from downtown Versailles. Versailles is about 20 minutes west of Lexington.

Schedule

The Bluegrass Scenic Railroad operates on weekends from the last weekend in May through the third weekend in October. The train departs at 10:30 a.m., 1:30 and 3:30 p.m. on Saturday and at 1:30 and 3:30 p.m. on Sunday.

Fares

The round trip fare for adults is $7.00 and $4.00 for children ages 2 through 12. Tickets for senior citizens aged 62 and over are $6.00. Children under 2 ride for free.

Ride Information

Bluegrass Railroad Museum
P.O. Box 27
Versailles, KY 40383
Phone: 800-755-2476 / 606-873-2476

Local Information

Woodford County Chamber of Commerce
P.O. Box 442
Versailles, KY 40383
Phone: 606-873-5122

Notes

Discounts for groups of 20 or more are available with advance notice. Weekday charters of non-scheduled trains are available to schools, churches, and private organizations. Tour buses are welcome. Coach rental is also available for birthday parties, weddings, etc. on regularly schedule trains. For more information contact the museum office.

SPECIAL EVENTS AND EXCURSIONS

CHILDREN'S DAY ✓
DINING:
    BRUNCH
    LUNCH
    DINNER
EASTER BUNNY
FAIRS/FESTIVALS
FALL FOLIAGE
FATHER'S DAY
GRANDPARENT'S DAY
HALLOWEEN ✓
INDEPENDENCE DAY
LABOR DAY
MEMORIAL DAY
MOONLIGHT
MOTHER'S DAY
MURDER MYSTERIES
NEW YEAR
SANTA CLAUS ✓
THANKSGIVING
TRAIN ROBBERIES ✓
VALENTINE'S DAY
VETERAN'S DAY

Call for current information, schedule and fares on the above special events.

KENTUCKY RAILWAY MUSEUM

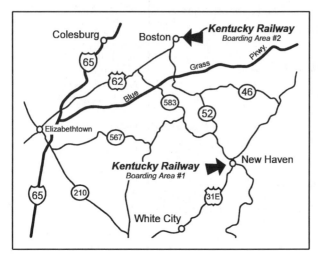

LOCATION
New Haven and Boston
SEASON
April - November
ROUND TRIP
22 Miles
FARES
Adult, $12.00

The Ride

The Kentucky Railway Museum operates a 22 mile scenic train ride through Kentucky's scenic and historic Rolling Fork River Valley, traveling through forests, fields, and farmland. The train ride takes about 1½ hours to complete including a 20 minute layover. Passengers can spend more time in either Boston or New Haven and catch a later train back. One-way trips are also available.

All Aboard

There are two areas in which passengers may board, in Boston and in New Haven. The station in New Haven is a replica of the original depot and is located at 136 South Main Street. The street address for the Boston departure location was not known at press time.

Schedule

The Train runs on weekends from April through November with additional train runs Tuesday through Friday from Memorial Day to Labor Day. Weekend departure times April 1 to May 26 and from November 11 through November 26 are 2:00 p.m. from New Haven and 3:00 p.m. from Boston. Weekday departure times are also 2:00 p.m. from New Haven and 3:00 p.m.

from Boston. From May 27 through November 5, Saturday departure times from New Haven are 11:00 a.m., 1:00 and 3:00 p.m.; Sunday 1:00 and 3:00 p.m. Departures from Boston are: Saturday 12:00 noon and 2:00 p.m.; Sunday 2:00 p.m. only.

Fares

Adult ticket prices for the train ride are $12.00, children ages 2 to 12 are $8.00. Children under 2 ride free. Admission to museum for adults is $3.00 and $2.00 for children 2 through 12. Discounts are available when museum and train ride tickets are purchased at the same time, please call or write for details.

Ride Information

Kentucky Railway Museum
P.O. Box 240
New Haven, KY 40051
Phone: 800-272-0152 / 502-549-5470

Local Information

LaRue County Chamber of Commerce
P.O. Box 176
Hodgenville, KY 42748
Phone: 502-358-3411

Bardstown - Nelson County Chamber of Commerce
P.O. Box 296
Bardstown, KY 40004
Phone: 502-348-9545
Fax: 502-348-9740

SPECIAL EVENTS AND EXCURSIONS	
CHILDREN'S DAY	
DINING:	
BRUNCH	
LUNCH	
DINNER	
EASTER BUNNY	
FAIRS/FESTIVALS	
FALL FOLIAGE	
FATHER'S DAY	✓
GRANDPARENT'S DAY	
HALLOWEEN	✓
INDEPENDENCE DAY	✓
LABOR DAY	✓
MEMORIAL DAY	✓
MOONLIGHT	
MOTHER'S DAY	✓
MURDER MYSTERIES	
NEW YEAR	
SANTA CLAUS	✓
THANKSGIVING	✓
TRAIN ROBBERIES	✓
VALENTINE'S DAY	
VETERAN'S DAY	

Call for current information, schedule and fares on the above special events.

Notes

The 3:00 p.m. departures from Boston are not round trip; passengers must provide there own transportation back to Boston. A steam locomotive powers the train on selected weekends and holidays only. Discounts for groups of 20 or more are available as are family packages and school field trip discounts. Special packages with local attractions are available for groups and charters.

BELFAST & MOOSEHEAD LAKE RR

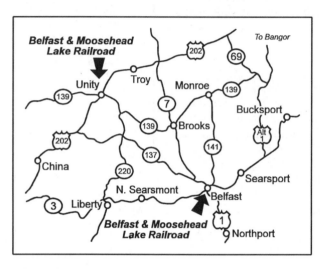

LOCATION
Belfast and Unity
SEASON
May - October
ROUND TRIP
Exc. #1, 24 Miles
Exc. #2, 18 Miles
FARES
Adult,
Exc. #1, $14.00
Exc. #2, $14.00

The Ride

Two different scenic excursion train rides are available for passengers to choose from. Both travel through the rolling fields and pristine woodlands of Waldo County. Both train rides can be coordinated with boat rides out of Belfast Harbor.

Belfast to Brooks (Excursion #1):
The diesel-powered train travels from Belfast to Brooks on a 24 mile round trip lasting approximately 1½ hours. The scenic ride follows the Passagassawakeag River through Maine's rolling farmland and over arched bridges. Passengers should always be on the lookout for the notorious "Waldo Station Gang" who have been known to rob the train.

Unity to Burnham Junction (Excursion #2):
This steam-powered excursion travels from the Victorian-style station in Unity to Burnham Junction and returns. Passengers are treated to both entertainment and a narrative history of the area on the 18 mile round trip. The train follows along Lake Winnecook and lasts for about 1½ hours.

All Aboard

Passengers may board the steam-powered excursion in Unity and the diesel-powered train ride in Belfast. The depot in Unity is located at 1 Depot Square and the Belfast depot is located at 11 Walter Street.

Schedule

Train rides operate daily June through August and the last week of September through the third week in October. Train operates on weekends through most of May and all of September. The diesel-powered train ride departs Belfast at 11:30 a.m. Steam trains departing from Unity leave at 11:30 a.m.

Fares

Fares for both excursions are the same. Adult ticket prices are $14.00, children aged 3 to 16 are $7.00. Children under 3 ride free.

Ride Information

Belfast & Moosehead Lake Railroad
One Depot Square
Unity, ME 04988
Phone: 800-392-5500 / 207-948-5500

Local Information

Belfast Area Chamber of Commerce
P.O. Box 58
Belfast, ME 04915
Phone: 207-338-5900

SPECIAL EVENTS AND EXCURSIONS	
CHILDREN'S DAY	✓
DINING:	
BRUNCH	✓
LUNCH	✓
DINNER	
EASTER BUNNY	
FAIRS/FESTIVALS	
FALL FOLIAGE	✓
FATHER'S DAY	✓
GRANDPARENT'S DAY	
HALLOWEEN	
INDEPENDENCE DAY	
LABOR DAY	
MEMORIAL DAY	
MOONLIGHT	
MOTHER'S DAY	✓
MURDER MYSTERIES	
NEW YEAR	
SANTA CLAUS	
THANKSGIVING	
TRAIN ROBBERIES	✓
VALENTINE'S DAY	
VETERAN'S DAY	

Call for current information, schedule and fares on the above special events.

Notes

First class, coach, and open-air cars available. Reservations recommended. Charters and group discounts available. Overnight getaway specials and combination train ride/riverboat excursions available. A gift shop is located at both the Unity and Belfast stations. Lunches are available on all trips.

Belfast	*Northport*	*N. Searsmont*

 110   129, 134   146   136

MAINE COAST RAILROAD

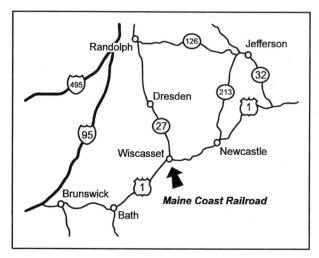

LOCATION
Wiscassett
SEASON
May - October
ROUND TRIP
14 Miles
FARES
Adult, $10.00

The Ride

This 1½ hour, 14 mile round trip ride from Wiscasset to Newcastle travels across tidal rivers and wildlife marshes of south-central Maine. In August and September "Rail & Sail" combination train ride and boat cruise are available. Passengers board the "Finback" for a narrated nature & history cruise down the Sheepscot River. The boat tour lasts about 1¼ hours.

All Aboard

The train departs the depot in Wiscasset located on Water Street just off U.S. Hwy. 1. Wiscasset is approximately 45 miles northeast of Portland.

Schedule

The train operates on weekends and holidays from Memorial Day weekend through late June and from early September through mid-October. From late June through Labor Day weekend the train operates daily. All departures times are 11:00 a.m. and 1:00 p.m. from Wiscasset.

Fares

For the train ride only the adult ticket price is $10.00 and $5.00 for children ages 5 through 15. Children 4 and under ride free. The senior citizen rate is $9.00. A family fare of $25.00 is available and applies to two adults and up to four children. Please call for the "Rail & Sail" fares and schedules.

Ride Information

Maine Coast Railroad
P.O. Box 614
Wiscasset, ME 04578
Phone: 800-795-5404 / 207-882-8000
Fax: 800-882-7699

Local Information

Wiscasset Regional Business Association
P.O. Box 150
Wiscasset, ME 04578

Damariscotta Region Chamber of Commerce
P.O. Box 13
Damariscotta, ME 04543
Phone: 207-563-8340

Boothbay Harbor Chamber of Commerce
P.O. Box 356
Boothbay Harbor, ME 04538
Phone: 207-633-2353
Fax: 207-633-7448

Boothbay Chamber of Commerce
P.O. Box 187
Boothbay, ME 04537
Phone: 207-633-4743

SPECIAL EVENTS AND EXCURSIONS	
CHILDREN'S DAY	
DINING:	
BRUNCH	
LUNCH	✓
DINNER	
EASTER BUNNY	✓
FAIRS/FESTIVALS	✓
FALL FOLIAGE	✓
FATHER'S DAY	
GRANDPARENT'S DAY	
HALLOWEEN	✓
INDEPENDENCE DAY	✓
LABOR DAY	✓
MEMORIAL DAY	✓
MOONLIGHT	
MOTHER'S DAY	
MURDER MYSTERIES	
NEW YEAR	
SANTA CLAUS	✓
THANKSGIVING	
TRAIN ROBBERIES	
VALENTINE'S DAY	
VETERAN'S DAY	

Call for current information, schedule and fares on the above special events.

Notes

Charter rates for any occasion are available as well as club and diner car for lunch or dinner service. Tour operator and group rates are also available.

WESTERN MARYLAND SCENIC RR

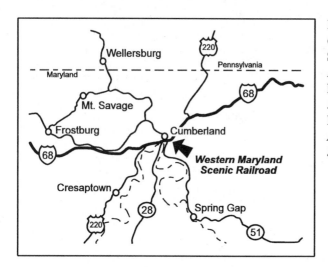

LOCATION
Cumberland
SEASON
May - December
ROUND TRIP
32 Miles
FARES
Adult,
$14.75 - $16.75

The Ride

This 32 mile, 3 hour round trip on the "Mountain Thunder" travels between Cumberland and Frostburg. Leaving Cumberland, the "Mountain Thunder" passes through a breach in the Allegheny Mountains known as The Narrows. While negotiating grades up to 2.8%, the ride continues over an iron truss bridge and around Helmstetter's Horseshoe Curve. The train finally arrives at the old depot center in Frostburg after passing through the 1000-foot long Brush Mountain Tunnel. Passengers will have a 1½ hour layover in Frostburg to enjoy a meal at the depot restaurant, shop in the old hotel or visit the Thrasher Carriage Museum. You also have the opportunity to watch the engine as it is moved onto the turntable and prepared for the return trip.

All Aboard

Passengers board the train at the Western Maryland Station Center located in Cumberland at 13 Canal Street.

Schedule

The train operates on weekends only during April and departs at 11:30 a.m.

The ride operates Tuesday through Sunday from May through September and departs at 11:30 a.m. The train departs at 11:00 a.m. and 4:00 p.m. Tuesday through Sunday in October. From November 1 through mid-December, the train operates on weekends only and departs at 11:30 a.m.

Fares

Adult ticket prices are $14.75 except in October and December when ticket prices are $16.75. Children ages 2 through 12 are $9.50 during the regular season and $10.50 in October and December. Children under 2 are free when not occupying a seat. Senior discounts available.

Ride Information

Western Maryland Scenic Railroad
13 Canal Street
Cumberland, MD 21502
Phone: 800-872-4650 / 301-759-4400
Fax: 301-759-1329

Local Information

Allegany County Chamber of Commerce
Bell Tower Building
Cumberland, MD 21502
Phone: 301-722-2820
Fax: 301-722-5995

SPECIAL EVENTS AND EXCURSIONS	
CHILDREN'S DAY	
DINING:	
BRUNCH	
LUNCH	
DINNER	
EASTER BUNNY	
FAIRS/FESTIVALS	✓
FALL FOLIAGE	✓
FATHER'S DAY	✓
GRANDPARENT'S DAY	
HALLOWEEN	✓
INDEPENDENCE DAY	
LABOR DAY	
MEMORIAL DAY	
MOONLIGHT	
MOTHER'S DAY	✓
MURDER MYSTERIES	✓
NEW YEAR	
SANTA CLAUS	✓
THANKSGIVING	
TRAIN ROBBERIES	
VALENTINE'S DAY	
VETERAN'S DAY	

Call for current information, schedule and fares on the above special events.

Notes

Group rates are available. Train charters, caboose rentals and school group pricing is also available. Please note that access for the physically challenged is limited, inform the railroad of your needs. A museum, gift shop, and restaurant are located at the depot.

 045 112

CAPE COD SCENIC RAILROAD

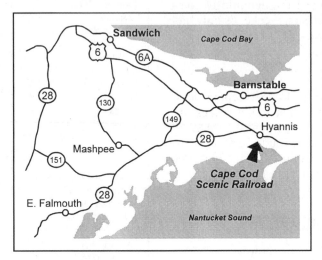

LOCATION
Hyannis
SEASON
May - October
ROUND TRIP
38 Miles
FARES
Adult, $11.50

The Ride

The Cape Cod Scenic Railroad operates a 38 mile scenic excursion on a vintage train through the heart of Cape Cod. The rail excursion begins in Hyannis and travels to the Cape Cod Canal with a stop in historic Sandwich Village. Passengers enjoy entertaining commentary on history, folklore, and facts about old Cape Cod on this 1¾ hour round trip through quaint villages, dunes and cranberry bogs. Passengers may stay in Sandwich Village to spend time visiting the many sites and board a later train back to Hyannis. Overnight packages are also available.

All Aboard

Passengers board the train at the Downtown Hyannis Station located at Main and Center streets.

Schedule

The Cape Cod Scenic Railroad operates weekends and holidays in May and daily except Monday from June through October. The train departs Hyannis at 10:00 a.m., 12:30 and 3:00 p.m.

Fares

Adult ticket prices are $11.50, children aged 3 through 12 $7.50. Senior discounts available.

Ride Information

Cape Cod Scenic Railroad
252 Main Street
Hyannis, MA 02601
Phone: 508-771-3788

Local Information

Cape Cod Chamber of Commerce
P.O. Box 16
Hyannis, MA 02601
Phone: 508-362-3225
Fax: 508-362-3698

Hyannis Area Chamber of Commerce
1481 Route 132
Hyannis, MA 02601
Phone: 508-362-5230
Fax: 508-362-9499

Cape Cod Canal Region Chamber of Commerce
70 Main Street
Buzzards Bay, MA 02532
Phone: 508-759-3122
Fax: 508-759-6965

SPECIAL EVENTS AND EXCURSIONS

CHILDREN'S DAY	
DINING:	
BRUNCH	
LUNCH	
DINNER	✓
EASTER BUNNY	
FAIRS/FESTIVALS	
FALL FOLIAGE	✓
FATHER'S DAY	✓
GRANDPARENT'S DAY	
HALLOWEEN	
INDEPENDENCE DAY	
LABOR DAY	
MEMORIAL DAY	
MOONLIGHT	
MOTHER'S DAY	✓
MURDER MYSTERIES	
NEW YEAR	✓
SANTA CLAUS	✓
THANKSGIVING	
TRAIN ROBBERIES	
VALENTINE'S DAY	✓
VETERAN'S DAY	

Call for current information, schedule and fares on the above special events.

Notes

The 3:00 p.m. train may be subject to a 45 minute layover at the canal on Sundays depending on Amtrak schedules. A dinner train operates year-round. Group rates and charters available. Food is available on all excursions.

 040   082

ADRIAN & BLISSFIELD RAILROAD

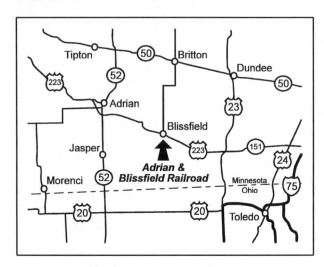

LOCATION
Blissfield
SEASON
Year-round
ROUND TRIP
18 Miles
FARES
Adult, $7.50

The Ride

Passengers begin their excursion in Blissfield for a leisurely ride on a segment of the Erie & Kalamazoo Railroad which began operations in 1836. The train travels through the rich farmland of southeastern Michigan to Lenawee Junction. The entire 18 mile round trip takes about 1½ hours to complete. The Adrian & Blissfield Railroad also offers a 2 to 2½ hour excursion aboard *The Old Road Dinner Train.* Passengers enjoy exquisite meals prepared and served in traditional, impeccable dining car style.

All Aboard

Passengers board the train at the Blissfield East Depot located on U.S. Highway 223 at Depot Street just east of downtown Blissfield or at the Blissfield West Platform located behind the Hathaway House Restaurant. Blissfield is located approximately 20 miles northwest of Toledo, Ohio.

Schedule

The Adrian & Blissfield Railroad operates on weekends from May through October. Additional rides are added on Tuesday and Thursday in July and

August. In November, the train runs only on Sunday. The train departs at 2:00 p.m. from the Blissfield East depot and approximately 10 minutes later from the Blissfield West platform. Special excursions operate January through April and in December.

Fares

The adult fare for the excursion train is $7.50 and $4.50 for children ages 3 to 12. Senior citizen tickets cost $6.50. Children under 3 years ride free. Fares for the dinner and special excursion trains vary. Please call or write for current information.

Ride Information

Adrian & Blissfield Railroad Co.
P.O. Box 95
Blissfield, MI 49228
Phone: 517-486-5979

Local Information

Blissfield Area Chamber of Commerce
P.O. Box 25
Blissfield, MI 49228
Phone: 517-486-3642 / 517-486-2236

SPECIAL EVENTS AND EXCURSIONS	
CHILDREN'S DAY	
DINING:	
BRUNCH	
LUNCH	
DINNER	✓
EASTER BUNNY	
FAIRS/FESTIVALS	
FALL FOLIAGE	✓
FATHER'S DAY	
GRANDPARENT'S DAY	
HALLOWEEN	✓
INDEPENDENCE DAY	
LABOR DAY	
MEMORIAL DAY	
MOONLIGHT	
MOTHER'S DAY	
MURDER MYSTERIES	✓
NEW YEAR	✓
SANTA CLAUS	✓
THANKSGIVING	
TRAIN ROBBERIES	✓
VALENTINE'S DAY	
VETERAN'S DAY	

Call for current information, schedule and fares on the above special events.

Notes

Group rates and charters available. Reservations are not required for the regular excursions but are required for the dinner train and special event runs.

🛏 077

COE RAIL SCENIC TRAIN

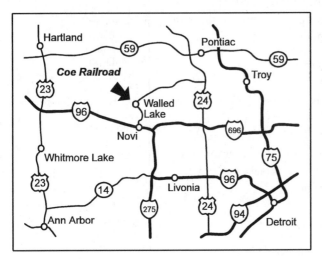

LOCATION
Walled Lake
SEASON
April - October
ROUND TRIP
10½ Miles
FARES
Adult, $7.00

The Ride

The Coe Rail Scenic Train offers a 10½ mile round trip ride through the scenic countryside of the West Bloomfield Bird Sanctuary and Wetlands. The entire round trip lasts approximately 1 hour.

All Aboard

The train departs Walled Lake from the depot located at 840 North Pontiac Trail. Walled Lake is approximately 30 miles northwest of downtown Detroit.

Schedule

The Coe Rail Scenic Train operates on Sunday only from April through October. The train departs at 1:00 p.m. and 2:30 p.m.

Fares

The adult ticket price is $7.00 and $6.00 for seniors aged 65 and over. Children ages 2 through 10 are $6.00. Children under 2 ride free.

Ride Information

Coe Railroad
840 North Pontiac Trail
Walled Lake, MI 48390
Phone: 810-960-9440

Local Information

Lakes Area Chamber of Commerce
305 North Pontiac Trail - #B
Walled Lake, MI 48390
Phone: 810-624-2826
Fax: 810-624-2892

Notes

Group discounts and chartered trips available. Facilities are accessible to the handicapped. Coe Railroad also operates the *Michigan Star Clipper Dinner Train.* Passengers enjoy a 3 hour scenic train ride while being treated to a 4-star, 5-course dinner prepared fresh on board. The dining excursion operates Tuesday through Sunday, year-round, with evening departures. It is also possible to reserve a private sleeping compartment for an overnight train experience. Proper attire and reservations are required. The dining excursion is for adults only.

SPECIAL EVENTS AND EXCURSIONS	
CHILDREN'S DAY	
DINING:	
BRUNCH	
LUNCH	✓
DINNER	✓
EASTER BUNNY	
FAIRS/FESTIVALS	
FALL FOLIAGE	✓
FATHER'S DAY	
GRANDPARENT'S DAY	
HALLOWEEN	✓
INDEPENDENCE DAY	
LABOR DAY	
MEMORIAL DAY	
MOONLIGHT	
MOTHER'S DAY	
MURDER MYSTERIES	✓
NEW YEAR	✓
SANTA CLAUS	
THANKSGIVING	
TRAIN ROBBERIES	
VALENTINE'S DAY	
VETERAN'S DAY	

Call for current information, schedule and fares on the above special events.

 047

COOPERSVILLE & MARNE RAILWAY

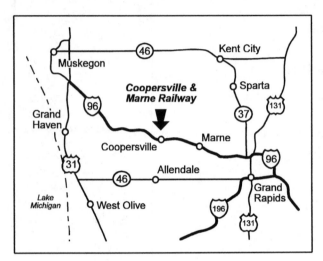

LOCATION
Coopersville
SEASON
July - December
ROUND TRIP
12 Miles
FARES
Adult, $7.50

The Ride

The Coopersville & Marne Railway operates a 12 mile round trip excursion through the woods and farmland of west-central Michigan. The train travels between the towns of Coopersville and Marne. The entire round trip ride takes about 1 hour to complete.

All Aboard

Passengers board the train at the depot in downtown Coopersville. The depot is located at the corner of Eastmanville and Danforth. Coopersville is about 15 miles west of Grand Rapids just off I-96. Follow the "Ride the Train" signs to the depot.

Schedule

The Coopersville & Marne Railway operates train rides on Saturdays only from early July through late September. The train departs the depot at 1:00 and 3:00 p.m. Additional runs are added on Sundays during October and December.

Fares

Ticket prices for adults are $7.50 and for children ages 3 through 13, $4.50. Senior citizens receive a $1.00 discount on the purchase price of their ticket. Children under 3 ride for free.

Ride Information

The Coopersville & Marne Railway Company
P.O. Box 55
Coopersville, MI 49404
Phone: 616-837-7000

Local Information

Coopersville Area Chamber of Commerce
P.O. Box 135
Coopersville, MI 49404
Phone: 616-837-9731

Notes

Group discounts are available and the entire train is available for charter. Reservations are not required for the regularly scheduled runs. Trains operate rain or shine. In Coopersville a railroad gift shop is located next to the depot in the "Yellow Caboose."

SPECIAL EVENTS AND EXCURSIONS

CHILDREN'S DAY	
DINING:	
BRUNCH	
LUNCH	
DINNER	✓
EASTER BUNNY	
FAIRS/FESTIVALS	✓
FALL FOLIAGE	
FATHER'S DAY	
GRANDPARENT'S DAY	
HALLOWEEN	✓
INDEPENDENCE DAY	
LABOR DAY	
MEMORIAL DAY	
MOONLIGHT	
MOTHER'S DAY	
MURDER MYSTERIES	✓
NEW YEAR	
SANTA CLAUS	✓
THANKSGIVING	✓
TRAIN ROBBERIES	✓
VALENTINE'S DAY	
VETERAN'S DAY	

Call for current information, schedule and fares on the above special events.

LITTLE RIVER RAILROAD

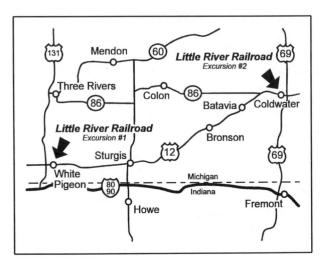

LOCATION
White Pigeon and Coldwater
SEASON
June - October
ROUND TRIP
Exc. #1, 25 Miles
Exc. #2, 10 Miles
FARES
Adult,
Exc. #1, $15.00
Exc. #2, $7.00

The Ride

White Pigeon to Sturgis (Excursion #1): This scenic train ride is a 25 mile, 2½ hour round trip beginning in White Pigeon and runs to Sturgis. Passengers layover in Sturgis for 30 minutes while the engine is serviced and switched for the return trip.

The Batavia Flyer (Excursion #2): This train ride begins in Coldwater and travels across farmland to Batavia. The 10 mile round trip takes approximately 1 hour and 20 minutes to complete.

All Aboard

Excursion #1: In White Pigeon, passengers board the train at the depot located at the intersection of W. Peck Street and St. Joseph Street.

Excursion #2: The depot for this excursion is located on Park Avenue, just east of Division Street in Coldwater.

Schedule

Excursion #1: Train rides operate on Sundays in June, July, and October and departs at 1:30 p.m.

Excursion #2: Train operates on Sundays in August and September and departs at 1:00 p.m. and 3:00 p.m.

Fares

Excursion #1: Adult ticket prices are $15.00, children ages 3 through 11 are $8.00. Special family rates are available.

Excursion #2: Adult tickets cost $7.00 and children 3 to 11, $4.00.

Ride Information

Little River Railroad
13187 State Route 120
Middlebury, IN 46540
Phone: 219-825-9182

Local Information

Excursion #1:
Sturgis Area Chamber of Commerce
P.O. Box 165
Sturgis, MI 49091
Phone: 616-651-5758
Fax: 616-651-4124

Excursion #2:
Coldwater/Branch County Chamber of Commerce
20 Division Street
Coldwater, MI 49036
Phone: 800-968-9333 / 517-278-5985
Fax: 517-278-8369

SPECIAL EVENTS AND EXCURSIONS	
CHILDREN'S DAY	
DINING:	
BRUNCH	
LUNCH	
DINNER	
EASTER BUNNY	
FAIRS/FESTIVALS	✓
FALL FOLIAGE	✓
FATHER'S DAY	✓
GRANDPARENT'S DAY	
HALLOWEEN	✓
INDEPENDENCE DAY	✓
LABOR DAY	
MEMORIAL DAY	✓
MOONLIGHT	
MOTHER'S DAY	
MURDER MYSTERIES	
NEW YEAR	
SANTA CLAUS	
THANKSGIVING	
TRAIN ROBBERIES	✓
VALENTINE'S DAY	
VETERAN'S DAY	

Call for current information, schedule and fares on the above special events.

Notes

Group rates and charters are available. Fares are slightly higher when train runs for special events. Facilities are accessible to the physically challenged.

Coldwater	*Union*
🛏 102	🛏 090

Southern Michigan Railroad

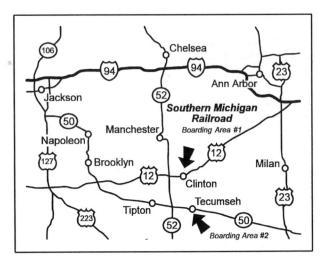

Location
Clinton and Tecumseh
Season
June - September
Round Trip
9 Miles
Fares
Adult, $7.00

The Ride

The Southern Michigan Railroad operates an excursion train between Clinton and Tecumseh during summer months. Passengers aboard the 9 mile round trip can begin their journey in either Clinton or Tecumseh. The route of the train travels through a wildlife area, crosses a wooden bridge over the Raisin River and the Evans Creek. The entire trip takes about 2 hours to complete. During the Fall, another excursion train runs from Tecumseh to Raisin Center.

All Aboard

Passengers can board in either Clinton or Tecumseh. The depot in Clinton is located at 320 South Division Street and the Tecumseh depot is at the northeast corner of Chicago Blvd. and Evans Street.

Schedule

The Southern Michigan Railroad operates on Sunday only from early June through mid-September. Departures from Clinton are 11:00 a.m., 1:00 and 3:00 p.m. The train departs from Tecumseh at 12:00 noon, 2:00 and 4:00

p.m. The 4:00 p.m. train is a one-way trip to Clinton. Passengers can also choose to stay longer in either Tecumseh or Clinton and take another train back to the origin of departure.

Fares

Adult tickets cost $7.00, children ages 2 through 12 are $4.00. Seniors over 65 receive a $1.00 discount.

Ride Information

Southern Michigan Railroad Society
P.O. Box K
Clinton, MI 49236
Phone: 517-423-7230

Local Information

Tecumseh Area Chamber of Commerce
P.O. Box 265
Tecumseh, MI 49286
Phone: 517-423-3740

Lenawee County Chamber of Commerce
202 North Main Street - Suite A
Adrian, MI 49221
Phone: 517-265-5141
Fax: 517-263-6065

SPECIAL EVENTS AND EXCURSIONS	
CHILDREN'S DAY	✓
DINING:	
BRUNCH	
LUNCH	
DINNER	
EASTER BUNNY	
FAIRS/FESTIVALS	✓
FALL FOLIAGE	✓
FATHER'S DAY	
GRANDPARENT'S DAY	
HALLOWEEN	✓
INDEPENDENCE DAY	
LABOR DAY	
MEMORIAL DAY	
MOONLIGHT	
MOTHER'S DAY	
MURDER MYSTERIES	
NEW YEAR	
SANTA CLAUS	
THANKSGIVING	
TRAIN ROBBERIES	
VALENTINE'S DAY	
VETERAN'S DAY	

Call for current information, schedule and fares on the above special events.

Notes

Group rates and charters are available. Children under 12 years old must be accompanied by an adult. A museum and gift shop are located in the Clinton depot.

Tecumseh

 031   126

BRANSON SCENIC RAILWAY

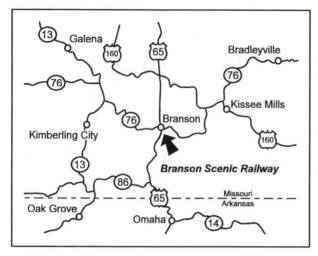

LOCATION
Branson
SEASON
March - December
ROUND TRIP
40 Miles
FARES
Adult, $18.50

The Ride

The Branson Scenic Railway excursion train departs from historic downtown Branson. The ride crosses rivers, high trestles and passes through tunnels as the train rolls through the Ozark hills and valleys. The entire trip is 40 miles long and takes approximately two hours to complete.

All Aboard

Passengers board the train at 206 E. Main Street, 5 blocks east of Highway 65 in downtown Branson.

Schedule

The Branson Scenic Railway operates Monday through Saturday from April through September. During the month of October, the train operates daily. In March, November and December, the train departs Wednesday through Saturday. Departure times are 8:30 a.m., 11:00 a.m., and 2:00 p.m. During the months of June, July, August, and October a 4:30 p.m. departure time is added.

Fares

Adult tickets are $18.50; children ages 3 to 12, $8.75; students aged 13 through 18, $13.50; seniors (55 and over) $17.50. Children under 3 ride free.

Ride Information

Branson Scenic Railway
206 East Main Street
Branson, MO 65616
Phone: 800-287-2462 / 417-334-6110
Fax: 417-336-3909

Local Information

Branson/Lakes Area Chamber of Commerce
P.O. Box 1897
Branson, MO 65615
Phone: 417-334-4136
Fax: 417-334-4139

Notes

Group rates and charters are available. Facilities are accessible to the physically challenged. All trains are non-smoking.

SPECIAL EVENTS AND EXCURSIONS

CHILDREN'S DAY
DINING:
    BRUNCH ✓
    LUNCH ✓
    DINNER
EASTER BUNNY
FAIRS/FESTIVALS
FALL FOLIAGE ✓
FATHER'S DAY
GRANDPARENT'S DAY
HALLOWEEN ✓
INDEPENDENCE DAY ✓
LABOR DAY ✓
MEMORIAL DAY ✓
MOONLIGHT
MOTHER'S DAY
MURDER MYSTERIES ✓
NEW YEAR
SANTA CLAUS ✓
THANKSGIVING
TRAIN ROBBERIES
VALENTINE'S DAY
VETERAN'S DAY ✓

Call for current information, schedule and fares on the above special events.

Smoky Hill Railway

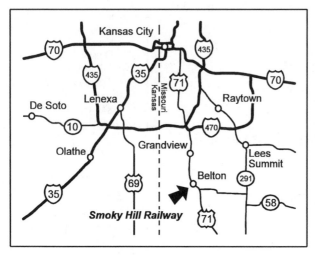

LOCATION
Belton
SEASON
April - October
ROUND TRIP
5 Miles
FARES
Adult, $5.75

The Ride

Passengers on the Smoky Hill Railway enjoy a 5 mile round trip on trackage originally built in 1871. Vintage passenger cars take travelers through the scenic woods and farmland of western Missouri. The entire round trip from Belton takes about 45 minutes to complete.

All Aboard

Passengers board the train from the depot in downtown Belton located at 502 Walnut Street. Belton is a community located on the southeastern edge of Kansas City.

Schedule

The Smoky Hill Railway operates on Saturdays, Sundays, and holidays from early April through October. The train departs at 2:00 p.m. Extra trains are frequently operated during the week, please call or write for schedule information.

Fares

The adult ticket price is $5.75 and $5.50 for seniors aged 55 and over. Tickets for children 12 and under cost $4.50. Tickets can be purchased at the depot which opens 1 hour before departure.

Ride Information

Smoky Hill Railway
502 Walnut Street
Belton, MO 64012
Phone: 816-331-0630

Local Information

Belton Chamber of Commerce
P.O. Box 350
Belton, MO 64012
Phone: 816-331-2420

Notes

Reservations are required for groups of 20 or more. Chartered trains available. Persons that are handicapped and require special services are asked to contact the manager 10 days prior to riding the train so arrangements may be made. A gift shop is located in a baggage car next to the depot. Displays of historic cars are on the grounds of the depot.

SPECIAL EVENTS AND EXCURSIONS

CHILDREN'S DAY
DINING:
    BRUNCH
    LUNCH
    DINNER
EASTER BUNNY
FAIRS/FESTIVALS
FALL FOLIAGE
FATHER'S DAY
GRANDPARENT'S DAY
HALLOWEEN   ✓
INDEPENDENCE DAY
LABOR DAY   ✓
MEMORIAL DAY   ✓
MOONLIGHT
MOTHER'S DAY
MURDER MYSTERIES
NEW YEAR
SANTA CLAUS
THANKSGIVING
TRAIN ROBBERIES
VALENTINE'S DAY
VETERAN'S DAY

Call for current information, schedule and fares on the above special events.

St. Louis, Iron Mountain

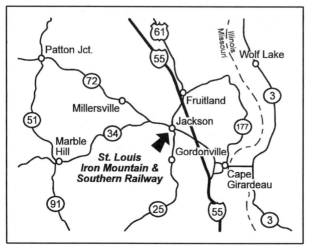

LOCATION
Jackson
SEASON
April - October
ROUND TRIP
10 Miles
FARES
Adult, $10.00

The Ride

The St. Louis, Iron Mountain & Southern Railway operates a 10 mile round trip excursion beginning in Jackson and traveling to the country stop in Gordonville where there is a 10 minute layover before the return trip. The train travels on track that is over one hundred years old through the scenic countryside of Cape Girardeau County in southeastern Missouri. The round trip takes approximately 1 hour and 20 minutes to travel. Longer dinner excursions to Dutchtown (16 miles) and Delta (36 miles) are also available.

All Aboard

All rides originate and end in Jackson. Passengers board the train in Jackson at the depot located at the intersection of U.S. Highway 61 and State Highway 25. Jackson is approximately 100 miles south of St. Louis.

Schedule

The St. Louis, Iron Mountain & Southern Railway operates on weekends from April through October. The train departs Jackson at 11:00 a.m. and 2:00 p.m. on Saturday and at 1:00 and 3:00 p.m. on Sunday. An additional train runs at 1:00 p.m. on Wednesday and Friday in June, July, and August.

Fares

Adult ticket price is $10.00 and $5.00 for children ages 3 through 12. Children 2 and under ride free.

Ride Information

St. Louis, Iron Mountain & Southern Railway
P.O. Box 244
Jackson, MO 63755
Phone: 800-455-7245 / 314-243-1688

Local Information

Jackson Chamber of Commerce
P.O. Box 352
Jackson, MO 63755
Phone: 314-243-8131

Notes

Group rates and weekday charters are available. Facilities are accessible to the physically challenged. Reservations are suggested for all excursions. Refreshments are available on the train. A gift shop and restaurant are located at the depot. A steam engine is used only during the warmer months.

SPECIAL EVENTS AND EXCURSIONS	
CHILDREN'S DAY	
DINING:	
BRUNCH	✓
LUNCH	✓
DINNER	✓
EASTER BUNNY	✓
FAIRS/FESTIVALS	✓
FALL FOLIAGE	✓
FATHER'S DAY	✓
GRANDPARENT'S DAY	
HALLOWEEN	✓
INDEPENDENCE DAY	
LABOR DAY	
MEMORIAL DAY	
MOONLIGHT	
MOTHER'S DAY	✓
MURDER MYSTERIES	✓
NEW YEAR	✓
SANTA CLAUS	✓
THANKSGIVING	
TRAIN ROBBERIES	✓
VALENTINE'S DAY	✓
VETERAN'S DAY	✓

Call for current information, schedule and fares on the above special events.

FREMONT & ELKHORN VALLEY RR

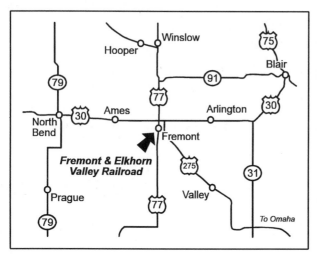

LOCATION
Fremont
SEASON
April - December
ROUND TRIP
30 Miles
FARES
Adult,
$11.00 - $14.00

The Ride

Passengers on this scenic train ride depart Fremont and travel to the historic town of Hooper, passing through the scenic Elkhorn Valley. Riding on rail cars dating from the 1920s, the 30 mile round trip lasts approximately 3 hours, including a 30 minute layover in Hooper. Hooper's 1890's Main Street is listed on the National Register of Historic Places. The Fremont and Elkhorn Valley Railroad also offers a shorter train ride to Nickerson, a 16 mile round trip from Fremont.

All Aboard

The Fremont & Elkhorn Valley Railroad depot is located at 1835 N. Somers Avenue in Fremont, about 35 miles northwest of Omaha.

Schedule

The train operates on Sundays in April, November, and December departing at 2:00 p.m. Train departs at 1:00 p.m. on Saturday and 2:00 p.m. on Sunday from May through October. Rides to Nickerson operate Monday through Friday from June through August; departure time is 2:00 p.m.

Fares

Adult ticket prices for the ride to Hooper are $11.00 and $14.00 (air-conditioned cars), children ages 3 to 12, $6.00 and $9.00. Prices for the 16 mile round trip to Nickerson are $6.50 for adults and $4.00 for children. Children under 3 ride free.

Ride Information

Fremont & Elkhorn Valley Railroad
1835 North Somers
Fremont, NE 68025
Phone: 800-942-7245 / 402-727-0615

Local Information

Fremont Area Chamber of Commerce
P.O. Box 182
Fremont, NE 68025
Phone: 402-721-2641
Fax: 402-721-9359

Notes

Group rates and charters are available. Special run times are possible. Please call for information and prices. Reservations are required during the months of April, November, and December. A museum and gift shop are located in the depot.

SPECIAL EVENTS AND EXCURSIONS	
CHILDREN'S DAY	
DINING:	
BRUNCH	
LUNCH	
DINNER	
EASTER BUNNY	
FAIRS/FESTIVALS	
FALL FOLIAGE	
FATHER'S DAY	
GRANDPARENT'S DAY	
HALLOWEEN	
INDEPENDENCE DAY	✓
LABOR DAY	✓
MEMORIAL DAY	✓
MOONLIGHT	
MOTHER'S DAY	
MURDER MYSTERIES	
NEW YEAR	
SANTA CLAUS	✓
THANKSGIVING	
TRAIN ROBBERIES	
VALENTINE'S DAY	
VETERAN'S DAY	

Call for current information, schedule and fares on the above special events.

 035

NEVADA NORTHERN RAILWAY

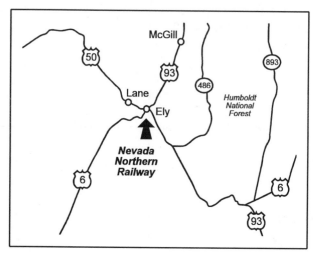

LOCATION
Ely
SEASON
May - September
ROUND TRIP
Exc. #1, 22 Miles
Exc. #2, 14 Miles
FARES
Adult,
Exc. #1, $14.00
Exc. #2, $10.00

The Ride

Hiliner Route (Excursion #1): The Hiliner Route is a 22 mile, 1¾ hour round trip that takes passengers from Ely to "Adverse" near McGill and offers views of the scenic Steptoe Valley from high in the foothills.

Keystone Route (Excursion #2): This 14 mile, 1½ hour round trip takes passengers through a curved tunnel (one of only a few curved tunnels in the world), the ghost town of Lane City, and up the Robinson Canyon to the historic mining district of Keystone.

All Aboard

All trains depart from the museum's depot located at Avenue A and 11th Street in Ely. Ely is in east-central Nevada.

Schedule

Excursion #1: The steam-powered train operates on Saturdays and some Sundays from late May to Labor Day. Departure times are 1:00 p.m. and 3:30 p.m.

Excursion #2: This diesel-powered excursion train operates on Saturdays only from late May to Labor Day. Departure time is 5:30 p.m.

Fares

Excursion #1: Adult ticket prices are $14.00; juniors (ages 12 to 18) $12.00; Seniors (age 65 and over) $12.00; children ages 5 to 11 are $6.00. Children under 5 ride free when accompanied by an adult.

Excursion #2: Adults, $10.00; juniors and seniors, $8.00; children, $4.00.

Ride Information

Nevada Northern Railway Museum
P.O. Box 150040
East Ely, NV 89315
Phone: 702-289-2085
Fax: 702-289-6284

Local Information

Excursions #1 and #2:
White Pine Chamber of Commerce
636 Aultman Street
Ely, NV 89301
Phone: 702-289-8877
Fax: 702-289-6144

SPECIAL EVENTS AND EXCURSIONS

CHILDREN'S DAY
DINING:
    BRUNCH
    LUNCH
    DINNER
EASTER BUNNY
FAIRS/FESTIVALS   ✓
FALL FOLIAGE
FATHER'S DAY
GRANDPARENT'S DAY
HALLOWEEN
INDEPENDENCE DAY   ✓
LABOR DAY   ✓
MEMORIAL DAY   ✓
MOONLIGHT
MOTHER'S DAY
MURDER MYSTERIES
NEW YEAR
SANTA CLAUS
THANKSGIVING
TRAIN ROBBERIES
VALENTINE'S DAY
VETERAN'S DAY

Call for current information, schedule and fares on the above special events.

Notes

Discounted prices available when both excursion tickets are purchased together. Group rates and charters are available. Facilities are accessible to the handicapped. Walking guided tours of the railroad facility and museum are offered. A gift shop is also located at the museum.

 046   087, 125   144

VIRGINIA & TRUCKEE RAILROAD

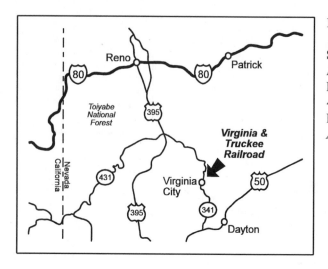

LOCATION
Virginia City
SEASON
May - October
ROUND TRIP
4 Miles
FARES
Adult, $4.50

The Ride

The Virginia & Truckee Railroad offers a 4 mile round trip beginning in Virginia City to the historic town of Gold Hill. The route of the steam train follows the original 126 year old right-of-way and passes through some of the most famous Comstock mines. Passengers can choose to stay in historic Gold Hill and return on the next train (except the last train of the day). The round trip lasts for approximately 35 minutes.

All Aboard

Passengers board the train at the depot in Virginia City located on "F" Street, one block south of Washington Street. Virginia City is located about 20 miles southeast of Reno.

Schedule

The round trip train ride operates daily from the end of May to the beginning of October. The train departs Virginia City approximately every 50 minutes starting at 10:30 a.m. through 5:45 p.m.

Fares

The round trip fare for adults is $4.50 and for children $2.25. An all day pass is available for $9.00.

Ride Information

Virginia & Truckee Railroad Company
P.O. Box 467
Virginia City, NV 89440
Phone: 702-847-0380

Local Information

Virginia City Chamber of Commerce
P.O. Box 464
Virginia City, NV 89440
Phone: 702-847-0311
Fax: 702-847-0999

Notes

Passengers can choose to ride in open-air cars or the caboose. A closed in car is available for cold weather days. Special excursion and chartered trains available. Group discounts are available. Facilities are accessible to the physically challenged. All trips are narrated by the conductor.

SPECIAL EVENTS AND EXCURSIONS
CHILDREN'S DAY
DINING:
BRUNCH
LUNCH
DINNER
EASTER BUNNY
FAIRS/FESTIVALS
FALL FOLIAGE
FATHER'S DAY
GRANDPARENT'S DAY
HALLOWEEN
INDEPENDENCE DAY
LABOR DAY ✓
MEMORIAL DAY ✓
MOONLIGHT ✓
MOTHER'S DAY
MURDER MYSTERIES
NEW YEAR
SANTA CLAUS
THANKSGIVING
TRAIN ROBBERIES
VALENTINE'S DAY
VETERAN'S DAY

Call for current information, schedule and fares on the above special events.

 024, 027

 050

CONWAY SCENIC RAILROAD

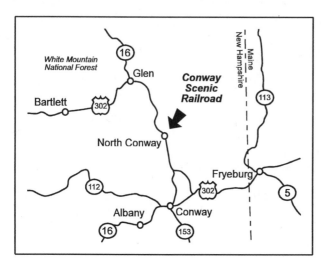

LOCATION
North Conway
SEASON
April - December
ROUND TRIP
Exc. #1, 11 Miles
Exc. #2, 21 Miles
Exc. #3, 50 Miles
FARES
Adult,
Exc. #1, $8.00
Exc. #2, $13.50
Exc. #3, $31.95

The Ride

The Conway Scenic Railroad offers rail excursions of varying duration aboard open-air and enclosed vintage coaches through the scenic Mt. Washington Valley countryside (the "Valley" Train) and through spectacular Crawford Notch (the "Notch" Train). The "Valley" Train carries passengers across several river and stream crossings, through scenic woodlands and fields offering views of the surrounding White Mountains. The "Notch" Train carries passengers through some of the finest scenery in the entire Northeast — steep ravines, cascading brooks and streams, wide mountain vistas and across the famed Frankenstein Trestle and Willey Brook Bridge.

Excursion #1: This 11 mile, 55 minute scenic round trip travels south to Conway, powered by steam or early diesel locomotive.

Excursion #2: Powered by early diesel locomotive, this 1¾ hour, 21 mile round trip travels to Bartlett and return.

Excursion #3: Powered by twin FP-9 locomotives, this 5 hour, 50 mile excursion travels through spectacular Crawford Notch to Crawford Notch Depot and return.

All Aboard

Passengers board all trains at the restored 1874 train station located in the heart of North Conway on Norcross Circle, off of U.S. Highway 302/New Hampshire Route 16.

Schedule

Excursion #1: Train operates on weekends from April 20 to May 17 with departure times of 12:00 noon and 2:00 p.m. The train departs daily at 12:00 noon from May 18 to June 14 except Memorial Day weekend when the train departs at 10:30 a.m., 1:30 p.m., and 4:30 p.m. From June 15 to October 20, the train operates daily and departs at 10:30 a.m., 1:30 p.m., and 4:30 p.m. The daily departure time from October 21 through October 27 is 12:00 noon. The train departs at 12:00 noon and 2:00 p.m. on weekends from November through mid-December.

Excursion #2: This train ride operates daily at 2:00 p.m. from May 18 to June 14 except on Memorial Day weekend when an 11:30 a.m. departure time is added. From June 15 to October 20, the train operates daily and departs at 11:30 a.m. and 2:30 p.m. A 6:30 p.m. departure time is added on certain dates from June through October, call for details.

Excursion #3: Train departs daily at 11:00 a.m. from June 22 to October 18, except Mondays in July and August.

Fares

Excursion #1: Adult coach class ticket prices are $8.00, first class $10.00; children ages 4 to 12 are $5.50 for coach and $7.50 first class; Children under 4 ride free in coach class, cost for first class is $4.00.

Excursion #2: Coach class adult ticket prices are $13.50, first class $16.50; children ages 4 to 12, coach $8.50, first class $11.50; children under 4 are $2.50 (coach) and $7.00 (first class)

Excursion #3: All fares are for coach class tickets. Adults $31.95; children ages 4 to 12 are $16.95; children under 4 are $4.95. Limited upgrade is available for an additional $5.00 per ticket.

Ride Information

Conway Scenic Railroad
P.O. Box 1947
North Conway, NH 03860
Phone: 603-356-5251

Local Information

Mt. Washington Valley Chamber
  of Commerce and Visitors Bureau
P.O. Box 2300
North Conway, NH 03860
Phone: 800-367-3364 / 603-356-3171
Fax: 603-356-7069

Notes

Group rates and charters available. Reservations are strongly recommended for Excursion #3. Reservations are available starting May 18. Facilities are accessible to the handicapped. A gift shop, snack bar, and free museum are located in the station. The Dining Car "Chocorua" offers lunch and dinner on the "Valley" train. Lunch is available Tuesday through Sunday, July 4 through October 20. Dinner is available on all "Sunset" departures, Tuesday through Saturday, July through Labor Day and on Thursday, Friday, and Saturday, Labor Day through October 19. Please call for schedule and menu.

SPECIAL EVENTS AND EXCURSIONS	
CHILDREN'S DAY	
DINING:	
BRUNCH	
LUNCH	✓
DINNER	✓
EASTER BUNNY	✓
FAIRS/FESTIVALS	✓
FALL FOLIAGE	✓
FATHER'S DAY	✓
GRANDPARENT'S DAY	
HALLOWEEN	✓
INDEPENDENCE DAY	
LABOR DAY	
MEMORIAL DAY	
MOONLIGHT	
MOTHER'S DAY	✓
MURDER MYSTERIES	
NEW YEAR	
SANTA CLAUS	✓
THANKSGIVING	✓
TRAIN ROBBERIES	
VALENTINE'S DAY	
VETERAN'S DAY	

Call for current information, schedule and fares on the above special events.

Mt. Washington Cog Railway

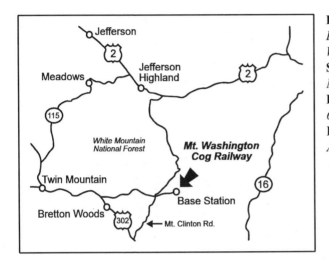

LOCATION
Base of Mt. Washington
SEASON
May - October
ROUND TRIP
6½ Miles
FARES
Adult, $35.00

The Ride

Built in 1869, the Mt. Washington Cog Railway was considered an engineering marvel in its time. This was the world's first mountain climbing cog railway and today it is the only one in operation powered completely by coal-fired steam. The 6½ mile round trip to the summit of Mt. Washington is the second steepest railway track in the world. Travelers cross "Jacob's Ladder", a trestle with an incredible 37% grade, as they ascend to the Northeast's highest peak on one of eight available trains. On some days, the view from the top spans four states, Canada and the Atlantic Ocean. The round trip takes 3 hours to complete, including a 20 minute stop at the summit.

All Aboard

Passengers board at the Base Station located east of U.S. Highway 302 on Base Station Road.

Schedule

The cog railway operates on weekends in May and daily from June through

October. The train departs hourly from early morning to late afternoon during summer. The spring and fall schedules may vary. Please call or write for complete details.

Fares

Adult ticket prices are $35.00; children ages 6 through 12, $24.00; seniors aged 62 and over are $32.00.

Ride Information

Mt. Washington Cog Railway
Route 302
Bretton Woods, NH 03589
Phone: 800-922-8825 ext. 6
          603-278-5404 ext. 6 (in NH)
Fax: 603-278-5830

Local Information

Twin Mountain - Bretton
   Woods Chamber of Commerce
P.O. Box 194
Twin Mountain, NH 03595
Phone: 800-245-8946

SPECIAL EVENTS AND EXCURSIONS
CHILDREN'S DAY
DINING:
BRUNCH
LUNCH ✓
DINNER
EASTER BUNNY
FAIRS/FESTIVALS
FALL FOLIAGE
FATHER'S DAY
GRANDPARENT'S DAY
HALLOWEEN
INDEPENDENCE DAY
LABOR DAY
MEMORIAL DAY
MOONLIGHT
MOTHER'S DAY
MURDER MYSTERIES
NEW YEAR
SANTA CLAUS
THANKSGIVING
TRAIN ROBBERIES
VALENTINE'S DAY
VETERAN'S DAY
Call for current information, schedule and fares on the above special events.

Notes

Group rates and charters are available. A gift shop, restaurant, and museum are located at the base of the mountain. Advance ticket purchase is strongly recommended. A jacket or sweater is recommended as well as a camera and lots of film. Passengers can return on a later train but your seats are only guaranteed for the train you go up on, if no seats are available on the next train you will have to stand on the way down, it takes around 1½ hours.

BLACK RIVER & WESTERN RR

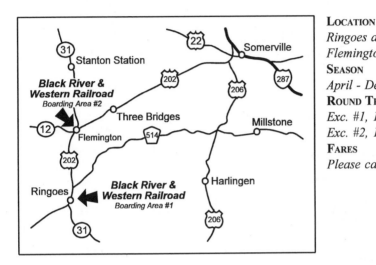

LOCATION
Ringoes and Flemington
SEASON
April - December
ROUND TRIP
Exc. #1, 10 Miles
Exc. #2, 14 Miles
FARES
Please call

The Ride

Ringoes To Flemington (Excursion #1):
This 10 mile round trip takes passengers through New Jersey's scenic farmland as it travels between Ringoes and Flemington.

Ringoes To Lambertville (Excursion #2):
This excursion train travels to Lambertville, which is situated near the Delaware River. The length of the round trip ride is 14 miles.

All Aboard

Excursion #1: Passengers may board at either the Ringoes Station or the Flemington Station. The Ringoes Station is located ¾ of a mile east of the junction of U.S. Highway 202 and State Highway 31 on County Road 579. The Flemington Station is located off State Highway 12 in Flemington.

Excursion #2: All train runs depart from the Ringoes Station described above.

Schedule

Excursion #1: Train operates on weekends only from April through December except in July and August when the train operates on Thursday and

Friday. Departure times from Ringoes are 10:45 a.m., 12:15, 1:45 and 3:15 p.m. Departures from Flemington are 11:30 a.m., 1:00 and 2:30 p.m.

Excursion #2: The train operates on Sundays only from May through October, departing from Ringoes at 12:30, 2:30 and 4:30 p.m.

Fares

Please call or write for current fares.

Ride Information

Black River & Western Railroad
P.O. Box 200
Ringoes, NJ 08551
Phone: 908-782-6622

Local Information

Excursions #1 and #2:
Hunterdon County Chamber of Commerce
2200 Route 31 - Suite 15
Lebanon, NJ 08833
Phone: 908-735-5955 *Fax:* 908-730-6580

Excursion #2:
Lambertville Area Chamber of Commerce
4 South Union Street
Lambertville, NJ 08530
Phone: 609-397-0055 *Fax:* 609-397-1530

SPECIAL EVENTS AND EXCURSIONS	
CHILDREN'S DAY	
DINING:	
BRUNCH	
LUNCH	
DINNER	✓
EASTER BUNNY	✓
FAIRS/FESTIVALS	✓
FALL FOLIAGE	✓
FATHER'S DAY	
GRANDPARENT'S DAY	
HALLOWEEN	✓
INDEPENDENCE DAY	✓
LABOR DAY	✓
MEMORIAL DAY	✓
MOONLIGHT	✓
MOTHER'S DAY	
MURDER MYSTERIES	✓
NEW YEAR	
SANTA CLAUS	✓
THANKSGIVING	
TRAIN ROBBERIES	✓
VALENTINE'S DAY	
VETERAN'S DAY	✓

Call for current information, schedule and fares on the above special events.

Notes

Groups rates and charters are available. The Ringoes to Flemington excursion operates evening trains on various days of the season, inquire for details. A museum and gift shop are located at the Ringoes Station and the Lambertville Station. One-way trips available except on Train Robbery and Santa Claus Train.

Flemington	*Ringoes*
🎁 132	🚩 012

CUMBRES & TOLTEC SCENIC RR

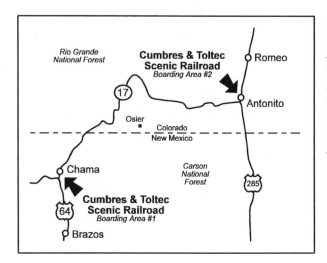

LOCATION
*Chama, NM and
Antonito, CO*
SEASON
May - October
ROUND TRIP
64 Miles
FARES
Adult, $34.00

The Ride

This authentic narrow-gauge steam excursion travels 64 miles through peaks and valleys of the scenic Rockies. The Cumbres & Toltec Scenic Railroad (the longest and highest narrow-gauge steam railroad in America) is a registered National Historic Site. Trains depart from Chama, New Mexico and from Antonito, Colorado and travel to the half-way point in Osier, Colorado. After a one hour layover in Osier, trains depart and return to your origin of departure. You can ride the entire route all in one trip by using their van service. You can choose to leave by train or van first from either Antonito or Chama.

All Aboard

Passengers may board the train in either Chama or Antonito. The Chama, New Mexico station is located at 500 S. Terrace Avenue and the Antonito, Colorado depot is located at the junction of U.S. Highway 285 and State Highway 17.

Schedule

The Cumbres & Toltec Scenic Railroad operates daily from Memorial Day weekend to mid-October. Passengers departing from Chama leave at 10:30 a.m. and return by 4:30 p.m. Passengers departing from Antonito leave at 10:00 a.m. and return at 5:00 p.m. Departure times vary when riding the entire length and returning by van, please inquire for details.

Fares

Adult ticket prices are $34.00 and children 11 years old and under are $17.00. The cost to travel the entire length by train with van service to origin of departure is $52.00 for adults and $27.00 for children. Ticket prices for those that ride the entire route and provide their own return transportation are $45.00 for adults and $21.00 for children.

Ride Information

Cumbres & Toltec Scenic Railroad
P.O. Box 789
Chama, NM 87520
Phone: 505-756-2151

Cumbres & Toltec Scenic Railroad
P.O. Box 668
Antonito, CO 81120
Phone: 719-376-5483

Local Information

Chama Valley Chamber of Commerce
P.O. Box 306
Chama, NM 87520
Phone: 800-477-0149 / 505-756-2306

Antonito Chamber of Commerce
P.O. Box 427
Antonito, CO 81120
Phone: 800-835-1098 / 719-376-5443

Notes

There are special coaches available with wheel-chair lifts for the physically challenged. Group rates for 21 or more and charter trains for up to 300 people are available. It is recommended that passengers prepare for cool weather by wearing a coat or jacket. Access to an open sight-seeing car is available to all passengers. Hot lunches are available at the layover in Osier or passengers may bring their own picnic lunch.

Chama

 036

 100, 101, 109

SPECIAL EVENTS AND EXCURSIONS	
CHILDREN'S DAY	
DINING:	
BRUNCH	
LUNCH	✓
DINNER	
EASTER BUNNY	
FAIRS/FESTIVALS	
FALL FOLIAGE	
FATHER'S DAY	✓
GRANDPARENT'S DAY	
HALLOWEEN	
INDEPENDENCE DAY	
LABOR DAY	
MEMORIAL DAY	
MOONLIGHT	✓
MOTHER'S DAY	
MURDER MYSTERIES	
NEW YEAR	
SANTA CLAUS	
THANKSGIVING	
TRAIN ROBBERIES	
VALENTINE'S DAY	
VETERAN'S DAY	

Call for current information, schedule and fares on the above special events.

SANTA FE SOUTHERN RAILWAY

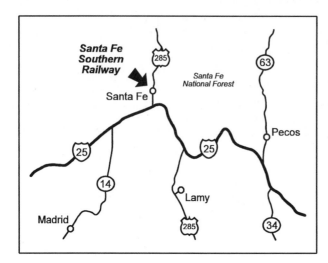

LOCATION
Santa Fe
SEASON
Year-round
ROUND TRIP
36 Miles
FARES
Adult, $21.00

The Ride

The Santa Fe Southern Railway operates a 36 mile round trip excursion beginning in Santa Fe and traveling south through the scenic northern New Mexico countryside to its destination in Lamy. Passengers can bring a picnic or make arrangements to have lunch at the historic Legal Tender Restaurant in Lamy. The entire round trip takes about 4 hours to complete.

All Aboard

Passengers board the train from the depot in Santa Fe located at 410 South Guadalupe Street. Santa Fe is located in north-central New Mexico, approximately 57 miles north of Albuquerque.

Schedule

The Santa Fe Southern Railway operates its scenic excursion year-round with runs on Tuesday, Thursday, and Saturday. The train departs from the depot at 10:30 a.m.

Fares

The adult fare is $21.00, $16.00 for children ages 7 through 13, and $5.00 for children aged 3 through 6. Children under 2 ride for free. Tickets for seniors aged 60 and up are $16.00.

Ride Information

Santa Fe Southern Railway
410 South Guadalupe Street
Santa Fe, NM 87501
Phone: 505-989-8600
Fax: 505-983-7620

Local Information

Santa Fe County Chamber of Commerce
P.O. Box 1928
Santa Fe, NM 87504
Phone: 505-988-3279
Fax: 505-984-2205

Notes

Group rates and charters are available. A gift shop with railroad memorabilia, books, models, and toys is located in the Santa Fe Southern Railway Depot. A special Sunset Train operates on Fridays from mid-May through September and departs one hour before sunset.

SPECIAL EVENTS AND EXCURSIONS

CHILDREN'S DAY
DINING:
    BRUNCH
    LUNCH ✓
    DINNER
EASTER BUNNY
FAIRS/FESTIVALS
FALL FOLIAGE
FATHER'S DAY
GRANDPARENT'S DAY
HALLOWEEN
INDEPENDENCE DAY
LABOR DAY
MEMORIAL DAY
MOONLIGHT
MOTHER'S DAY
MURDER MYSTERIES
NEW YEAR ✓
SANTA CLAUS ✓
THANKSGIVING ✓
TRAIN ROBBERIES
VALENTINE'S DAY
VETERAN'S DAY

Call for current information, schedule and fares on the above special events.

 063, 076

ADIRONDACK SCENIC RAILROAD

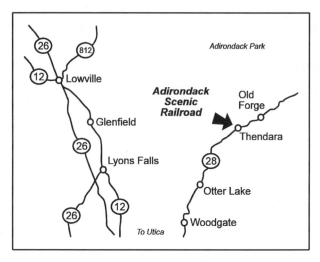

LOCATION
Thendara
SEASON
May - November
ROUND TRIP
9 Miles
FARES
Adult, $6.00

The Ride

Passengers aboard this 9 mile scenic train excursion travel in open-window coaches along the Moose River through the woods into some of the most scenic beauty of the Adirondack Park. The entire round trip takes about one hour to complete.

All Aboard

The train departs from the depot in Thendara located on State Highway 28 (one mile south of Old Forge). Thendara is approximately 45 miles northeast of Utica.

Schedule

The Adirondack Scenic Railroad operates on weekends only from the first weekend in May to Memorial Day and departs at 10:00 and 11:30 a.m., 1:00, 2:30 and 4:00 p.m. From Memorial Day weekend through mid-June, the train operates daily except on Thursday and Friday. The train departs at the same times listed above. From mid-June to late October, excursions are offered daily except on Friday with departure times being the same as above.

From late October to late November, the train operates on weekends only and departs Thendara at 11:30 a.m. and 2:30 p.m. only.

Fares

Adult ticket prices are $6.00 and for children ages 2 through 12, $4.00. Children under 2 ride for free.

Ride Information

Adirondack Scenic Railroad
P.O. Box 84
Thendara, NY 13472
Phone: 315-369-6290

Local Information

Central Adirondack Association
P.O. Box 68
Old Forge, NY 13420
Phone: 315-369-6983

Herkimer County Chamber of Commerce
P.O. Box 129
Mohawk, NY 13407
Phone: 315-866-7820
Fax: 315-866-7833

SPECIAL EVENTS AND EXCURSIONS	
CHILDREN'S DAY	
DINING:	
BRUNCH	
LUNCH	
DINNER	
EASTER BUNNY	
FAIRS/FESTIVALS	✓
FALL FOLIAGE	✓
FATHER'S DAY	✓
GRANDPARENT'S DAY	
HALLOWEEN	✓
INDEPENDENCE DAY	✓
LABOR DAY	✓
MEMORIAL DAY	✓
MOONLIGHT	
MOTHER'S DAY	✓
MURDER MYSTERIES	✓
NEW YEAR	
SANTA CLAUS	✓
THANKSGIVING	✓
TRAIN ROBBERIES	✓
VALENTINE'S DAY	
VETERAN'S DAY	

Call for current information, schedule and fares on the above special events.

Notes

A museum and gift shop are located at the station. The railroad station and passenger cars are accessible to the handicapped. Charters and group rates for 15 or more persons are available. All trains are diesel powered. Outdoor enthusiasts can canoe down the Moose River and be picked up at the Minnehana Loading Platform for a ride back on the train.

ARCADE & ATTICA RAILROAD

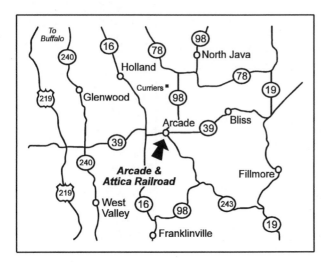

LOCATION
Arcade
SEASON
May - December
ROUND TRIP
14 Miles
FARES
Adult, $8.50

The Ride

The Arcade & Attica Railroad takes passengers through green meadows and woodlands as it travels the 7 miles of track between Arcade and the Curriers Station Stop. The 14 mile round trip lasts for approximately 90 minutes including a 20 minute layover in Curriers. There, passengers can watch the locomotive be prepared for its return trip or browse through the small museum.

All Aboard

The train departs Arcade from the depot located at 278 Main Street, three miles east of New York State Route 16. Arcade is about 40 miles southeast of Buffalo.

Schedule

The Arcade & Attica Railroad operates train rides from Memorial Day weekend through the last weekend in October with special runs in December and March. Departure times on Saturdays and Sundays are 12:30 and 3:00 p.m. During the months of July and August, the train runs on Wednesdays at

12:30 and 3:00 p.m. and on Fridays at 1:00 p.m. Contact for complete schedule.

Fares

Adult ticket prices are $8.50, children aged 3 to 11, $5.00. Discounts for senior citizens offered.

Ride Information

Arcade & Attica Railroad
P.O. Box 246
Arcade, NY 14009
Phone: 716-492-3100

Local Information

Arcade Area Chamber of Commerce
278 Main Street
Arcade, NY 14009
Phone: 716-492-2114

Notes

Group rates are available. No reservations will be taken except for groups of 25 or more. Tick-

SPECIAL EVENTS AND EXCURSIONS	
CHILDREN'S DAY	✓
DINING:	
BRUNCH	
LUNCH	
DINNER	
EASTER BUNNY	
FAIRS/FESTIVALS	✓
FALL FOLIAGE	✓
FATHER'S DAY	
GRANDPARENT'S DAY	
HALLOWEEN	✓
INDEPENDENCE DAY	✓
LABOR DAY	
MEMORIAL DAY	✓
MOONLIGHT	
MOTHER'S DAY	
MURDER MYSTERIES	✓
NEW YEAR	
SANTA CLAUS	✓
THANKSGIVING	
TRAIN ROBBERIES	
VALENTINE'S DAY	
VETERAN'S DAY	

Call for current information, schedule and fares on the above special events.

ets are on sale in Arcade up until train time on a first come, first served basis. The "Civil War Train Capture" takes place the third weekend in August. Please note that the special events and excursions usually need reservations. Trains operate rain or shine.

 147   044

CHAMPAGNE TRAIL

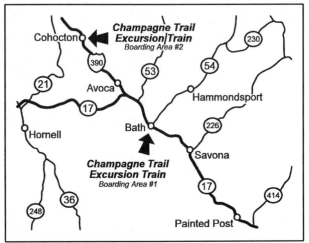

LOCATION
Bath and Cohocton
SEASON
May - October
ROUND TRIP
15 Miles
FARES
Adult, $10.00

The Ride

The Champagne Trail rail excursion travels between Bath and Cohocton through the scenic hills of the beautiful Finger Lakes wine country. Passengers may board at either location for the 15 mile round trip. All passengers leaving from Bath will have a 45 minute layover in Cohocton, allowing time to browse through the Cohocton Valley Farm Museum. The entire round trip lasts for about 2¾ hours including the layover. One-way trips from either location are available.

All Aboard

Passengers may board the train at either the Bath Station or Cohocton Depot. The Bath Station is located at 31 Lackawanna Avenue and the Cohocton Depot is at 55 Maple Avenue.

Schedule

Train excursions operate Friday through Sunday from May through June and during September and October. Departure times from Bath are 8:00 and 11:30 a.m., and 3:00 p.m. The train departs Cohocton at 10:00 a.m., 1:30

and 5:00 p.m. During the months of July and August, train rides are added on Wednesdays with departure times remaining the same.

Fares

Adult ticket prices are $10.00; children, $5.00. One way tickets are available for $6.00. Seniors (60 and over) receive a 10% discount on Friday runs.

Ride Information

Champagne Trail Excursion Train
31 Lackawanna Ave.
Bath, NY 14810
Phone: Bath, 607-776-1616
       Cohocton, 716-384-9187

Local Information

Greater Bath Area Chamber of Commerce
10 Pulteney Square West
Bath, NY 14810
Phone: 607-776-7122
Fax: 607-776-1260

SPECIAL EVENTS AND EXCURSIONS
CHILDREN'S DAY
DINING:
BRUNCH
LUNCH
DINNER
EASTER BUNNY
FAIRS/FESTIVALS
FALL FOLIAGE
FATHER'S DAY
GRANDPARENT'S DAY
HALLOWEEN
INDEPENDENCE DAY
LABOR DAY
MEMORIAL DAY
MOONLIGHT
MOTHER'S DAY
MURDER MYSTERIES
NEW YEAR
SANTA CLAUS
THANKSGIVING
TRAIN ROBBERIES
VALENTINE'S DAY
VETERAN'S DAY

NONE

Call for current information, schedule and fares on the above special events.

Notes

All facilities are accessible to the physically challenged. Group packages available for 25 or more. Refreshments are available on the train. A restaurant and lounge is located at the railroad headquarters in Bath.

Bath

 004

DELAWARE & ULSTER RAIL RIDE

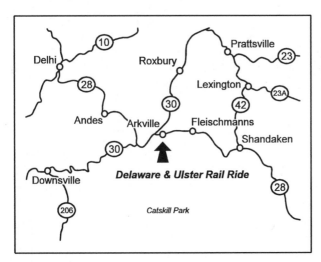

LOCATION
Arkville
SEASON
May - October
ROUND TRIP
10 Miles
FARES
Adult, $7.00

The Ride

The Delaware & Ulster Rail Ride takes passengers on a scenic 10 mile round trip from Arkville to Fleischmanns. The train's vintage coaches, some open-air, travel through the colorful Catskill Mountains. The entire round trip takes approximately 1 hour to complete.

All Aboard

Passengers board the train at the depot in Arkville on State Highway 28. Arkville is located approximately 70 miles southwest of Albany.

Schedule

The Delaware & Ulster Rail Ride operates on weekends and holidays from Memorial Day weekend through October. The train runs Wednesday through Sunday from the first week in July to Labor Day. All trains depart from the Arkville Depot at 11:00 a.m., 1:00 p.m., and 3:00 p.m.

Fares

Round trip fare for adults is $7.00 and $4.00 for children ages 5 through 11. Children under 5 ride for free. The ticket price for senior citizens is $5.50.

Ride Information

Delaware & Ulster Rail Ride
P.O. Box 310
Stamford, NY 12167
Phone: 800-225-4132 / 914-586-3877

Local Information

Delaware County Chamber of Commerce
97 Main Street
Delhi, NY 13753
Phone: 800-642-4443 / 607-746-2281
Fax: 607-746-3571

Notes

Group discounts for 20 or more people are available. A gift shop, picnic tables, and train exhibits are located on the depot area. A private dining car with catering is available for charter. Heated coaches are also available. Facilities are accessible to the handicapped.

SPECIAL EVENTS AND EXCURSIONS	
CHILDREN'S DAY	✓
DINING:	
BRUNCH	
LUNCH	✓
DINNER	
EASTER BUNNY	
FAIRS/FESTIVALS	✓
FALL FOLIAGE	✓
FATHER'S DAY	✓
GRANDPARENT'S DAY	✓
HALLOWEEN	✓
INDEPENDENCE DAY	✓
LABOR DAY	✓
MEMORIAL DAY	✓
MOONLIGHT	
MOTHER'S DAY	
MURDER MYSTERIES	
NEW YEAR	
SANTA CLAUS	
THANKSGIVING	
TRAIN ROBBERIES	✓
VALENTINE'S DAY	
VETERAN'S DAY	

Call for current information, schedule and fares on the above special events.

NEW YORK & LAKE ERIE RAILROAD

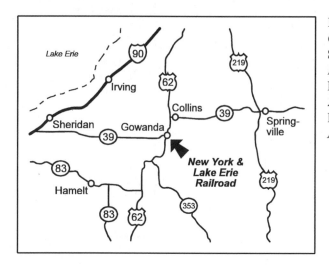

LOCATION
Gowanda
SEASON
May - October
ROUND TRIP
20 Miles
FARES
Adult, $8.50

The Ride

Passengers aboard "The Flyer" are taken from Gowanda across scenic rural countryside over the historic Erie Railroad trackage. The train begins its journey by climbing one of the steepest grades east of the Mississippi. Near the top of the grade you will pass through an old stone tunnel that dates back to 1865. Your destination is South Dayton, where a short layover allows passengers enough time to visit the gift shop inside the depot. The round trip excursion is 20 miles in length and lasts for 2½ hours, including the layover.

All Aboard

Passengers board the train at the depot in Gowanda located at 50 Commercial Street. Gowanda is about 35 miles south of Buffalo.

Schedule

The train departs the depot at 1:00 p.m. on Saturday and Sunday from Memorial Day weekend through September. In October the train departs at 1:00 p.m. and 3:45 p.m. on weekends. A 12:00 noon departure time is added on Wednesdays and Fridays during the months of July and August.

Fares

Round trip fares for adults are $8.50, senior citizens $7.50, children 3 to 11 are $4.00. Children under 3 ride free when not occupying a seat.

Ride Information

New York & Lake Erie Railroad
P.O. Box 309
Gowanda, NY 14070
Phone: 716-532-5716

Local Information

Gowanda Area Chamber of Commerce
P.O. Box 45
Gowanda, NY 14070
Phone: 716-532-2834
Fax: 716-532-2779

Notes

Group discounts and charters available. Snacks and beverages are available on the train. Passengers are permitted to bring their own food on board. Reservations are accepted only for groups of 10 or more. The New York & Lake Erie Railroad also offers *The Blue Diamond Dinner Train.* This scenic four hour round trip goes to Cherry Creek, New York. Reservations are required.

SPECIAL EVENTS AND EXCURSIONS	
CHILDREN'S DAY	✓
DINING:	
BRUNCH	✓
LUNCH	
DINNER	✓
EASTER BUNNY	✓
FAIRS/FESTIVALS	
FALL FOLIAGE	✓
FATHER'S DAY	✓
GRANDPARENT'S DAY	
HALLOWEEN	✓
INDEPENDENCE DAY	
LABOR DAY	
MEMORIAL DAY	
MOONLIGHT	
MOTHER'S DAY	✓
MURDER MYSTERIES	✓
NEW YEAR	✓
SANTA CLAUS	✓
THANKSGIVING	
TRAIN ROBBERIES	✓
VALENTINE'S DAY	✓
VETERAN'S DAY	

Call for current information, schedule and fares on the above special events.

TIOGA SCENIC RAILROAD

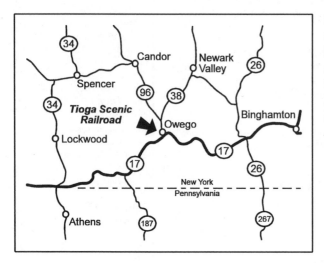

LOCATION
Owego
SEASON
May - October
ROUND TRIP
22 Miles
FARES
Adult, $7.00

The Ride

Your scenic excursion aboard the Tioga Scenic Railroad begins in Owego and travels north through the scenic countryside to the destination of Newark Valley. Passengers can enjoy the outdoors aboard the late 1800's open-air car or on early 1900's vintage railroad cars. This unique 22 mile round trip takes approximately 2 hours to complete.

All Aboard

All excursion trains begin at the depot in Owego located at 25 Delphine Street. Owego is located approximately 20 miles west of Binghamton in south-central New York.

Schedule

The Tioga Scenic Railroad operates excursions on Saturdays and Sundays from Memorial Day weekend through the last weekend in October. Departure times are 12:00 noon and 3:00 p.m. Additional rides operate most holidays, call for more information.

Fares

Ticket prices for adults are $7.00 and for children 4 to 11, $5.00. Senior citizen tickets are $6.50. Children under 3 ride for free.

Ride Information

Tioga Scenic Railroad
25 Delphine Street
Owego, NY 13827
Phone: 800-428-4642 / 607-687-6786

Local Information

Tioga County Chamber of Commerce
188 Front Street
Owego, NY 13827
Phone: 607-687-2020

Notes

Group rates for 30 or more available upon request. A museum with displays including a large HO scale train layout is located at the Owego Depot. An ice cream and gift shop are also located at the Owego Depot. Facilities are accessible to the handicapped. Please contact the Tioga Scenic Railroad for details on the many special events and excursions offered throughout the year.

SPECIAL EVENTS AND EXCURSIONS	
CHILDREN'S DAY	
DINING:	
BRUNCH	✓
LUNCH	✓
DINNER	✓
EASTER BUNNY	✓
FAIRS/FESTIVALS	
FALL FOLIAGE	✓
FATHER'S DAY	✓
GRANDPARENT'S DAY	
HALLOWEEN	✓
INDEPENDENCE DAY	
LABOR DAY	
MEMORIAL DAY	
MOONLIGHT	
MOTHER'S DAY	✓
MURDER MYSTERIES	✓
NEW YEAR	✓
SANTA CLAUS	✓
THANKSGIVING	✓
TRAIN ROBBERIES	✓
VALENTINE'S DAY	
VETERAN'S DAY	

Call for current information, schedule and fares on the above special events.

 028, 058

 130

GREAT SMOKY MOUNTAINS RAILWAY

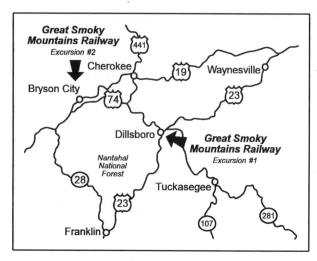

LOCATION
*Dillsboro and
Bryson City*
SEASON
April - December
ROUND TRIP
*Exc. #1, 34 Miles
Exc. #2, 44 Miles*
FARES
*Adult,
Exc. #1, $18.00
Exc. #2, $19.00*

The Ride

The Great Smoky Mountains Railway offers several scenic train ride options. Passengers can choose to ride in Open Cars, Coaches, Crown Coach, Club Car, or the Caboose. Many of the rides can be combined with lunch or dinner service. Two of the six regularly scheduled excursions are described here. Call or write for their comprehensive brochure detailing the complete schedule of all excursions.

Tuckasegee River (Excursion #1):
This 34 mile round trip departs Dillsboro and travels alongside the Tuckasegee River, crosses several trestles, and offers spectacular views of the Great Smoky Mountains. Passengers also pass a train wreck site from the movie, "The Fugitive." The entire trip takes about 3½ hours to complete, including a one hour layover in Bryson City for shopping and dining opportunities.

Nantahala Gorge (Excursion #2):
This scenic train ride begins in Bryson City and travels to the spectacular Nantahala Gorge and back. The gorge is a popular area for whitewater rafting, kayaking, and canoeing. The length of the entire round trip is 44

miles and takes approximately 4½ hours to complete. Passengers have 1 hour at the gorge to view the whitewater activities or take in the scenery. A raft and rail excursion is available on morning departures.

All Aboard

Excursion #1:
Passengers board the scenic train ride in Dillsboro from the depot located at One Front Street. Dillsboro is about 50 miles west of Asheville.

Excursion #2:
Boarding for this ride takes place at the depot in Bryson City located on the corner of Depot and Everett Streets.

Schedule

The Great Smoky Mountains Railway operates several hundred excursion runs at various times from April through December. Please refer to their brochure for specific information.

Fares

Excursion #1:
For the diesel engine, adult ticket prices are $18.00 and children 2 to 12 are $9.00. For the steam-powered excursion train, adult tickets cost $23.00 and children $9.00. Children under the age of 2 ride for free.

Excursion #2:
Ticket prices for adults aboard the diesel-powered train are $19.00 and $9.00 for children. For the steam locomotive, the adult ticket price is $24.00 and for children, $9.00.

Please see brochure for dates and times regarding steam or diesel powered excursion runs.

SPECIAL EVENTS AND EXCURSIONS

CHILDREN'S DAY	
DINING:	
BRUNCH	
LUNCH	✓
DINNER	✓
EASTER BUNNY	✓
FAIRS/FESTIVALS	
FALL FOLIAGE	✓
FATHER'S DAY	✓
GRANDPARENT'S DAY	
HALLOWEEN	✓
INDEPENDENCE DAY	
LABOR DAY	
MEMORIAL DAY	
MOONLIGHT	
MOTHER'S DAY	✓
MURDER MYSTERIES	✓
NEW YEAR	✓
SANTA CLAUS	✓
THANKSGIVING	
TRAIN ROBBERIES	
VALENTINE'S DAY	
VETERAN'S DAY	

Call for current information, schedule and fares on the above special events.

Ride Information

Great Smoky Mountains Railway
P.O. Box 397
Dillsboro, NC 28725
Phone: 800-872-4681 / 704-586-8811

Local Information

Swain County Chamber of Commerce
P.O. Box 509
Bryson City, NC 28713
Phone: 800-867-9246 / 704-488-3681

Jackson County Chamber of Commerce
18 Central Street
Sylva, NC 28779
Phone: 800-962-1911 / 704-586-2155

Notes

Snacks and beverages are available on all trains. Charters and group rates
for 20 or more are available. Group discounts apply to train fare portion
only on any excursion. No group discounts are available on the special excursions. Gift certificates are available in any amount. Open-air cars are
available on each excursion. A museum displaying thousands of railroad
memorabilia articles and a variety of scale model trains is located next to the
depot in Dillsboro. Admission to the museum: adults $3.00; children $2.00;
children 2 and under are free. Accessibility for the physically challenged is
limited.

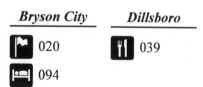

Bryson City	*Dillsboro*
020	039
094	

ASHTABULA, CARSON & JEFFERSON

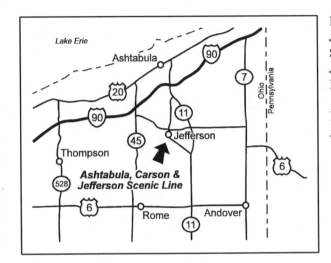

LOCATION
Jefferson
SEASON
June - October
ROUND TRIP
12 Miles
FARES
Adult, $6.50

The Ride

The Ashtabula, Carson & Jefferson Scenic Line operates a 12 mile scenic excursion through the woodlands and farmland of northeastern Ohio. The train departs Jefferson and travels to Carson, a staging yard for Conrail's coal and iron ore operations in Ashtabula Harbor. The 12 mile round trip takes about 1 hour to complete.

All Aboard

The train departs from the Jefferson Depot platform located on East Jefferson Street, two blocks east of State Highway 46. The town of Jefferson is approximately 40 miles north of Youngstown in northeastern Ohio.

Schedule

This scenic train ride operates on Saturdays and Sundays only, no holidays, from Father's Day weekend to the last Sunday in October. The train departs at 12:30, 2:00 and 3:30 p.m.

Fares

Adult ticket prices are $6.50 and $5.50 for seniors aged 60 and over. Ticket prices for children ages 3 through 12 are $4.50. Children under 3 ride free when not occupying a seat.

Ride Information

Ashtabula, Carson & Jefferson Scenic Line
P.O. Box 222
Jefferson, OH 44047
Phone: 216-576-6346

Local Information

Ashtabula County Convention
    and Visitors Bureau
36 West Walnut St.
Jefferson, OH 44047
Phone: 800-337-6746 / 216-576-4707

Notes

Group discounts for 15 or more are available with reservations. Week day charters available, inquire on rates and times. Reservations are required only in October when Fall foliage is at its peak. Souvenirs and snacks are sold at the ticket booth and on the train. No pets are permitted on premises.

SPECIAL EVENTS AND EXCURSIONS

CHILDREN'S DAY
DINING:
    BRUNCH
    LUNCH
    DINNER
EASTER BUNNY
FAIRS/FESTIVALS
FALL FOLIAGE ✓
FATHER'S DAY ✓
GRANDPARENT'S DAY
HALLOWEEN ✓
INDEPENDENCE DAY
LABOR DAY
MEMORIAL DAY
MOONLIGHT
MOTHER'S DAY
MURDER MYSTERIES ✓
NEW YEAR
SANTA CLAUS
THANKSGIVING
TRAIN ROBBERIES
VALENTINE'S DAY
VETERAN'S DAY

Call for current information, schedule and fares on the above special events.

CUYAHOGA VALLEY SCENIC RR

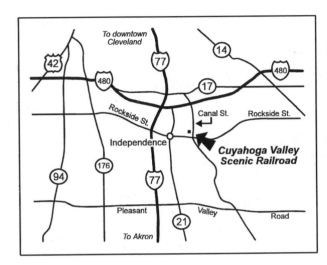

LOCATION
Independence
SEASON
May - October
ROUND TRIP
52 Miles
FARES
Adult, $20.00

The Ride

The Cuyahoga Valley Scenic Railroad operates several different excursions throughout the year. The Cuyahoga Limited excursion to Akron is described here. Passengers aboard this scenic train travel through the heart of the 33,000-acre Cuyahoga Valley National Recreation Area, which is administered by the National Park Service, and follow alongside the Ohio & Erie Canal before reaching their destination in downtown Akron. Passengers are given 3½ hours to shop at the nearby Quaker Square or visit the Inventure Place (Inventor's Hall of Fame and Museum) and the Akron Art Museum before returning to Independence. The entire 52 mile trip takes approximately 6½ hours to complete, including the layover in Akron.

All Aboard

This scenic train ride departs from the depot in Independence located on Old Rockside Road.

Schedule

This scenic train operates Wednesday through Sunday from late May through August with departures at 10:00 a.m. on Wednesday and Thursday and 11:00 a.m. on the weekend. The ride operates on weekends only during the month of September and daily in October. The train departs at 11:00 a.m. during September. In October, the weekday departure time is 10:00 a.m. and on weekends, 11:00 a.m.

Fares

Adult tickets are $20.00 and children ages 3 through 12 are $12.00. Children under 3 are free when not occupying a seat. Senior citizen discounts are available.

Ride Information

Cuyahoga Valley Scenic Railroad
P.O. Box 158
Peninsula, OH 44264
Phone: 800-468-4070

Local Information

Independence Chamber of Commerce
P.O. Box 31326
Independence, OH 44131
Phone: 216-573-2707
Fax: 216-838-1738

Greater Cleveland C & VB
3100 Tower City Center
Cleveland, OH 44113
Phone: 216-621-4110

SPECIAL EVENTS AND EXCURSIONS	
CHILDREN'S DAY	
DINING:	
BRUNCH	
LUNCH	
DINNER	
EASTER BUNNY	✓
FAIRS/FESTIVALS	
FALL FOLIAGE	✓
FATHER'S DAY	
GRANDPARENT'S DAY	
HALLOWEEN	
INDEPENDENCE DAY	✓
LABOR DAY	✓
MEMORIAL DAY	✓
MOONLIGHT	
MOTHER'S DAY	
MURDER MYSTERIES	
NEW YEAR	
SANTA CLAUS	✓
THANKSGIVING	
TRAIN ROBBERIES	
VALENTINE'S DAY	✓
VETERAN'S DAY	

Call for current information, schedule and fares on the above special events.

Notes

Advance reservations are requested for all trips. Discounts available for groups of 15 or more. Charters are available. No cash refunds are given for cancellations; reservations can be exchanged for another date or a gift certificate if cancellation notice is given 72 hours before departure. Smoking is not permitted on board. Please write or call for information on their other scenic excursions.

HOCKING VALLEY SCENIC RAILWAY

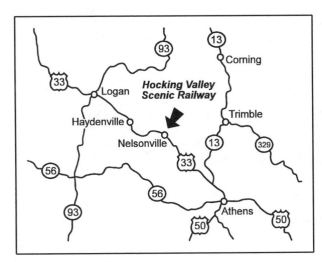

LOCATION
Nelsonville
SEASON
May - October
ROUND TRIP
Exc. #1, 12 Miles
Exc. #2, 25 Miles
FARES
Adult,
Exc. #1, $6.50
Exc. #2, $9.50

The Ride

The Hocking Valley Scenic Railway offers two train rides through south-eastern Ohio's rolling hills. The historic locomotives and passenger coaches take you on a ride over a century old right-of-way that is listed on the National Register of Historic Places. The train rides also include a visit to Robbins Crossing, an 1860's settlers' village museum.

Nelsonville to Haydenville (Excursion #1):
This scenic 12 mile round trip takes about 1½ hours to complete.

Nelsonville to Logan (Excursion #2):
This 25 mile round trip excursion takes approximately 2½ hours to complete.

All Aboard

Both trains leave the depot in Nelsonville at U.S. Hwy. 33 and Hocking Parkway Drive. Nelsonville is about 90 miles southeast of Columbus. The depot is listed on the National Register of Historic Places.

Schedule

Both trains operate on Saturdays, Sundays and major holidays from Memorial Day through October. Train to Haydenville (Excursion #1) departs at 12:00 noon. The train to Logan (Excursion #2) departs Nelsonville at 2:30 p.m.

Fares

Excursion #1: The adult ticket price is $6.50 and for children 2 to 12, $4.00

Excursion #2: Round trip adult fare is $9.50 and for children ages 2 through 12, $6.50

Ride Information

Hocking Valley Scenic Railway
P.O. Box 427
Nelsonville, OH 45764
Phone: 513-335-0382 (weekdays)
          614-753-9531 (weekends)

Local Information

Athens County Convention & Visitors Bureau
P.O. Box 1019
667 East State Street
Athens, OH 45701
Phone: 800-878-9767
Fax: 614-593-7365

Hocking Hills Regional Welcome Center
P.O. Box 350
Logan, OH 43138
Phone: 800-462-5464 / 614-385-9706

Notes

Group discounts and charters available. Facilities accessible to the physically challenged. Reservations are not required, but recommended. The Hocking Valley Scenic Railway also offers the "Canal Winchester Steam-Diesel Specials", a 100 mile round trip. Please call for details.

SPECIAL EVENTS AND EXCURSIONS

CHILDREN'S DAY
DINING:
    BRUNCH
    LUNCH
    DINNER
EASTER BUNNY
FAIRS/FESTIVALS ✓
FALL FOLIAGE ✓
FATHER'S DAY
GRANDPARENT'S DAY
HALLOWEEN
INDEPENDENCE DAY
LABOR DAY
MEMORIAL DAY
MOONLIGHT
MOTHER'S DAY
MURDER MYSTERIES
NEW YEAR
SANTA CLAUS ✓
THANKSGIVING
TRAIN ROBBERIES
VALENTINE'S DAY
VETERAN'S DAY

Call for current information, schedule and fares on the above special events.

I & O Scenic Railway

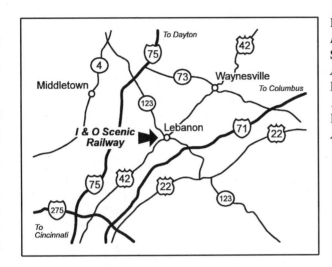

LOCATION
Lebanon
SEASON
April - December
ROUND TRIP
14 Miles
FARES
Adult, $9.00

The Ride

The I & O Scenic Railway offers a 14 mile round trip excursion beginning in Lebanon. The train follows an old stage coach route as it passes through meadows and pastures. Narration of the local history is provided on the train. The entire round trip lasts for approximately 1 hour.

All Aboard

The train departs from the Lebanon Station located at 198 South Broadway. Lebanon is in southwest Ohio about 30 miles northeast of Cincinnati.

Schedule

The I & O Scenic Railway operates from April through December. In April, November, and December, the train operates on weekends only. From May through October, the train operates on Wednesday, Friday, Saturday, and Sunday. Departure times on Wednesdays and Fridays are 10:30 a.m. and 12:00 noon. Departure times on Saturdays are 10:30 a.m., 12:00 noon, 1:30 and 3:00 p.m. The Sunday departures are 12:00 noon, 1:30 and 3:00 p.m.

Fares

The ticket price for adults is $9.00 and for seniors, $8.00. Children ticket prices are $5.00 for children ages 3 through 12. Children under 3 ride free.

Ride Information

I & O Scenic Railway
198 South Broadway
Lebanon, OH 45036
Phone: 513-398-8584

Local Information

Lebanon Area Chamber of Commerce
120 East South Street - #201
Lebanon, OH 45036
Phone: 513-932-1100

Notes

Group discounts available for when there are 20 or more people in the group. Chartered trains also available. A snack bar is on board. No restrooms are on the train. An open-air car is pulled with each excursion.

SPECIAL EVENTS AND EXCURSIONS	
CHILDREN'S DAY	✓
DINING:	
BRUNCH	
LUNCH	
DINNER	✓
EASTER BUNNY	✓
FAIRS/FESTIVALS	✓
FALL FOLIAGE	✓
FATHER'S DAY	✓
GRANDPARENT'S DAY	✓
HALLOWEEN	
INDEPENDENCE DAY	✓
LABOR DAY	✓
MEMORIAL DAY	✓
MOONLIGHT	
MOTHER'S DAY	✓
MURDER MYSTERIES	✓
NEW YEAR	
SANTA CLAUS	✓
THANKSGIVING	
TRAIN ROBBERIES	
VALENTINE'S DAY	
VETERAN'S DAY	

Call for current information, schedule and fares on the above special events.

 033, 059

 153

OHIO CENTRAL RAILROAD

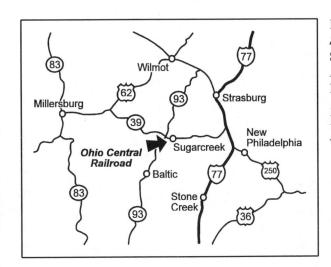

LOCATION
Sugarcreek
SEASON
May - October
ROUND TRIP
12 Miles
FARES
Adult, $7.00

The Ride

The Ohio Central Railroad takes passengers on a 12 mile scenic excursion through the rolling hills and farmland of northeastern Ohio. The journey begins in Sugarcreek, also known as "The Little Switzerland of Ohio", and travels through the heart of the largest Amish community in the world. The round trip ride takes approximately 1 hour to complete. Extra trains run at various times throughout the year including "all day" trips.

All Aboard

The train departs from the Ohio Central Station located at 111 Factory Street in Sugarcreek. Sugarcreek is approximately 30 miles southwest of Canton.

Schedule

The Ohio Central Railroad operates excursions daily except on Sunday from May through October. Departure times are 11:00 a.m., 12:30, 2:00 and 3:30 p.m. Monday through Saturday. Additional departure times of 9:30 a.m. and 5:00 p.m. are added on Saturdays in July, August, and October.

Fares

Adult ticket prices are $7.00 and for children ages 3 to 12, the fare is $4.00. Children under 3 ride for free.

Ride Information

Ohio Central Railroad, Inc.
P.O. Box 427
Sugarcreek, OH 44681
Phone: 216-852-4676
Fax: 216-852-2989

Local Information

Tuscarawas County Chamber of Commerce
P.O. Box 232
New Philadelphia, OH 44663
Phone: 216-343-4474
Fax: 216-343-6526

Notes

Discounts available for groups of 20 or more persons. A gift shop is located in the depot. Facilities are accessible to the physically challenged.

SPECIAL EVENTS AND EXCURSIONS

CHILDREN'S DAY
DINING:
  BRUNCH
  LUNCH
  DINNER
EASTER BUNNY
FAIRS/FESTIVALS ✓
FALL FOLIAGE ✓
FATHER'S DAY
GRANDPARENT'S DAY
HALLOWEEN
INDEPENDENCE DAY ✓
LABOR DAY ✓
MEMORIAL DAY ✓
MOONLIGHT
MOTHER'S DAY
MURDER MYSTERIES
NEW YEAR
SANTA CLAUS ✓
THANKSGIVING
TRAIN ROBBERIES
VALENTINE'S DAY
VETERAN'S DAY

Call for current information, schedule and fares on the above special events.

TOLEDO, LAKE ERIE & WESTERN

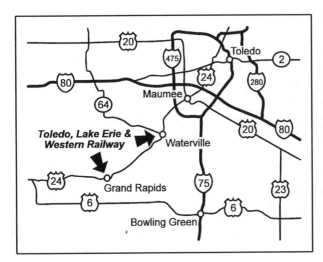

LOCATION
Waterville and Grand Rapids
SEASON
May - October
ROUND TRIP
20 Miles
FARES
Adult, $8.00

The Ride

Passengers aboard the Bluebird Passenger Train are taken on a 20 mile round trip through farmland between Waterville and Grand Rapids. The train rides alongside the Maumee River and crosses it on a 900-foot bridge near Grand Rapids. Passengers can choose between the 20 mile round trip or a one-way trip. Passengers may also layover and catch the next train back. The trip takes 45 minutes each way.

All Aboard

Passengers may board the train either at the depot in Waterville or in Grand Rapids. The Waterville Depot is at 49 North Sixth Street and the Grand Rapids Depot is located at Third and Mill Streets.

Schedule

This train ride operates on weekends and holidays from the first weekend in May through the last weekend in October. The train leaves Waterville at 1:00 and 4:00 p.m. Departures from Grand Rapids are 2:30 and 5:30 p.m. Beginning in June and lasting through August, additional train runs are offered on Tuesdays and Thursdays. Departure times from Waterville are 10:30 a.m. and 1:30 p.m. and from Grand Rapids at 11:45 a.m. and 2:45 p.m.

Fares

Round trip adult tickets are $8.00 and one-way tickets are $5.50. For children ages 3 through 12, the round trip fare is $4.50 and $3.25 for one-way. Seniors aged 65 and up receive a discount of $1.00 on the round trip fare and .50¢ for a one-way ticket.

Ride Information

Toledo, Lake Erie & Western Railway
P.O. Box 168
Waterville, OH 43566
Phone: 419-878-2177

Local Information

Waterville Chamber of Commerce
P.O. Box 74
Waterville, OH 43566
Phone: 419-878-5188

Grand Rapids Chamber of Commerce
P.O. Box 391
Grand Rapids, OH 43522
Phone: 419-832-1106

Notes

Passengers may ride in Caboose and Parlor Car seats for an additional charge. Group rates are available and Coach reservations are accepted for groups of 20 or more. Charters are also available.

Waterville

 038

SPECIAL EVENTS AND EXCURSIONS	
CHILDREN'S DAY	
DINING:	
BRUNCH	
LUNCH	
DINNER	
EASTER BUNNY	
FAIRS/FESTIVALS	✓
FALL FOLIAGE	
FATHER'S DAY	✓
GRANDPARENT'S DAY	
HALLOWEEN	
INDEPENDENCE DAY	
LABOR DAY	✓
MEMORIAL DAY	✓
MOONLIGHT	
MOTHER'S DAY	✓
MURDER MYSTERIES	
NEW YEAR	
SANTA CLAUS	
THANKSGIVING	
TRAIN ROBBERIES	
VALENTINE'S DAY	
VETERAN'S DAY	

Call for current information, schedule and fares on the above special events.

HUGO HERITAGE RAILROAD

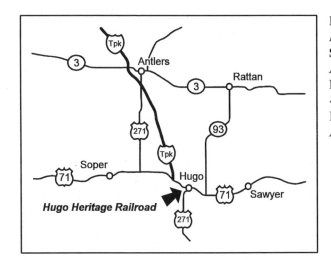

LOCATION
Hugo
SEASON
April - November
ROUND TRIP
45 Miles
FARES
Adult, $15.00

The Ride

The Hugo Heritage Railroad offers passengers a 2½ hour excursion through the Red River Valley, crossing streams and creeks, wooded areas and pastures of southeastern Oklahoma. Dogwoods and Redwoods bring magnificent colors to the area in spring. The train departs Hugo, known as Circus City U.S.A., and travels to historic Antlers, named for the piles of deer antlers hunters would leave behind. The 45 mile round trip includes a 30 minute layover in Antlers, giving passengers the opportunity to browse through the museum located there.

All Aboard

Passengers board the train at the Hugo Depot located just west of downtown at 300 West Jackson. Hugo is in southeastern Oklahoma.

Schedule

The Hugo Heritage Railroad operates on Saturdays only from April through November. The train departs Hugo at 2:00 p.m.

Fares

Ticket prices for adults are $15.00 and for children ages 2 through 11, tickets are $10.00. Children under 2 ride for free.

Ride Information

Hugo Heritage Railroad
P.O. Box 577
Hugo, OK 74743
Phone: 405-326-6630

Local Information

Hugo Chamber of Commerce
200 South Broadway
Hugo, OK 74743
Phone: 405-326-7511
Fax: 405-326-7767

Notes

Charters are available. No carry on food or drinks are permitted on board. A museum is located in the depot and displays include railroad artifacts and a miniature train exhibit. The Harvey House restaurant, one of only two in its original location, is also in the depot. Discounts are offered for groups. Railroad Days are held in October.

SPECIAL EVENTS AND EXCURSIONS	
CHILDREN'S DAY	
DINING:	
BRUNCH	
LUNCH	
DINNER	
EASTER BUNNY	
FAIRS/FESTIVALS	
FALL FOLIAGE	✓
FATHER'S DAY	
GRANDPARENT'S DAY	
HALLOWEEN	
INDEPENDENCE DAY	
LABOR DAY	
MEMORIAL DAY	
MOONLIGHT	
MOTHER'S DAY	
MURDER MYSTERIES	
NEW YEAR	
SANTA CLAUS	
THANKSGIVING	
TRAIN ROBBERIES	
VALENTINE'S DAY	
VETERAN'S DAY	

Call for current information, schedule and fares on the above special events.

 118

MT. HOOD RAILROAD

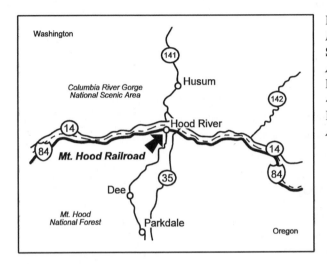

LOCATION
Hood River
SEASON
April - December
ROUND TRIP
44 Miles
FARES
Adult, $21.95

The Ride

The Mt. Hood Railroad begins in Hood River in the heart of the Columbia River Gorge National Scenic Area and travels south to the town of Parkdale. The route climbs a 3% grade through steep canyons to a switchback, one of a few remaining railroad switchbacks, as it continues its ascent up the Hood River Valley. The scenic train ride offers beautiful views of Mt. Hood and Mt. Adams. The 44 mile round trip takes approximately 4 hours to complete.

All Aboard

Excursions begin in Hood River and depart from the Mt. Hood Railroad Depot located at 110 Railroad Avenue. The depot, built in 1911, has been designated a National Historic Site.

Schedule

There are two departure times for the Mt. Hood Railroad. The morning train departs at 10:00 a.m. and the afternoon train leaves at 3:00 p.m. The afternoon train runs on weekends only from mid-April through October. The morning train operates Wednesday through Sunday from mid-April through October. An additional morning train run is added on Tuesday during July and August. The schedule will vary in November and December.

Fares

Adult tickets are $21.95, children ages 2 through 11 $13.95. Senior citizens aged 60 and over receive a $3.00 discount. A discount is given on weekday excursions in April, May and October through December.

Ride Information

Mount Hood Railroad
110 Railroad Avenue
Hood River, OR 97031
Phone: 800-872-4661

Local Information

Hood River County Chamber of Commerce
Port Marina Park
Hood River, OR 97031
Phone: 800-366-3530 / 503-386-2000
Fax: 503-386-2057

Notes

Group discounts and charters are available. Facilities are accessible to the physically challenged.

SPECIAL EVENTS AND EXCURSIONS

CHILDREN'S DAY	
DINING:	
BRUNCH	
LUNCH	
DINNER	
EASTER BUNNY	✓
FAIRS/FESTIVALS	✓
FALL FOLIAGE	✓
FATHER'S DAY	✓
GRANDPARENT'S DAY	
HALLOWEEN	✓
INDEPENDENCE DAY	✓
LABOR DAY	✓
MEMORIAL DAY	✓
MOONLIGHT	
MOTHER'S DAY	✓
MURDER MYSTERIES	
NEW YEAR	
SANTA CLAUS	✓
THANKSGIVING	✓
TRAIN ROBBERIES	✓
VALENTINE'S DAY	
VETERAN'S DAY	

Call for current information, schedule and fares on the above special events.

SUMPTER VALLEY RAILROAD

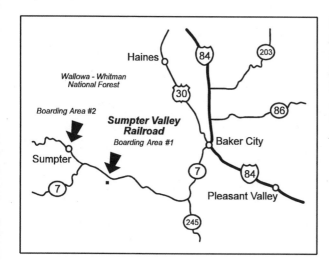

LOCATION
Sumpter Valley
SEASON
May - September
ROUND TRIP
10 Miles
FARES
Adult, $8.00

The Ride

Passengers aboard this 10 mile round trip travel through the scenic Sumpter Valley with views of the surrounding Elkhorn Mountains, through a County Game Habitat to the historic mining town of Sumpter. The entire round trip takes about 2 hours to complete including a layover in either Sumpter or at the McEwen Station. Passengers can spend more time at the layover site and take a later train back. One-way trips are also offered.

All Aboard

Passengers may board at the McEwen Station (Boarding Area #1 on the map) or in Sumpter. The McEwen Station is in the Baker County Day Park on Dredge Loop Road, off of State Highway 7. The Sumpter Depot is located on the eastern edge of town.

Schedule

The Sumpter Valley Railroad operates train rides from Memorial Day weekend through September on Saturday, Sunday, and holidays. The train departs from McEwen Station at 10:00 a.m., 12:30 and 3:00 p.m. Departures from the Sumpter Depot are 11:00 a.m., 1:30 p.m., and 4:00 p.m. The 4:00 p.m. departure is a one-way trip only.

Fares

Round trip fare for adults is $8.00 and for children ages 6 to 16, $6.00. One-way tickets are also available for $5.00 and $4.00 respectively. Family rates are available and cost $20.00 for the round trip and $13.00 for the one-way trip.

Ride Information

Sumpter Valley Railroad Restoration Inc.
P.O. Box 389
Baker City, OR 97814
Phone: 503-894-2268

Local Information

Baker County Visitor & Convention Bureau
490 Campbell Street
Baker City, OR 97814
Phone: 503-523-3356 / 800-523-1235

Notes

Discounts for groups and charters are available. Facilities are handicap accessible. Several pieces of historic rail equipment are on display at the McEwen Station. New additions are planned for the Sumpter Depot in 1996 including a large museum and gift shop.

SPECIAL EVENTS AND EXCURSIONS

CHILDREN'S DAY
DINING:
    BRUNCH
    LUNCH
    DINNER
EASTER BUNNY
FAIRS/FESTIVALS
FALL FOLIAGE
FATHER'S DAY
GRANDPARENT'S DAY
HALLOWEEN
INDEPENDENCE DAY ✓
LABOR DAY ✓
MEMORIAL DAY ✓
MOONLIGHT ✓
MOTHER'S DAY
MURDER MYSTERIES
NEW YEAR
SANTA CLAUS
THANKSGIVING
TRAIN ROBBERIES
VALENTINE'S DAY
VETERAN'S DAY

Call for current information, schedule and fares on the above special events.

BELLEFONTE HISTORICAL RAILROAD

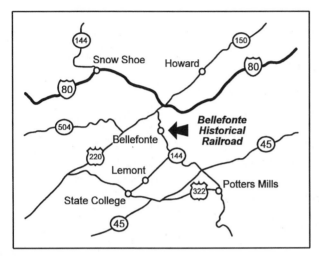

LOCATION
Bellefonte
SEASON
June - August
ROUND TRIP
15 Miles
FARES
Adult,
$6.00 - $8.00

The Ride

The Bellefonte Historical Railroad offers a variety of train excursions along its 60 miles of track through scenic and historic central Pennsylvania. Two of the most common routes are described here. Both trains depart from Bellefonte and travel about 15 miles round trip. Both excursions take approximately 1 hour to complete, including a short layover at either destination. The Saturday train goes to Lemont and the Sunday run travels to Howard.

All Aboard

Boarding for all train excursions are at the depot in Bellefonte located at 320 West High Street. Bellefonte is located about 45 miles northeast of Altoona in central Pennsylvania.

Schedule

Trains operate on weekends and holidays from June through August. The ride to Lemont departs Bellefonte on Saturdays at 1:00 and 3:30 p.m. The train to Howard leaves on Sundays at 1:00, 2:30 and 4:00 p.m.

Fares

The adult fare for the excursion to Lemont is $6.00 and $3.00 for children. Adult ticket prices for the excursion to Howard are $8.00 and $4.00 for children.

Ride Information

Bellefonte Historical Railroad Society
320 West High Street
Bellefonte, PA 16823
Phone: 814-355-0311
         814-355-2392 (charters)

Local Information

Bellefonte Area Chamber of Commerce
Train Station
320 West High Street
Bellefonte, PA 16823
Phone: 814-355-2917
Fax: 814-355-2761

Chamber of Business &
   Industry of Centre County
200 Innovation Blvd. - #201
State College, PA 16803
Phone: 814-234-1829
Fax: 814-234-5869

SPECIAL EVENTS AND EXCURSIONS	
CHILDREN'S DAY	
DINING:	
BRUNCH	
LUNCH	
DINNER	✓
EASTER BUNNY	
FAIRS/FESTIVALS	
FALL FOLIAGE	✓
FATHER'S DAY	
GRANDPARENT'S DAY	
HALLOWEEN	
INDEPENDENCE DAY	✓
LABOR DAY	✓
MEMORIAL DAY	✓
MOONLIGHT	
MOTHER'S DAY	
MURDER MYSTERIES	
NEW YEAR	
SANTA CLAUS	✓
THANKSGIVING	
TRAIN ROBBERIES	
VALENTINE'S DAY	
VETERAN'S DAY	

Call for current information, schedule and fares on the above special events.

Notes

Facilities are accessible to the handicapped. Beverages available on the train. Chartered trains available year-round. Please call or write for schedule and fares on Bellefonte Historical Railroad's other scenic excursions.

GETTYSBURG RAILROAD

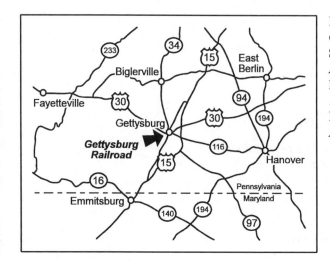

LOCATION
Gettysburg
SEASON
April - October
ROUND TRIP
16 Miles
FARES
Adult, $7.50

The Ride

This 16 mile round trip ride takes passengers past the first-day Civil War battlefields into the scenic countryside of Adams County before reaching the destination of Biglerville. This scenic excursion takes about 1½ hours to complete. Passengers can enjoy a longer 50 mile round trip that travels to Mt. Holly Springs.

All Aboard

Passengers board the train in Gettysburg at the depot located at 106 North Washington Street. Gettysburg is in south-central Pennsylvania about 15 miles north of the Maryland border.

Schedule

The Gettysburg Railroad operates on weekends in April with departure times of 1:00 and 3:00 p.m. In May and June, the train departs at 10:00 a.m. and 12:30 p.m. on Thursday and Friday and at 1:00 and 3:00 p.m. on weekends. During July and August, the train operates weekdays at 11:00 a.m. and 1:00 p.m. and on weekends at 11:00 a.m., 1:00 and 3:00 p.m. Departures in

September and October are 11:00 a.m. and 1:00 p.m. on Thursday and Friday and 11:00 a.m., 1:00 and 3:00 p.m. on Saturday and Sunday.

Fares

Adult fare is $7.50, children 3 to 12 years old are $3.50. The fare for senior citizens aged 65 and over is $7.00.

Ride Information

Gettysburg Railroad Passenger Services
106 N. Washington Street
Gettysburg, PA 17325
Phone: 717-334-6932

Local Information

Gettysburg - Adams County Area
Chamber of Commerce
33 York Street
Gettysburg, PA 17325
Phone: 717-334-8151
Fax: 717-334-3368

SPECIAL EVENTS AND EXCURSIONS	
CHILDREN'S DAY	
DINING:	
BRUNCH	
LUNCH	
DINNER	✓
EASTER BUNNY	✓
FAIRS/FESTIVALS	
FALL FOLIAGE	✓
FATHER'S DAY	
GRANDPARENT'S DAY	
HALLOWEEN	✓
INDEPENDENCE DAY	
LABOR DAY	✓
MEMORIAL DAY	
MOONLIGHT	✓
MOTHER'S DAY	
MURDER MYSTERIES	
NEW YEAR	
SANTA CLAUS	✓
THANKSGIVING	
TRAIN ROBBERIES	✓
VALENTINE'S DAY	
VETERAN'S DAY	

Call for current information, schedule and fares on the above special events.

Notes

Reservations for the 16 mile round trip are not required, but are recommended for the 50 mile round trip. Group rates and charters are available. Alcoholic beverages are not permitted on train. Facilities are accessible to the handicapped. A gift shop is located in the depot.

 069, 074, 083, 121

KNOX & KANE RAILROAD

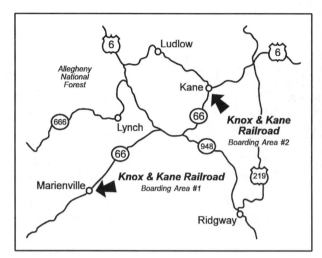

LOCATION
*Marienville and
Kane*
SEASON
June - October
ROUND TRIP
32 or 96 Miles
FARES
*Adult,
$14.00 - $20.00*

The Ride

The Knox & Kane Railroad offers a scenic excursion through the peaks and valleys of the Allegheny National Forest. The ride takes passengers to the Kinzua Bridge, one of the highest railroad bridges in the world, then back to their origin of departure. The Kinzua Bridge stands 301 feet above the Kinzua Creek Valley and was designated a Historic Civil Engineering Landmark in 1982. The bridge is also listed on the National Register of Historic Places. Passengers may choose to begin their train ride in either Marienville or Kane. The trip is a 96 mile, 8 hour round trip for those departing from Marienville and a 32 mile, 3½ hour trip for those departing from Kane. There is a 30 minute layover at the bridge.

All Aboard

Passengers departing from Marienville board the train at the depot located on South Forest Street. For those passengers departing from Kane, the depot is located on Route 321.

Schedule

The Knox & Kane Railroad operates on Friday, Saturday, and Sunday during June and September. In July and August, the train runs Tuesday through

Sunday. For the first two weeks in October, the train runs Wednesday through Sunday and on weekends only for the last two weeks. The train leaves Marienville at 8:30 a.m. and departs Kane at 10:45 a.m.

Fares

The adult ticket price for passengers departing from Marienville is $20.00 and $14.00 for those departing from Kane. The fare for children ages 3 through 12 is $13.00 and $8.00. Children under the age of 3 ride for free.

Ride Information

Knox & Kane Railroad Co.
P.O. Box 422
Marienville, PA 16239
Phone: 814-927-6621

Local Information

Kane Chamber of Commerce
14 Greeves Street
Kane, PA 16735
Phone: 814-837-6565

Forest County Tourist Promo Agency
P.O. Box 366
Tionesta, PA 16353
Phone: 814-927-8266 / 800-222-1706 (in Pennsylvania)

Notes

A snack bar is available on the train. Group rates and charters are available. The Knox & Kane Railroad recommends that advance reservations be made. Box lunches are available for a $3.75 fee per person.

SPECIAL EVENTS AND EXCURSIONS

CHILDREN'S DAY
DINING:
    BRUNCH
    LUNCH
    DINNER
EASTER BUNNY
FAIRS/FESTIVALS
FALL FOLIAGE
FATHER'S DAY
GRANDPARENT'S DAY
HALLOWEEN
INDEPENDENCE DAY
LABOR DAY
MEMORIAL DAY
MOONLIGHT
MOTHER'S DAY
MURDER MYSTERIES
NEW YEAR
SANTA CLAUS
THANKSGIVING
TRAIN ROBBERIES
VALENTINE'S DAY
VETERAN'S DAY

NONE

Call for current information, schedule and fares on the above special events.

Kane

 097

MIDDLETOWN & HUMMELSTOWN RR

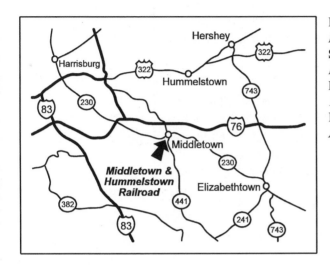

LOCATION
Middletown
SEASON
May - October
ROUND TRIP
11 Miles
FARES
Adult, $6.00

The Ride

This scenic 11 mile 1¼ hour round trip begins in Middletown and travels to Hummelstown at the Indian Echo Caverns. The train follows alongside the Swatara Creek as a narrator speaks of the history of Union Canal and the railroad. The train takes passengers across a 35-foot high bridge above the creek. On the return trip, a musician leads passengers in sing-a-longs and invites everyone to join the crew in performing the chicken dance. Passengers can choose to take a 45 minute tour of Indian Echo Caverns for an additional fee. Passengers should allow 3 hours for the train/cavern combination.

All Aboard

Boarding takes place at the Race Street Station, 6½ blocks south of Main Street (PA 230) in Middletown. Middletown is located a few miles southeast of Harrisburg.

Schedule

The Middletown & Hummelstown Railroad operates from May through

October on Saturdays, Sundays, and some holidays. The train departs Middletown at 11:00 a.m., 1:00, 2:30 and 4:00 p.m. During the months of July and August, the train also operates Tuesday through Friday with departure times of 11:00 a.m., 1:00 and 2:30 p.m.

Fares

Round trip fares for adults are $6.00 for the train ride only and $13.00 for the train ride/cavern tour combination. Tickets for children ages 3 to 11 are $3.00 and $6.50. Children under 3 ride free when not occupying a seat.

Ride Information

Middletown & Hummelstown Railroad
136 Brown Street
Middletown, PA 17057
Phone: 717-944-4435

Local Information

Capital Region Chamber of Commerce
P.O. Box 969
Harrisburg, PA 17108
Phone: 717-232-4121

Notes

Special events operate throughout the year, please call or write for complete details. The number of train/cavern combination tickets on any train is limited and subject to Caverns' capacity. In addition, cavern tours are not available on the last train ride of each operating day. Snacks and beverages are available on board as is a gift shop. Group discounts available.

SPECIAL EVENTS AND EXCURSIONS

CHILDREN'S DAY	
DINING:	
BRUNCH	
LUNCH	
DINNER	✓
EASTER BUNNY	✓
FAIRS/FESTIVALS	
FALL FOLIAGE	✓
FATHER'S DAY	✓
GRANDPARENT'S DAY	
HALLOWEEN	✓
INDEPENDENCE DAY	✓
LABOR DAY	✓
MEMORIAL DAY	✓
MOONLIGHT	
MOTHER'S DAY	✓
MURDER MYSTERIES	
NEW YEAR	✓
SANTA CLAUS	✓
THANKSGIVING	
TRAIN ROBBERIES	
VALENTINE'S DAY	✓
VETERAN'S DAY	

Call for current information, schedule and fares on the above special events.

NEW HOPE & IVYLAND RAIL ROAD

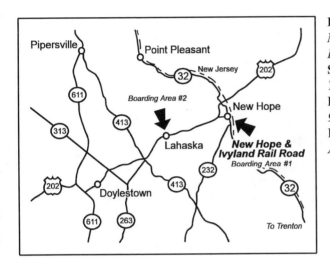

LOCATION
*New Hope and
Lahaska*
SEASON
Year Round
ROUND TRIP
9 Miles
FARES
Adult, $7.95

The Ride

The New Hope & Ivyland Rail Road operates a narrated, 9 mile scenic steam train ride through the rolling hills and valleys of eastern Pennsylvania between New Hope and Lahaska. Passengers traveling from either location may layover and catch a later train back to their original point of departure. The entire round trip takes about one hour to complete.

All Aboard

Passengers may board at the New Hope Station in downtown New Hope or at the Lahaska Station, east of U.S. Highway 202 on Street Road. New Hope is approximately 35 miles north of Philadelphia on the Delaware River.

Schedule

The New Hope & Ivyland Rail Road operates on weekends and holidays from November through early April. Daily departures take place mid-April through October except for Tuesdays and Wednesdays from late April through late May. Departure times for all rides are 11:00 a.m., 12:00 noon, 1:00, 2:00, 3:00, 4:00 and 5:15 p.m. from the New Hope Station and 11:30 a.m.,

12:30, 1:30, 2:30, 3:30, 4:30 and 5:50 p.m. from the Lahaska Station. The 4:30 and 5:50 trains from Lahaska are one-way trips to New Hope only.

Fares

Round trip fare for adults is $7.95 and $6.95 for seniors. The ticket price for children ages 2 through 11 is $3.95, under 2 is $1.00.

Ride Information

New Hope & Ivyland Rail Road
P.O. Box 634
New Hope, PA 18938
Phone: 215-862-2332
Fax: 215-862-2150

Local Information

Central Bucks Chamber of Commerce
115 West Court Street
Doylestown, PA 18901
Phone: 215-348-3913 / 215-345-7051
Fax: 215-348-7154

SPECIAL EVENTS AND EXCURSIONS

CHILDREN'S DAY	
DINING:	
BRUNCH	✓
LUNCH	✓
DINNER	✓
EASTER BUNNY	✓
FAIRS/FESTIVALS	
FALL FOLIAGE	✓
FATHER'S DAY	
GRANDPARENT'S DAY	
HALLOWEEN	✓
INDEPENDENCE DAY	✓
LABOR DAY	✓
MEMORIAL DAY	✓
MOONLIGHT	
MOTHER'S DAY	
MURDER MYSTERIES	
NEW YEAR	✓
SANTA CLAUS	✓
THANKSGIVING	
TRAIN ROBBERIES	
VALENTINE'S DAY	
VETERAN'S DAY	

Call for current information, schedule and fares on the above special events.

Notes

Discounts available for large groups. Facilities at the New Hope Station are accessible to the handicapped. A gift shop is located at the New Hope Station and a picnic area is located at the Lahaska Station. Brunch, lunch, and dinner trains operate year-round, please contact for details.

OIL CREEK & TITUSVILLE RAILROAD

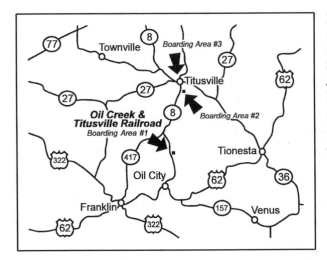

LOCATION
Oil City and Titusville
SEASON
June - October
ROUND TRIP
27 Miles
FARES
Adult, $9.00

The Ride

This 27 mile round trip takes passengers through the Oil Creek Valley, where oil was first extracted from the ground in 1859. Fortune seekers flocked here during the world's first oil boom. You'll see the sites of towns that grew up overnight and then vanished just as quickly when the oil ceased flowing. Volunteer guides provide historical information and tales of the area circa 1859. The entire round trip takes about 2½ hours to complete.

All Aboard

Passengers can board the train at three locations. The Perry Street Station located at 409 S. Perry Street in Titusville, the Drake Well Station just outside the city limits of Titusville at the Drake Well Museum and the Rynd Farm Station located about 4 miles north of Oil City off State Highway 8.

Schedule

The Oil Creek & Titusville Railroad operates train rides from mid-June through late October. Trains departing from the Perry Street Station leave at 11:45 a.m. and 3:15 p.m. on weekends and at 2:00 p.m. Wednesday through Friday. Passengers departing from the Drake Well Station leave at 12:00 noon and 3:30 p.m. on weekends and at 2:15 p.m. Wednesday through Friday. There is only one round trip departure from the Rynd Farm Station on Saturday and Sunday at 1:15 p.m. One-way departures are available from this station at 4:30 p.m. on weekends and 3:00 p.m. Wednesday, Thursday, and Friday.

Fares

Ticket prices for adults are $9.00, children (3 to 17) $5.00. Seniors aged 60 and up are $8.00.

Ride Information

Oil Creek & Titusville Railroad
P.O. Box 68
Oil City, PA 16301
Phone: 814-676-1733
Fax: 814-677-2192

Local Information

Oil City Area Chamber of Commerce
P.O. Box 376
Oil City, CA 16301
Phone: 814-676-8521
Fax: 814-676-8185

Titusville Area Chamber of Commerce
116 West Central Avenue
Titusville, PA 16354
Phone: 814-827-2941
Fax: 814-827-2914

SPECIAL EVENTS AND EXCURSIONS	
CHILDREN'S DAY	
DINING:	
BRUNCH	
LUNCH	
DINNER	✓
EASTER BUNNY	✓
FAIRS/FESTIVALS	✓
FALL FOLIAGE	
FATHER'S DAY	
GRANDPARENT'S DAY	
HALLOWEEN	✓
INDEPENDENCE DAY	
LABOR DAY	✓
MEMORIAL DAY	✓
MOONLIGHT	✓
MOTHER'S DAY	
MURDER MYSTERIES	✓
NEW YEAR	
SANTA CLAUS	✓
THANKSGIVING	
TRAIN ROBBERIES	
VALENTINE'S DAY	
VETERAN'S DAY	

Call for current information, schedule and fares on the above special events.

Notes

Car level platforms with wheelchair ramps are available at the three stations mentioned. October train tickets should be purchased a minimum of 14 days in advance. Refreshments are available on the train. Box lunches are offered with advance notification and payment. Group discounts for 20 or more and charters are available.

Titusville

 051   108

Rail Tours

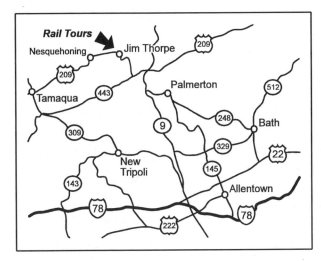

LOCATION
Jim Thorpe
SEASON
May - September
ROUND TRIP
Exc. #1, 8 Miles
Exc. #2, 20 Miles
FARES
Adult,
Exc. #1, $5.00
Exc. #2, $8.00

The Ride

Yesterday's Train Today (Excursion #1): This 8 mile round trip begins in Jim Thorpe and takes passengers to Nesquehoning (milepost 5). The trip takes about 40 minutes to complete.

Lake Hauto Specials (Excursion #2): This scenic train ride travels beyond Nesquehoning and takes passengers to scenic Lake Hauto. The 20 mile round trip takes approximately 1 hour and 45 minutes to complete.

All Aboard

Both scenic excursions begin at the depot in Jim Thorpe located along U.S. Highway 209 across from the Carbon County court house. Jim Thorpe is approximately 26 miles northwest of Allentown in eastern Pennsylvania.

Schedule

Excursion #1: This excursion operates on weekends and holidays from early May through September. The train departs at 12:00 noon, 1:00 p.m., and 2:00 p.m. A 3:00 p.m. departure is added after Labor Day for the remaining weekends in September.

Excursion #2: This scenic train ride operates on Sundays and holidays only from Memorial Day weekend through Labor Day weekend. The train departs at 3:00 p.m.

Fares

Excursion #1: Round trip fare for adults is $5.00 and for children ages 2 through 11, $3.00. Children under 2 ride free.

Excursion #2: Adult tickets for the round trip are $8.00. Children ages 2 through 11 are $4.00. Children under 2 ride free.

Ride Information

Rail Tours, Inc.
P.O. Box 285
Jim Thorpe, PA 18229
Phone: 717-325-4606

Local Information

Lehighton Chamber of Commerce
364 North First Street
Lehighton, PA 18235
Phone: 610-377-2191

SPECIAL EVENTS AND EXCURSIONS	
CHILDREN'S DAY	
DINING:	
BRUNCH	
LUNCH	
DINNER	
EASTER BUNNY	✓
FAIRS/FESTIVALS	
FALL FOLIAGE	✓
FATHER'S DAY	
GRANDPARENT'S DAY	
HALLOWEEN	
INDEPENDENCE DAY	
LABOR DAY	
MEMORIAL DAY	
MOONLIGHT	
MOTHER'S DAY	
MURDER MYSTERIES	
NEW YEAR	
SANTA CLAUS	✓
THANKSGIVING	
TRAIN ROBBERIES	
VALENTINE'S DAY	
VETERAN'S DAY	

Call for current information, schedule and fares on the above special events.

Notes

Discounts given to groups of 20 or more. Chartered trains available. Facilities are accessible to the physically challenged. Special Fall Foliage runs operate on weekends in October and take about 2¾ hours to complete the 34 mile round trip.

002, 003, 016, 021

080

STRASBURG RAIL ROAD

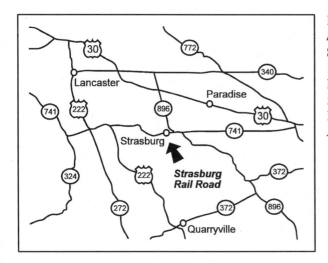

LOCATION
Strasburg
SEASON
Year-round
ROUND TRIP
9 Miles
FARES
Adult, $7.50

The Ride

This 9 mile scenic train ride begins in Strasburg and travels to the town of Paradise and back. You'll travel aboard one of America's oldest steam trains through farmlands and wooded areas. Often times Amish families can be seen working their farms using age-old methods. The entire round trip takes approximately 45 minutes to complete. Passengers may choose to ride in the parlor car, open-air observation cars, or restored wooden coaches, all restored to their original splendor. When available, passengers can combine the train ride with lunch or dinner service.

All Aboard

Passengers board the train on the grounds of the Strasburg Rail Road at the century-old depot located on State Highway 741. Strasburg is located approximately 10 miles southeast of Lancaster.

Schedule

The Strasburg Rail Road operates excursions year-round with various departure times depending on the season. A detailed schedule is available by calling or writing the ride operation. Only the summer schedule is given here.

From May 1st to Memorial Day weekend the train operates daily. Monday through Friday departures are at 11:00 a.m., 12:00 noon, 1:00, 2:00 and 3:00 p.m. On Saturdays, 4:00, 5:00 and 7:00 p.m. departures are added. On Sundays the 11:00 a.m. departure is omitted.

The train operates Monday through Friday from Memorial Day weekend through June with departures at 11:00 a.m., 12:00 noon, 1:00, 2:00, 3:00 and 4:00 p.m. On Saturdays and Sundays, additional departures at 5:00 and 7:00 p.m. are added. The 11:00 a.m. departure is omitted on Sundays.

From July through Labor Day, excursions operate Monday through Saturday with departures every half hour starting at 11:00 a.m. through 4:00 p.m. An early 10:00 a.m. and two evening runs at 5:00 and 7:00 p.m. are also available. On Sundays, the train operates every half hour from noon through 4:00 p.m. Two evening train rides depart at 5:00 and 7:00 p.m.

SPECIAL EVENTS AND EXCURSIONS	
CHILDREN'S DAY	
DINING:	
BRUNCH	
LUNCH	
DINNER	✓
EASTER BUNNY	✓
FAIRS/FESTIVALS	
FALL FOLIAGE	
FATHER'S DAY	
GRANDPARENT'S DAY	
HALLOWEEN	✓
INDEPENDENCE DAY	
LABOR DAY	✓
MEMORIAL DAY	✓
MOONLIGHT	
MOTHER'S DAY	
MURDER MYSTERIES	
NEW YEAR	
SANTA CLAUS	✓
THANKSGIVING	
TRAIN ROBBERIES	
VALENTINE'S DAY	
VETERAN'S DAY	

Call for current information, schedule and fares on the above special events.

Fares

Round trip tickets for adults are $7.50 and for children ages 3 through 11, $4.00. Children under 3 ride for free. Additional charges apply when passengers choose to ride in the parlor car or the dining car. An All Day Fare with unlimited rides is available for $15.00 per person.

Ride Information

Strasburg Rail Road Company
P.O. Box 96
Strasburg, PA 17579
Phone: 717-687-7522

Local Information

Pennsylvania Dutch Convention and Visitor's Bureau
501 Greenfield Road
Lancaster, PA 17601
Phone: 717-299-8901
Fax: 717-299-0470

Notes

Trains operate rain or shine except January through March. A gift shop and restaurant are located on the grounds. Boxed lunches are available at the restaurant for those planning a picnic at Groff's Grove along the train route. Group rates for 20 or more are available. Bus and tour groups are welcome. The Railroad Museum of Pennsylvania is just across the road from the Strasburg Rail Road. The museum houses one of the largest collections of locomotives and passenger coaches in the country.

 072

OLD COLONY & NEWPORT RAILWAY

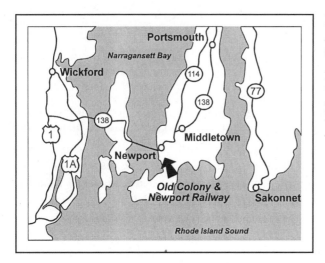

LOCATION
Newport
SEASON
May - November
ROUND TRIP
21 Miles
FARES
Adult, $6.00

The Ride

The Old Colony & Newport Railway offers a 21 mile, 3 hour round trip ride from downtown Newport to the Green Animals Topiary Gardens. The scenic train ride follows the natural rocky beaches of the Narragansett Bay, offering views of ships sailing in the bay and the Newport Naval Base. The 3 hour ride includes a one hour layover at the Green Animals Topiary Gardens. An additional fee is charged for admission or passengers may choose to stay on the train. The Old Colony & Newport Railway also offers a shorter 10 mile, one hour round trip ride from Newport during the summer months.

All Aboard

Passengers board the train at the depot in downtown Newport located at 19 America's Cup Avenue, next to the Newport Tourist Center.

Schedule

The 21 mile round trip operates on Sundays and holidays from May through mid-November and departs at 12:30 p.m. The shorter 10 mile round trip operates on Wednesday, Thursday, Saturday, Sunday, and holidays from July through Labor Day. Departure times are 11:00 a.m., 12:30 and 2:00 p.m.

Fares

Adult ticket prices for the 3 hour trip are $6.00 and $5.00 for the 1 hour trip. Children under 14 are $4.00 and $3.00. Senior citizen ticket prices are $5.00 and $4.00. Family rates are available. Tickets for riding in the parlor car on the 3 hour trip are $9.00 and $7.00 for the shorter trip.

Ride Information

Old Colony & Newport Railway
P.O. Box 343
Newport, RI 02840
Phone: 401-624-6951

Local Information

Newport County Chamber of Commerce
45 Valley Road
Newport, RI 02842
Phone: 401-847-1600
Fax: 401-849-5848

SPECIAL EVENTS AND EXCURSIONS
CHILDREN'S DAY
DINING:
BRUNCH
LUNCH
DINNER
EASTER BUNNY
FAIRS/FESTIVALS
FALL FOLIAGE ✓
FATHER'S DAY
GRANDPARENT'S DAY
HALLOWEEN
INDEPENDENCE DAY
LABOR DAY ✓
MEMORIAL DAY ✓
MOONLIGHT
MOTHER'S DAY
MURDER MYSTERIES
NEW YEAR
SANTA CLAUS ✓
THANKSGIVING
TRAIN ROBBERIES
VALENTINE'S DAY
VETERAN'S DAY
Call for current information, schedule and fares on the above special events.

Notes

Group discounts and charters are available. Train facilities are accessible to the physically challenged.

 005, 011

 049

 068, 081, 092

BLACK HILLS CENTRAL RAILROAD

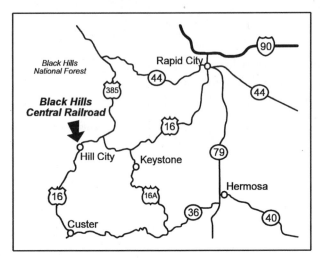

LOCATION
*Hill City and
Keystone Jct.*
SEASON
May - September
ROUND TRIP
20 Miles
FARES
Adult, $14.00

The Ride

The Black Hills Central Railroad offers a scenic 20 mile round trip that climbs steep grades as it winds through the Black Hills National Forest in western South Dakota. Spectacular mountain scenery, including the highest point between the Swiss Alps and the Rocky Mountains, are offered from the cars of this 1880's steam train. Mount Rushmore National Memorial is nearby. Allow 2 hours for the round trip ride.

All Aboard

Passengers have the option of boarding in either Hill City or near Keystone. The depot in Hill City is located on U.S. Highways 16 and 385. The Keystone boarding area is located at the Keystone junction on U.S. Highway 16A.

Schedule

The Black Hills Central Railroad operates train runs daily from mid-May through September. Before June and after Labor Day the schedule is reduced, please inquire for details. The train departs Hill City at 8:00 a.m. (except weekends), 10:15 a.m., 1:30 and 3:45 p.m. From Keystone Junction, the train leaves at 9:00 a.m. (except weekends), 11:15 a.m., 2:30 and

4:45 p.m. The 4:45 p.m. train from Keystone Junction is one-way only. Additional evening trains run in July and August.

Fares

The round trip fare for adults is $14.00, children 4 through 14 are $9.00. One-way ticket prices for adults are $10.00 and $6.50 for children. Children 3 and under ride free when not occupying a seat.

Ride Information

Black Hills Central Railroad
P.O. Box 1880
Hill City, SD 57745
Phone: 605-574-2222
Fax: 605-574-4915

Local Information

Hill City Area Chamber of Commerce
P.O. Box 253
Hill City, SD 57745
Phone: 800-888-1798

Rapid City Chamber of Commerce
P.O. Box 747
Rapid City, SD 57709
Phone: 605-343-1744
Fax: 605-343-1916

Notes

Groups of 20 or more receive discount prices. A snack bar and gift shop are located in the Hill City Depot area.

Keystone

 007, 014

 119, 128

SPECIAL EVENTS AND EXCURSIONS
CHILDREN'S DAY
DINING:
BRUNCH
LUNCH
DINNER
EASTER BUNNY
FAIRS/FESTIVALS
FALL FOLIAGE
FATHER'S DAY
GRANDPARENT'S DAY
HALLOWEEN
INDEPENDENCE DAY
LABOR DAY ✓
MEMORIAL DAY
MOONLIGHT ✓
MOTHER'S DAY
MURDER MYSTERIES
NEW YEAR
SANTA CLAUS
THANKSGIVING
TRAIN ROBBERIES
VALENTINE'S DAY
VETERAN'S DAY

Call for current information, schedule and fares on the above special events.

TENNESSEE VALLEY RAILROAD

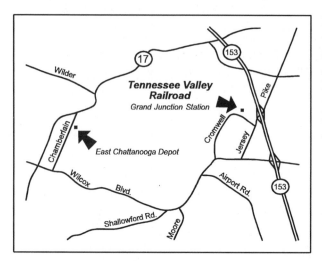

LOCATION
Chattanooga
SEASON
April - November
ROUND TRIP
6 Miles
FARES
Adult, $8.50

The Ride

The Tennessee Valley Railroad operates this 6 mile round trip between the Grand Junction Station and East Chattanooga Depot. The 1930's steam train travels across wooded areas, crossing the Chickamauga Creek and through the 986-foot Missionary Ridge Tunnel. The entire round trip takes approximately 45 minutes to complete.

All Aboard

Passengers may board at either depot. The Grand Junction Station is located at 4119 Cromwell Road and the East Chattanooga Depot is at 2200 North Chamberlain Avenue.

Schedule

The Tennessee Valley Railroad operates weekdays between 10:00 a.m. and 2:00 p.m. in April, May, September, and October and between 10:00 a.m. and 5:00 p.m. during the summer months. Weekend train rides operate between 10:00 a.m and 5:00 p.m. on Saturday and 12:00 noon and 5:00 p.m. on Sunday from April through November. Departure times from the East

Chattanooga Depot are 10:30 and 11:40 a.m., 12:55, 2:10, 3:25 and 4:35 p.m. Departures from the Grand Junction Station are 11:00 a.m., 12:15, 1:35, 2:45, 4:00 and 5:00 p.m.

Fares

Round trip fare for adults is $8.50 and for children ages 3 through 12, $4.50

Ride Information

Tennessee Valley Railroad
4119 Cromwell Road
Chattanooga, TN 37421
Phone: 423-894-8028
Fax: 423-894-8029

Local Information

Chattanooga Area Chamber of Commerce
1001 Market Street
Chattanooga, TN 37402
Phone: 423-756-2121
Fax: 423-267-7242

SPECIAL EVENTS AND EXCURSIONS

CHILDREN'S DAY	
DINING:	
BRUNCH	
LUNCH	✓
DINNER	✓
EASTER BUNNY	
FAIRS/FESTIVALS	
FALL FOLIAGE	✓
FATHER'S DAY	✓
GRANDPARENT'S DAY	✓
HALLOWEEN	✓
INDEPENDENCE DAY	✓
LABOR DAY	✓
MEMORIAL DAY	✓
MOONLIGHT	
MOTHER'S DAY	✓
MURDER MYSTERIES	
NEW YEAR	
SANTA CLAUS	
THANKSGIVING	
TRAIN ROBBERIES	
VALENTINE'S DAY	
VETERAN'S DAY	

Call for current information, schedule and fares on the above special events.

Notes

The Tennessee Valley Railroad also operates the "Downtown Arrow" during the summer months between the Grand Junction Station and Chattanooga Choo Choo Holiday Inn. Facilities are accessible to the handicapped. Group discounts and charters available. The Tennessee Valley Railroad also operates special excursion runs April through October.

AUSTIN STEAM TRAIN

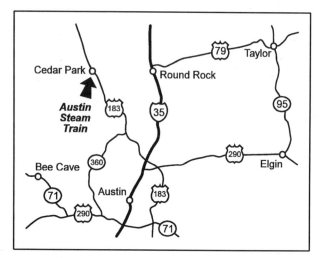

LOCATION
Cedar Park
SEASON
March - December
ROUND TRIP
66 Miles
FARES
Adult, $24.00

The Ride

Passengers board the Hill Country Flyer in Cedar Park and travel northwest to historic Burnet. This 66 mile round trip travels through Short Creek Canyon, crosses the South San Gabriel River, and then descends into the Hamilton Creek Valley before reaching Burnet. A 3 hour layover in Burnet gives passengers the opportunity to shop and explore historic Burnet. Passengers are treated to an Old West gun fight before the train leaves Burnet. The entire round trip, including layover, lasts about 7½ hours. One-way trips are also available.

All Aboard

The Hill Country Flyer departs Cedar Park from the depot located at the intersection of U.S. Highway 183 and F.M. 1431 at the Capital Metro Park and Ride. Cedar Park is about 4 miles northwest of Austin.

Schedule

This excursion train runs from March through December on weekends only. The train leaves Cedar Park at 10:00 a.m. and returns by 5:30 p.m. from

March through November 24. From November 30 through the last weekend in December, the train departs at 2:30 p.m. and returns by 9:30 p.m.

Fares

Ticket prices for adults, coach class, are $24.00 and $10.00 for children 2 through 13. Senior citizens receive a 10% discount. First class fare for adults is $38.00 and $19.00 for children. Children under 2 ride free.

Ride Information

Austin Steam Train Association
P.O. Box 1632
Austin, TX 78767
Phone: 512-477-8468 / 512-477-6377

Local Information

Cedar Park Chamber of Commerce
P.O. Box 1464
Cedar Park, TX 78630
Phone: 512-258-8007 / 512-258-8023

Burnet Chamber of Commerce
705 Buchanan Drive
Burnet, TX 78611
Phone: 512-756-4297

Notes

A shorter 2 hour excursion run is available in the evening on selected Saturdays. Reservations are required as seating is limited. First class passengers are provided complimentary snacks and soft drinks. Group discounts and charters are available. Passengers can choose to stay overnight in Burnet and catch a later train back to Cedar Park.

SPECIAL EVENTS AND EXCURSIONS	
CHILDREN'S DAY	
DINING:	
BRUNCH	
LUNCH	
DINNER	
EASTER BUNNY	✓
FAIRS/FESTIVALS	✓
FALL FOLIAGE	
FATHER'S DAY	✓
GRANDPARENT'S DAY	✓
HALLOWEEN	✓
INDEPENDENCE DAY	
LABOR DAY	
MEMORIAL DAY	
MOONLIGHT	
MOTHER'S DAY	✓
MURDER MYSTERIES	✓
NEW YEAR	✓
SANTA CLAUS	✓
THANKSGIVING	
TRAIN ROBBERIES	✓
VALENTINE'S DAY	
VETERAN'S DAY	

Call for current information, schedule and fares on the above special events.

TEXAS STATE RAILROAD

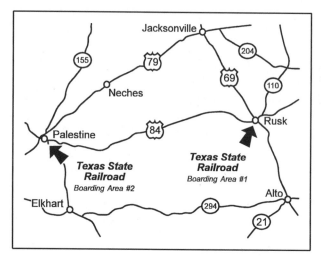

LOCATION
Palestine and Rusk
SEASON
March - November
ROUND TRIP
50 Miles
FARES
Adult, $15.00

The Ride

Passengers aboard the Texas State Railroad travel 50 miles round trip through
the pine and hardwood forests of eastern Texas between Palestine and Rusk.
There are some 30 bridges that the train crosses, the longest being 1,100 feet
spanning the Neches River. The train ride takes about 4 hours to complete,
including a 1 hour layover in either Palestine or Rusk, depending on which
town you depart from. One-way trips are also available.

All Aboard

Passengers can choose to begin their train ride in either Palestine or Rusk.
The Palestine depot is located on U.S. Highway 84, about 3 miles east of
town. The Rusk depot is about 2 miles west of town on U.S. Highway 84.

Schedule

The Texas State Railroad operates on weekends only from mid-March through
May and from early August through November. Additional train rides are
added on Thursday and Friday in June and July. The train leaves at 11:00
a.m. from both depot locations.

Fares

Round trip fares for adults are $15.00 and for children ages 3 to 12, $9.00. One-way tickets are also available and the cost to adults is $10.00 and for children, $6.00.

Ride Information

Texas State Railroad
P.O. Box 39
Rusk, TX 75785
Phone: 903-683-2561
          800-442-8951 (in Texas)

Local Information

Palestine Chamber of Commerce
P.O. Box 1177
Palestine, TX 75802
Phone: 800-659-3484 / 903-729-6066
Fax: 903-729-2083

Rusk Chamber of Commerce
P.O. Box 67
Rusk, TX 75785
Phone: 903-683-4242

SPECIAL EVENTS AND EXCURSIONS	
CHILDREN'S DAY	
DINING:	
BRUNCH	
LUNCH	
DINNER	
EASTER BUNNY	
FAIRS/FESTIVALS	✓
FALL FOLIAGE	✓
FATHER'S DAY	
GRANDPARENT'S DAY	
HALLOWEEN	
INDEPENDENCE DAY	
LABOR DAY	✓
MEMORIAL DAY	✓
MOONLIGHT	✓
MOTHER'S DAY	
MURDER MYSTERIES	✓
NEW YEAR	
SANTA CLAUS	
THANKSGIVING	
TRAIN ROBBERIES	✓
VALENTINE'S DAY	
VETERAN'S DAY	

Call for current information, schedule and fares on the above special events.

Notes

Reservations are recommended. Tickets may be picked up at the depot at least one hour before departure. An engine cab tour is offered before the train departs. Snacks, ice cream, beverages, and souvenirs are sold on the train. An evening train runs from the Rusk depot on selected nights in May and October. Special school discounts available. Group rates and charters are available.

Palestine

 135

HEBER VALLEY RAILROAD

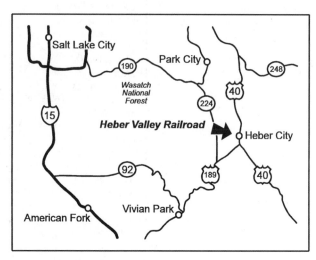

LOCATION
Heber City
SEASON
May - October
ROUND TRIP
32 Miles
FARES
Adult,
$14.00 - $16.00

The Ride

Passengers aboard the Heber Valley Railroad begin their 32 mile, 3½ hour round trip in Heber City. The train travels through high mountain meadows, across streams and rivers, and through the Provo River Canyon before reaching the destination of Vivian Park. There is a 30 minute layover in Vivian Park or you can stay longer and return on a later train. One-way trips are also available, however, passengers must provide return or continuing transportation.

All Aboard

Passengers board at the depot in Heber City located at 450 South 600 West. Heber City is approximately 25 miles northeast of Provo and 44 miles southeast of Salt Lake City.

Schedule

The Heber Valley Railroad operates weekends and holidays in May and October and daily from June through September. Departure times are 10:00 a.m. and 2:30 p.m. An evening train departs at 7:00 p.m. on Saturdays from late June through September. The Heber Valley Railroad also operates from Thanksgiving weekend to mid-March and departs from the Heber Depot at 1:30 p.m. on Friday, Saturday and Sunday.

Fares

Fares will vary depending on which locomotive is used. For the steam-powered train, adult round trip tickets are $16.00 and $14.00 for trains pulled by the diesel locomotive. Children ages 3 through 12 are $10.00 and $8.00. Children 2 and under ride free. Discounted prices for senior citizens are offered.

Ride Information

Heber Valley Railroad
P.O. Box 641
Heber City, UT 84032
Phone: 801-654-5601 (Heber City)
            801-581-9980 (Salt Lake City)

Local Information

Heber Valley Chamber of Commerce
P.O. Box 427
Heber City, UT 84032
Phone: 801-654-3666
Fax: 801-654-1479

SPECIAL EVENTS AND EXCURSIONS	
CHILDREN'S DAY	
DINING:	
BRUNCH	
LUNCH	
DINNER	
EASTER BUNNY	
FAIRS/FESTIVALS	
FALL FOLIAGE	✓
FATHER'S DAY	✓
GRANDPARENT'S DAY	
HALLOWEEN	
INDEPENDENCE DAY	✓
LABOR DAY	✓
MEMORIAL DAY	✓
MOONLIGHT	✓
MOTHER'S DAY	✓
MURDER MYSTERIES	
NEW YEAR	
SANTA CLAUS	✓
THANKSGIVING	
TRAIN ROBBERIES	
VALENTINE'S DAY	
VETERAN'S DAY	

Call for current information, schedule and fares on the above special events.

Notes

Reservations are strongly recommended. Discounts for groups of 25 or more available. Charters available. Box lunches can be ordered with reservation. Access for the physically challenged is limited. Souvenirs are sold on the train and at the Heber City Depot. Passengers have access to open-air observation cars.

GREEN MOUNTAIN RAILROAD

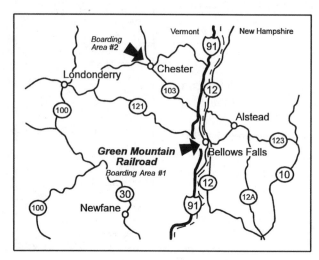

LOCATION
*Bellows Falls and
Chester*
SEASON
June - October
ROUND TRIP
26 Miles
FARES
Adult, $11.00

The Ride

The Green Mountain Railroad operates the Green Mountain Flyer excursion train between Bellows Falls and Chester. The route follows alongside the Connecticut and Williams Rivers. Passengers are treated to views of the Brockway Mills Gorge, covered bridges, and the rolling Vermont countryside. The 26 mile round trip takes about 2 hours to complete. One-way trips are also available.

All Aboard

Passengers may board the train in either Bellows Falls or Chester. The depot in Bellows Falls is located east of U.S. Highway 5 on Depot Street at the Amtrak station. The station in Chester is located on State Highway 103, where the tracks cross the highway.

Schedule

The Green Mountain Flyer operates on weekends in late June, Tuesday through Sunday (open on Monday if a holiday) in July, August, and early September. The train runs daily from mid-September through mid-October.

The train ride also operates Labor Day weekend. There are two departures from Bellows Falls, one at 11:00 a.m. and one at 2:00 p.m. There is only one departure from Chester at 12:10 p.m.

Fares

Round trip fares for adults are $11.00, one-way tickets $7.00. For children ages 3 to 12, round trip fare is $7.00 and $5.00 for the one-way trip. Children under 3 ride free when not occupying a seat.

Ride Information

Green Mountain Railroad Corp.
P.O. Box 498
Bellows Falls, VT 05101
Phone: 802-463-3069

Local Information

Greater Falls Region Chamber of Commerce
P.O. Box 554
Bellows Falls, VT 05101
Phone: 802-463-4280

Chester Chamber of Commerce
P.O. Box 623
Chester, VT 05143
Phone: 802-875-2939

Notes

For groups of 30 or more, discounted prices are available. Advance reservations required for group rates. Chartered operations are also available. Trains run rain or shine.

SPECIAL EVENTS AND EXCURSIONS

Children's Day
Dining:
   Brunch
   Lunch
   Dinner
Easter Bunny ✓
Fairs/Festivals
Fall Foliage ✓
Father's Day ✓
Grandparent's Day
Halloween
Independence Day ✓
Labor Day ✓
Memorial Day ✓
Moonlight ✓
Mother's Day ✓
Murder Mysteries
New Year
Santa Claus ✓
Thanksgiving
Train Robberies
Valentine's Day ✓
Veteran's Day

Call for current information, schedule and fares on the above special events.

CHEHALIS - CENTRALIA RAILROAD

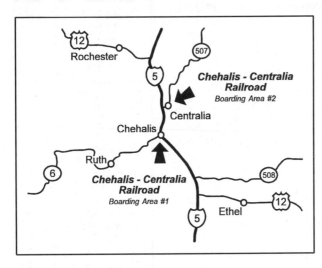

LOCATION
Chehalis and Centralia
SEASON
May - September
ROUND TRIP
Exc. #1, 12 Miles
Exc. #2, 18 Miles
FARES
Adult,
Exc. #1, $7.00
Exc. #2, $11.00

The Ride

The Chehalis - Centralia Railroad offers two excursions through the countryside of southwestern Washington. The steam-powered train travels through rural farmlands and the Chehalis River Valley.

Chehalis and Centralia (Excursion #1): This 12 mile round trip between the towns of Chehalis and Centralia takes approximately 2 hours to complete. One-way trips are also available.

Chehalis to Ruth (Excursion #2): This 18 mile round trip travels from Chehalis south to the town of Ruth. Allow 2½ to 3 hours for the round trip.

All Aboard

Excursion #1: Passengers can board in either Chehalis or in Centralia. The depot in Chehalis is located on Main Street, one block east of I-5. The Centralia depot is also located east of I-5 on Main Street in Centralia.

Excursion #2: Boarding for this excursion is only available in Chehalis, on Main Street.

Schedule

Excursion #1: This scenic excursion operates on weekends only from Memorial Day weekend through Labor Day weekend. The train departs Chehalis at 1:00 and 3:00 p.m. and from Centralia at 2:00 and 4:00 p.m. The 4:00 p.m. departure from Centralia is a one-way trip only.

Excursion #2: This ride operates on Saturdays only from Memorial Day weekend through Labor Day weekend and departs at 5:00 p.m.

Fares

Excursion #1: Round trip fares for adults are $7.00 and $3.50 for one-way tickets. Children ages 3 through 16 are $5.00 and $2.50 for one-way trips. Children under 3 ride free.

Excursion #2: Round trip fare for adults is $11.00 and $9.00 for children ages 3 to 16. Children under 3 ride free.

Ride Information

Chehalis - Centralia Railroad Association
1945 South Market Blvd.
Chehalis, WA 98532
Phone: 360-748-9593

Local Information

Twin Cities Chamber of Commerce
500 N.W. Chamber Way
Chehalis, WA 98532
Phone: 800-525-3323 / 360-748-8885
Fax: 360-748-8763

Notes

Group rates and charters are available.

SPECIAL EVENTS AND EXCURSIONS	
CHILDREN'S DAY	
DINING:	
BRUNCH	
LUNCH	
DINNER	✓
EASTER BUNNY	
FAIRS/FESTIVALS	
FALL FOLIAGE	
FATHER'S DAY	
GRANDPARENT'S DAY	
HALLOWEEN	
INDEPENDENCE DAY	
LABOR DAY	✓
MEMORIAL DAY	✓
MOONLIGHT	
MOTHER'S DAY	
MURDER MYSTERIES	
NEW YEAR	
SANTA CLAUS	
THANKSGIVING	
TRAIN ROBBERIES	
VALENTINE'S DAY	
VETERAN'S DAY	

Call for current information, schedule and fares on the above special events.

LAKE WHATCOM RAILWAY

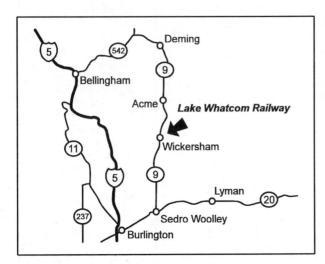

LOCATION
Wickersham
SEASON
July - August
ROUND TRIP
7 Miles
FARES
Adult, $10.00

The Ride

The Lake Whatcom Railway operates a 7 mile scenic excursion ride from Wickersham to the shores of Lake Whatcom. The steam-powered train takes passengers through a tunnel and travels along Mirror Lake through the scenic countryside of northwestern Washington. Allow approximately one hour to complete the round trip.

All Aboard

Passengers board the train at the depot in downtown Wickersham. Wickersham is about 10 miles north of Sedro Woolley and 30 miles south of the Canadian border.

Schedule

The Lake Whatcom Railway operates on Saturdays and Tuesdays only from the first of July through the end of August. The train departs Wickersham Junction at 11:00 a.m. and 1:00 p.m.

Fares

The adult ticket price is $10.00 and for children ages 2 through 17, $5.00.

Ride Information

Lake Whatcom Railway
P.O. Box 91
Acme, WA 98220
Phone: 360-595-2218

Local Information

Bellingham - Whatcom Chamber of Commerce
P.O. Box 958
Bellingham, WA 98227
Phone: 360-734-1330
Fax: 360-734-1332

Notes

Railroad facilities are accessible to the physically challenged. Group discounts are available. The train may be chartered year-round. Refreshments are available on the train.

SPECIAL EVENTS AND EXCURSIONS

CHILDREN'S DAY
DINING:
    BRUNCH
    LUNCH
    DINNER
EASTER BUNNY ✓
FAIRS/FESTIVALS
FALL FOLIAGE ✓
FATHER'S DAY
GRANDPARENT'S DAY
HALLOWEEN
INDEPENDENCE DAY ✓
LABOR DAY
MEMORIAL DAY
MOONLIGHT
MOTHER'S DAY
MURDER MYSTERIES
NEW YEAR
SANTA CLAUS ✓
THANKSGIVING
TRAIN ROBBERIES
VALENTINE'S DAY ✓
VETERAN'S DAY

Call for current information, schedule and fares on the above special events.

LEWIS & CLARK RAILWAY

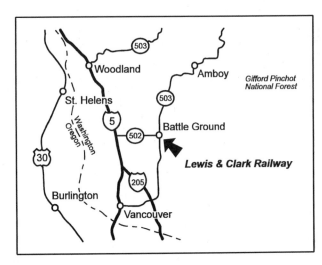

LOCATION
Battle Ground
SEASON
May - October
ROUND TRIP
20 Miles
FARES
Adult, $10.00

The Ride

This 20 mile round trip begins in Battle Ground and travels to the Moulton Falls County Park. Passengers aboard this scenic train ride travel through southwestern Washington's forests and farmlands, passing through the Yacolt Mountain Tunnel and crossing the East Fork of the Lewis River. The trip lasts approximately 2½ hours. Passengers can choose to ride in open-air observation cars, coaches, or the caboose.

All Aboard

Passengers board the train at the depot located in downtown Battle Ground at 1000 East Main Street. Battle Ground is about 15 miles north of Portland, Oregon.

Schedule

The Lewis & Clark Railway operates on Saturdays and Sundays from late May through early September with departure times of 10:00 a.m. and 1:30 p.m. From early September through October, the train operates on weekends and departs at 1:30 p.m. only.

Fares

Adult tickets cost $10.00, children ages 3 through 15 are $5.00. Ticket prices for seniors aged 60 and over are $9.00.

Ride Information

Lewis & Clark Railway Company
P.O. Box 604
Battle Ground, WA 98604
Phone: 360-687-2626

Local Information

Battle Ground Chamber of Commerce
1012 East Main Street
Battle Ground, WA 98604
Phone: 360-687-1510
Fax: 360-687-4505

Notes

Chartered trips are available. Special runs are offered for Spring, Fall and Christmas. Facilities are accessible to the handicapped. A gift shop and picnic area are located at the depot site.

SPECIAL EVENTS AND EXCURSIONS

CHILDREN'S DAY	
DINING:	
BRUNCH	
LUNCH	
DINNER	
EASTER BUNNY	
FAIRS/FESTIVALS	
FALL FOLIAGE	✓
FATHER'S DAY	
GRANDPARENT'S DAY	
HALLOWEEN	
INDEPENDENCE DAY	✓
LABOR DAY	✓
MEMORIAL DAY	✓
MOONLIGHT	
MOTHER'S DAY	
MURDER MYSTERIES	
NEW YEAR	
SANTA CLAUS	✓
THANKSGIVING	
TRAIN ROBBERIES	
VALENTINE'S DAY	
VETERAN'S DAY	

Call for current information, schedule and fares on the above special events.

MOUNT RAINIER SCENIC RAILROAD

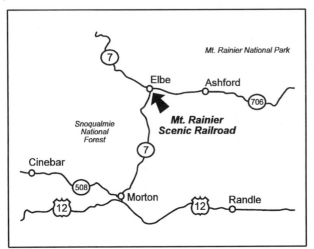

LOCATION
Elbe
SEASON
May - September
ROUND TRIP
14 Miles
FARES
Adult, $8.50

The Ride

This scenic train ride takes its passengers from Elbe to Mineral Lake through forests and farmland, crosses the Nisqually River, and offers views of the 14,410-foot high Mt. Rainier. Passengers are treated to live entertainment as they travel the 14 mile round trip. The entire ride takes about 1½ hours to complete, including a 20 minute layover at Mineral Lake. Passengers may also stay at Mineral Lake and catch a later train back to Elbe.

All Aboard

Passengers board the train in Elbe at the depot located on State Highway 7. Elbe is about 42 miles southeast of Tacoma.

Schedule

Mount Rainier Scenic Railroad operates daily from mid-June through Labor Day and on weekends from Memorial Day through the end of September. The train departs Elbe at 11:00 a.m., 1:15 p.m., and 3:30 p.m.

Fares

Adult ticket prices are $8.50. For children under the age of 12, the ticket price is $5.50 and for juniors (ages 12 to 17), $6.50. Seniors receive a $1.00 discount.

Ride Information

Mount Rainier Scenic Railroad
P.O. Box 921
Elbe, WA 98330
Phone: 360-569-2588
Fax: 360-569-2438

Local Information

Morton Chamber of Commerce
P.O. Box 10
Morton, WA 98356
Phone: 360-496-6086

Notes

Group rates and charters are available. Facilities are accessible to the physically challenged.
A gift shop is located at the station site. The Mount Rainier Scenic Railroad also operates a 25 and 40 mile round trip dinner train April through November; please call or write for more details. Open-air cars are available.

SPECIAL EVENTS AND EXCURSIONS	
CHILDREN'S DAY	
DINING:	
BRUNCH	
LUNCH	
DINNER	✓
EASTER BUNNY	
FAIRS/FESTIVALS	
FALL FOLIAGE	
FATHER'S DAY	✓
GRANDPARENT'S DAY	
HALLOWEEN	
INDEPENDENCE DAY	
LABOR DAY	✓
MEMORIAL DAY	✓
MOONLIGHT	
MOTHER'S DAY	✓
MURDER MYSTERIES	
NEW YEAR	
SANTA CLAUS	✓
THANKSGIVING	
TRAIN ROBBERIES	
VALENTINE'S DAY	
VETERAN'S DAY	

Call for current information, schedule and fares on the above special events.

 052

 117

PUGET SOUND & SNOQUALMIE

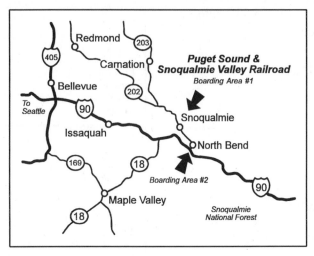

LOCATION
Snoqualmie and North Bend
SEASON
April - October
ROUND TRIP
10 Miles
FARES
Adult, $7.00

The Ride

The Puget Sound & Snoqualmie Valley Railroad offers a 10 mile round trip between the towns of Snoqualmie and North Bend, traveling through the scenic countryside of west-central Washington. The diesel-powered round trip takes approximately 1 hour and 15 minutes to complete. Passengers may layover in either town and take a later train back to their origin of departure.

All Aboard

Passengers may board the train in either Snoqualmie or North Bend. Both stations are located just off Interstate 90. The depot in Snoqualmie (built in 1890 and listed on the National Register of Historic Places) is located at 38625 S.E. King Street. The North Bend Station is located at 205 McLeland Street.

Schedule

The Puget Sound & Snoqualmie Valley Railroad operates on Saturdays from Memorial Day weekend through September and on Sundays from April through October. Departures times from Snoqualmie are 11:00 a.m., 12:30, 2:00, 3:30 and 5:00 p.m. The train departs from North Bend at 11:30 a.m., 1:00, 2:30 and 4:00 p.m.

Fares

Round trip fares for adults are $7.00 and for seniors aged 62 and older, $6.00. Fares for children ages 3 through 12 are $5.00. Children under 3 ride free.

Ride Information

Puget Sound Railway Historical Association
P.O. Box 459
Snoqualmie, WA 98065
Phone: 206-746-4025

Local Information

Upper Snoqualmie Valley Chamber of Commerce
P.O. Box 357
North Bend, WA 98045
Phone: 206-888-4440
Fax: 206-888-2427

SPECIAL EVENTS AND EXCURSIONS

CHILDREN'S DAY
DINING:
    BRUNCH
    LUNCH
    DINNER
EASTER BUNNY
FAIRS/FESTIVALS ✓
FALL FOLIAGE
FATHER'S DAY
GRANDPARENT'S DAY
HALLOWEEN ✓
INDEPENDENCE DAY
LABOR DAY
MEMORIAL DAY
MOONLIGHT
MOTHER'S DAY
MURDER MYSTERIES
NEW YEAR
SANTA CLAUS ✓
THANKSGIVING
TRAIN ROBBERIES
VALENTINE'S DAY
VETERAN'S DAY

Call for current information, schedule and fares on the above special events.

Notes

Group rates are available for 20 or more persons. Charters are also available. A gift shop and museum are located in the Snoqualmie depot. Open-air cars are available.

TOPPENISH, SIMCOE & WESTERN

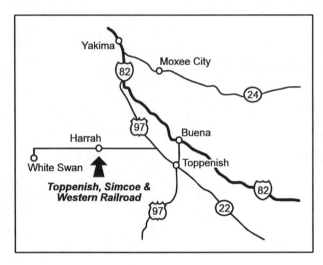

LOCATION
Harrah
SEASON
June - October
ROUND TRIP
20 Miles
FARES
Adult, $5.00

The Ride

The Toppenish, Simcoe & Western Railroad operates on the former Northern Pacific White Swan branch line. The 20 mile scenic train ride travels between Harrah and White Swan in south-central Washington. Allow about two hours for the complete round trip. One-way trips are also available.

All Aboard

Passengers board the train in Harrah which is located about 25 miles south of Yakima.

Schedule

The Toppenish, Simcoe & Western Railroad operates on Saturday and Sunday only from June through October. The train departs at 2:00 p.m. each day.

Fares

Round trip fare for adults is $5.00 and for children, $3.00.

Ride Information

Yakima Valley Rail & Steam Museum
P.O. Box 889
Toppenish, WA 98948
Phone: 509-865-1911

Local Information

Toppenish Chamber of Commerce
P.O. Box 28
Toppenish, WA 98948
Phone: 509-865-3262
Fax: 509-865-2532

Wapato Chamber of Commerce
P.O. Box 157
Wapato, WA 98951

Notes

Facilities are accessible to the physically challenged. Chartered trains are available year-
round. Group rates are also available. A gift
shop and the Yakima Valley Rail & Steam
Museum are located at 10 Asotin Avenue in
Toppenish, Washington. The museum is open
7 days a week, May through October, except for some holidays, and on
weekends all winter.

SPECIAL EVENTS AND EXCURSIONS	
CHILDREN'S DAY	
DINING:	
BRUNCH	
LUNCH	
DINNER	
EASTER BUNNY	✓
FAIRS/FESTIVALS	
FALL FOLIAGE	
FATHER'S DAY	
GRANDPARENT'S DAY	
HALLOWEEN	✓
INDEPENDENCE DAY	✓
LABOR DAY	
MEMORIAL DAY	
MOONLIGHT	
MOTHER'S DAY	
MURDER MYSTERIES	
NEW YEAR	
SANTA CLAUS	✓
THANKSGIVING	
TRAIN ROBBERIES	
VALENTINE'S DAY	
VETERAN'S DAY	

*Call for current information,
schedule and fares on the
above special events.*

Cass Scenic Railroad

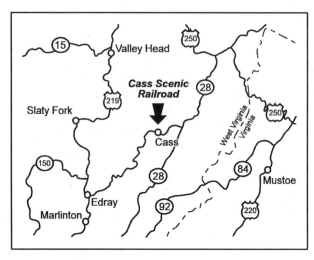

Location
Cass
Season
May - October
Round Trip
Exc. #1, 8 Miles
Exc. #2, 22 Miles
Fares
Adult,
Exc. #1, $11.00
Exc. #2, $15.00

The Ride

The Cass Scenic Railroad offers two excursions, from the town of Cass to Whittaker Station and from Cass to Bald Knob. On both excursions, passengers climb an 11% grade as the train negotiates two switchbacks. Both excursions are powered by a steam locomotive. Passengers enjoy the view from open-air cars.

Whittaker Station (Excursion #1):
This 8 mile round trip begins in the historic town of Cass and takes passengers to Whittaker Station where visitors will have the opportunity to disembark and enjoy the views of the surrounding wilderness area. The round trip takes about 1½ hours to complete.

Bald Knob (Excursion #2):
This 22 mile, 4½ hour round trip also begins in Cass and travels beyond the Whittaker Station to the summit of Bald Knob. At 4,842 feet (the second highest point in West Virginia), the Bald Knob overlook provides views into two states.

All Aboard

Passengers board the train at the depot in Cass located on Front Street.

Schedule

Excursion #1:

The train operates Tuesday through Sunday from Memorial Day to Labor Day and the first two weeks in October. In September, the train operates Friday through Sunday. An additional run is added on Thursday the last two weeks in October. All departure times are 12:00 noon.

Excursion #2:

This scenic excursion runs daily from Memorial Day to Labor Day and for the first two weeks in October. The train operates Friday through Sunday in September and Thursday through Sunday the last two weeks in October. All departure times are 11:00 a.m., 1:00 and 3:00 p.m.

Fares

Excursion #1:

Adult ticket prices are $10.00 during the week and $11.00 on weekends. Children ages 5 through 12 are $6.00 on weekdays and $7.00 on the weekends.

Excursion #2:

Weekday ticket prices for adults are $14.00 and $15.00 on weekends. Child ticket prices (ages 5 through 12) are $8.00 during the week and $9.00 on the weekends.

SPECIAL EVENTS AND EXCURSIONS

CHILDREN'S DAY
DINING:
    BRUNCH
    LUNCH
    DINNER   ✓
EASTER BUNNY
FAIRS/FESTIVALS
FALL FOLIAGE   ✓
FATHER'S DAY
GRANDPARENT'S DAY
HALLOWEEN   ✓
INDEPENDENCE DAY   ✓
LABOR DAY   ✓
MEMORIAL DAY   ✓
MOONLIGHT
MOTHER'S DAY
MURDER MYSTERIES
NEW YEAR
SANTA CLAUS
THANKSGIVING
TRAIN ROBBERIES
VALENTINE'S DAY
VETERAN'S DAY

Call for current information, schedule and fares on the above special events.

Ride Information

Cass Scenic Railroad State Park
P.O. Box 107
Cass, WV 24927
Phone: 800-225-5982 / 304-456-4300

Local Information

Marlinton Chamber of Commerce
1010 3rd Avenue
Marlinton, WV 24954
Phone: 304-799-4048

Notes

Train ticket includes admission to Cass Showcase, Wildlife Museum and Historical Museum. Train reservations are available for tickets only and do not guarantee seats. There is an additional charge of $1.50 per ticket for reservations. Group rates for 25 or more persons are available. Charters are available May through October on all days regular runs are not scheduled. Dinner trains operate on selected Saturday nights during the summer months.

POTOMAC EAGLE

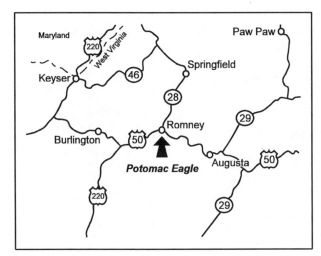

LOCATION
Romney
SEASON
May - October
ROUND TRIP
35 Miles
FARES
Adult,
$16.00 - $19.00

The Ride

This 3 hour narrated scenic excursion travels through pasture land filled with wildflowers and passes farms dating back to the early 1700's along the South Branch of the Potomac River. Passengers on this 35 mile round trip travel through a narrow valley known as "The Trough". It is through this remote region where several Bald Eagles have made their nests and can be seen quite frequently.

All Aboard

Passengers board the train at the Wappocomo Station which is located on State Highway 28, about one mile north of Romney.

Schedule

The train operates on weekends from Memorial Day through Labor Day, departing at 1:00 p.m. Two additional departure times of 10:00 a.m. and 2:00 p.m. are added in September. During October, the train operates on weekdays, departing at 1:00 p.m. and on the weekends at 10:00 a.m. and 2:00 p.m.

Fares

From May through September, the adult ticket price is $16.00. In October the adult fare is $19.00. For children ages 3 to 12, the ticket price is $10.00 and $12.00 in October. Children under 3 ride for free. Senior citizens (aged 60 and over) receive a $1.00 discount from May through September and a $2.00 discount in October.

Ride Information

Potomac Eagle
P.O. Box 657
Romney, WV 26757
Phone: 800-223-2453 (tickets)
           304-822-7464 (information)

Local Information

Hampshire County Chamber of Commerce
HC 74 - Box 2000
Sunrise Professional Bldg.
Romney, WV 26757
Phone: 304-822-7221

SPECIAL EVENTS AND EXCURSIONS	
CHILDREN'S DAY	
DINING:	
BRUNCH	
LUNCH	✓
DINNER	✓
EASTER BUNNY	
FAIRS/FESTIVALS	✓
FALL FOLIAGE	✓
FATHER'S DAY	
GRANDPARENT'S DAY	
HALLOWEEN	
INDEPENDENCE DAY	
LABOR DAY	✓
MEMORIAL DAY	✓
MOONLIGHT	
MOTHER'S DAY	
MURDER MYSTERIES	
NEW YEAR	
SANTA CLAUS	
THANKSGIVING	
TRAIN ROBBERIES	
VALENTINE'S DAY	
VETERAN'S DAY	

Call for current information, schedule and fares on the above special events.

Notes

Passengers may choose to ride in the "Classic Club" for an additional fee which includes lunch. Reservations are recommended for the Fall excursions. Train facilities are handicapped accessible. Snacks and beverages are available on all trains. Chartered trips are available.

 078

MID-CONTINENT RAILWAY

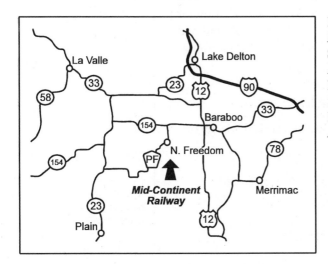

LOCATION
North Freedom
SEASON
May - October
ROUND TRIP
7 Miles
FARES
Adult, $8.00

The Ride

The Mid-Continent Railway offers a steam-powered excursion on the former branch of the Chicago & North Western Railroad built in 1903. The 7 mile excursion begins in North Freedom and travels through the woods and farmland of the Baraboo River Valley. The entire round trip takes nearly one hour to complete.

All Aboard

All trains depart from the restored 1894 depot in North Freedom located on Diamond Hill Road. North Freedom is approximately 50 miles northwest of Madison.

Schedule

Scenic train rides of the Mid-Continent Railway operate daily from mid-May through Labor Day and on weekends after Labor Day through October. Trains depart North Freedom at 10:30 a.m., 12:30, 2:00 and 3:00 p.m.

Fares

The round trip fare for adults is $8.00 and $7.00 for seniors over 62 years old. Children ages 3 through 12 are $4.50, under 3 ride for free. A family rate of $22.00 is offered and includes tickets for 2 adults and 2 or more children.

Ride Information

Mid-Continent Railway Historical Society Inc.
P.O. Box 358
North Freedom, WI 53951
Phone: 800-930-1385 / 608-522-4261
Fax: 608-522-4490

Local Information

Baraboo Area Chamber of Commerce
P.O. Box 442
Baraboo, WI 53913
Phone: 800-227-2266 / 608-356-8333
Fax: 608-356-8422

Reedsburg Area Chamber of Commerce
P.O. Box 142
Reedsburg, WI 53959
Phone: 800-844-3507 / 608-524-2850

SPECIAL EVENTS AND EXCURSIONS	
CHILDREN'S DAY	
DINING:	
BRUNCH	✓
LUNCH	
DINNER	✓
EASTER BUNNY	
FAIRS/FESTIVALS	
FALL FOLIAGE	✓
FATHER'S DAY	
GRANDPARENT'S DAY	
HALLOWEEN	
INDEPENDENCE DAY	✓
LABOR DAY	✓
MEMORIAL DAY	
MOONLIGHT	
MOTHER'S DAY	
MURDER MYSTERIES	
NEW YEAR	
SANTA CLAUS	✓
THANKSGIVING	
TRAIN ROBBERIES	
VALENTINE'S DAY	
VETERAN'S DAY	

Call for current information, schedule and fares on the above special events.

Notes

First class, brunch, and dinner trains run at various times of the year, call or write for details. Group rates available for groups of 15 or more. Charters are also available. The museum located at the depot site includes exhibits of steam locomotives, vintage railroad coaches, freight cars, and cabooses. Facilities are not accessible to the handicapped.

OSCEOLA & ST. CROIX VALLEY

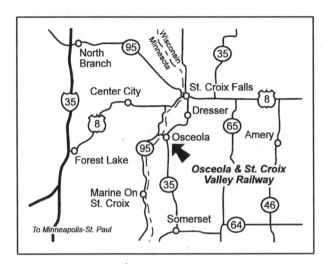

LOCATION
Osceola
SEASON
May - October
ROUND TRIP
Exc. #1, 10 Miles
Exc. #2, 23 Miles
FARES
Adult,
Exc. #1, $7.00
Exc. #2, $10.00

The Ride

The Osceola & St. Croix Valley Railway provides diesel and steam excursions and special event rail trips. Coach Attendants aboard the train provide information on the history of the route and the railroad as well as points of interest and scenic highlights along the way. Passengers on either excursion described below can spend additional time at the destination site and return on a later train.

Osceola To Dresser (Excursion #1):
Passengers aboard this train begin their journey in Osceola and travel 5 miles through the St. Croix River Valley to Dresser, Wisconsin. The entire 10 mile round trip takes about 45 minutes to complete including a 15 to 20 minute layover in Dresser.

Osceola To Marine On St. Croix (Excursion #2):
Passengers on this scenic train ride are taken from Osceola south through the beautiful St. Croix River Valley and cross the St. Croix River before arriving in Marine On St. Croix in Minnesota. The 90 minute round trip travels a total distance of 23 miles. There is a 15 to 20 minute layover in Marine On St. Croix.

All Aboard

Excursions #1 and #2:
Passengers taking either excursion board the train at the historic Osceola Depot located just off Wisconsin State Highway 35, on Depot Street. Osceola is in Polk County in northwestern Wisconsin about one hour northeast of Minneapolis and St. Paul.

Schedule

Excursion #1:
This scenic train ride operates weekends and holidays May through September. In May, June, July, August and October the train departs at 12:45 and 3:45 p.m. In September the departure times are 12:45, 1:45, and 3:45 p.m.

Excursion #2:
This excursion operates on weekends and holidays from May through October. The train departs the depot at 11:00 a.m. and 2:00 p.m. in May, June, July, August, and October. In September, the train departs at 11:00 a.m., 1:00 and 3:00 p.m.

Fares

Excursion #1:
The adult ticket price is $7.00; children aged 5 to 15 are $3.00. Children under 5 ride free. The family rate (2 adults and 2 to 5 children) is $20.00.

Excursion #2:
Adult ticket price is $10.00; children, $6.00. The family rate is $30.00.

Ride Information

Osceola & St. Croix Valley Railway
P.O. Box 176
Osceola, WI 54020
Phone: 800-643-7412
          612-228-0263 (recorded information)

Local Information

Osceola Business Association
P.O. Box 251
Osceola, WI 54020
Phone: 715-755-3300

Saint Croix Falls
P.O. Box 178
Saint Croix Falls, WI 54024
Phone: 715-483-3929

Notes

Group rates available for groups of 15 or more.
Chartered trains available. Special train runs
to Amery, Wisconsin available at various times
of the year. First class service is available and
may be reserved in advance. Facilities are accessible to the physically challenged.

 086

 148

SPECIAL EVENTS AND EXCURSIONS	
CHILDREN'S DAY	
DINING:	
BRUNCH	
LUNCH	
DINNER	
EASTER BUNNY	
FAIRS/FESTIVALS	
FALL FOLIAGE	✓
FATHER'S DAY	
GRANDPARENT'S DAY	
HALLOWEEN	
INDEPENDENCE DAY	✓
LABOR DAY	✓
MEMORIAL DAY	✓
MOONLIGHT	
MOTHER'S DAY	
MURDER MYSTERIES	
NEW YEAR	
SANTA CLAUS	
THANKSGIVING	
TRAIN ROBBERIES	
VALENTINE'S DAY	
VETERAN'S DAY	

*Call for current information,
schedule and fares on the
above special events.*

TRAVELER'S DIRECTORY

This exclusive *Traveler's Directory* will help you plan and enjoy your visit to the local communities where each scenic train ride operates.

Area businesses were contacted and offered the opportunity to participate in this directory. Those establishments that elected to be included supplied information on their business including a brief "welcome message" they wanted to relay to you about their establishment.

For easy reference, the Traveler's Directory is divided into five main headings and then into several subheadings. The following page lists the different headings used as well as the page number where each heading starts in the directory. Each listing is assigned a three digit reference number and arranged alphabetically by business name under each heading.

For your convenience, the Traveler's Directory is cross referenced with the train ride descriptions allowing you to use this directory in two ways:

Train Rides — After the description of each ride, if a local business is in the Traveler's Directory, you will find an icon(s) representing one of the *main headings* used in the directory. Following the icon(s) is the three digit reference number you use to quickly locate that business in the Traveler's Directory.

Traveler's Directory — Following the reference number of each listing is the page number where you will find the train ride description associated with the listing.

We would like to thank all the participating businesses for providing you the opportunity to receive more enjoyment from your "riding the rails" experience. Please show your appreciation for their support by paying them a visit next time you are in their town. Be sure to tell them *Riding The Rails* sent you!

Attention Business Owners

If you would like to let travelers know about your establishment, please contact us about being included in the next edition of *Riding The Rails*.

Roundabout Publications, 2767 S. Parker Rd. - Suite 240, Aurora CO 80014
Phone: 800-800-6727

Attractions / Recreation

Art Gallery, *210*
Bicycle Tours / Rental, *210*
Garden, *210*
Golf Course, *210*
Historical Place / Museum, *211*
Miniature Golf, *211*
Tours / Sight-seeing, *211*
Transportation / Taxi, *212*
Whitewater Rafting, *212*

Entertainment

Comedy Club, *213*
Old Tyme Photos, *213*
Skating, *213*
Theatre - Live / Dinner, *213*

Food / Beverage

Afternoon Tea, *214*
Bakery, *214*
Bar / Night Club, *214*
Fast Food, *214*
Ice Cream Parlor, *214*
Restaurant, *215*

Lodging

Bed & Breakfast / Inns, *218*
Cabin / Cottage / Guest Ranch, *223*
Campground / RV Park, *223*
Hotel / Motel, *224*
Resort, *227*

Shopping

Antiques, *227*
Book Store / Newsstand, *228*
Crafts, *228*
Dollhouses, *229*
Gift Shop, *229*
Kitchen / Gourmet, *230*
Miniatures, *231*
Specialty Shop, *231*

Attractions / Recreation

Art Gallery

•001• *Page #26*
Arts Center of the Ozarks
214 South Main
Springdale, AR 72765
Phone: 501-751-5441

Visit Northwest Arkansas' oldest art institution. Programming in theatre, music, visual arts, and dance. Art galleries and theatre open Monday through Saturday. Call for schedule of events.

•002• *Page #167*
Cat's Paw Gallery
31 Race Street
Jim Thorpe, PA 18229-2003
Phone: 717-325-4041

Devoted to the domestic feline image in fine art and original studio craft work by American artists. For art lovers fond of felines. Internationally recognized.

Bicycle Tours / Rental

•003• *Page #167*
Jim Thorpe River Adventures, Inc.
1 Adventure Lane
Jim Thorpe, PA 18229
Phone: 717-325-2570
        717-325-4960
Reservations only: 800-424-RAFT

25 mile self-guided mountain bike tour. Ideal opportunity to explore the beautiful scenery through the Lehigh Gorge State Park.

•004• *Page #126*
Wheels Unlimited
20 West Steuben St.
Bath, NY 14810
Phone: 607-776-6609

Sales, service and rental of top quality bikes — Giant, GT, Ross, Trek. Prompt service for all tourists.

Garden

•005• *Page #172*
Willows of Newport
   Romantic Inn & Garden
8 & 10 Willow St., Historic Point
Newport, RI 02840-1927
Phone: 401-846-5486

Cut flowers, turned-down brass canopy beds, breakfast in bed! 3 blocks to waterfront, Best Garden award in '94 & '95. Private bath & parking, A/C. ✶ ✶ ✶ Mobile Award. Award of excellence AB&BA. 'Best Places To Kiss'

Golf Course

•006• *Page #57*
Bonita Springs Golf Club
10200 Maddox Lane
Bonita Springs, FL 33923
Phone: 941-992-2800

Par 72 championship course. Long beautiful tree lined fairways. Open to the public. Located 2½ miles north of dog track off Old 41. Tee times required.

Historical Place / Museum

•007• *Page #174*
Big Thunder Gold Mine
604 Blair Street (P.O. Box 459)
Keystone, SD 57751
Phone: 605-666-4847

Experience 1880's gold mining—receive a <u>free</u> gold ore sample on the underground mine tour. Historical film & gold panning with guaranteed gold. Gift shop.

•008• *Page #68*
Boone County Museum
1004 Story Street
Boone, IA 50036
Phone: 515-432-1730

Many American Indian artifacts including replica of Indian Longhouse, turn of century F.W. Fitch Barbershop, primitives and old tools. 4,000 square feet on one floor.

•009• *Page #43*
Full Circle Cafe
P.O. Box 639
511 Rose Street
Georgetown, CO 80444
Phone: 303-569-3404

Built in 1873 by Theo F. Simmon. Part of the historic Hamill block. Many historic items on display. We also have ghosts.

•010• *Page #70*
Museum of Independent Telephony
412 South Campbell
Abilene, KS 67410
Phone: 913-263-2681

History of the telephone from 1876 to 1994.

•011• *Page #172*
Willows of Newport
Romantic Inn & Garden
8 & 10 Willow St., Historic Point
Newport, RI 02840-1927
Phone: 401-846-5486

Cut flowers, turned-down brass canopy beds, breakfast in bed! 3 blocks to waterfront, Best Garden award in '94 & '95. Private bath & parking, A/C. ✶✶✶ Mobile Award. Award of excellence AB&BA. 'Best Places To Kiss'

Miniature Golf

•012• *Page #115*
Pine Creek Miniature Golf
394 Route 31 North
Ringoes, NJ 08551
Phone: 609-466-3803

Two challenging 18-hole courses roll over acres of beautiful countryside. "You'll have to see this place to believe it!" — *Hunterdon County Democrat*

Tours / Sight-seeing

•013• *Page #15*
All Alaska Tours, Inc.
406 "G" Street, Suite 209
P.O. Box 10-0036
Anchorage, AK 99510
Phone: 907-272-8687
Fax: 907-272-2532
E-Mail: aat@touchngo.com

Year-round, professional tour planning services for groups and individuals. Custom tour specialists, Alaska Railroad, Whitepass and Yukon Route.

•014• *Page #174*
Big Thunder Gold Mine
604 Blair Street (P.O. Box 459)
Keystone, SD 57751
Phone: 605-666-4847

Experience 1880's gold mining—receive a <u>free</u> gold ore sample on the underground mine tour. Historical film & gold panning with guaranteed gold. Gift shop.

•015• *Page #45*
Dee Hive Tours
506 Harrison Avenue
Leadville, CO 80461
Phone: 719-486-2339

Scenic and historic 4x4 or Van tours of Leadville, Lake County and surrounding areas including high passes. ½-day and all day tours, advance reservations.

•016• *Page #167*
Jim Thorpe River Adventures, Inc.
1 Adventure Lane
Jim Thorpe, PA 18229
Phone: 717-325-2570
        717-325-4960
Reservations only: 800-424-RAFT

Whitewater rafting through the scenic Lehigh Gorge State Park. Variety of skill levels. Fun for everyone. Free cookout after weekend trips. Group rates.

•017• *Page #15*
Kenai Coastal Tours
319 F Street
Anchorage, AK 99501
Phone: 800-770-9119
        907-277-2131

Cruise in style aboard the M/V Kenai Explorer for an exciting 6-hour glacier and wildlife tour from Seward. Rail packages available from Anchorage, includes lunch.

•018• *Page #15*
Kenai Fjords Tours, Ltd.
P.O. Box 1889
Seward, AK 99664
Phone: 800-478-8068
        907-224-8068

Cruise Kenai Fjords National Park! Discover massive tidewater glaciers, abundant wildlife, unique seabirds. New, comfortable vessels. Since 1974, daily departures from Seward, April through October.

Transportation / Taxi

•019• *Page #45*
Dee Hive Transportation
506 Harrison Avenue
Leadville, CO 80461
Phone: 719-486-2339

Taxi Service throughout Lake County. Transportation to all points in Colorado including airports. 4x4 service available to trailheads year-round for bikers, hikers, and skiers.

Whitewater Rafting

•020• *Page #134*
Carolina Outfitters
    Whitewater Rafting
12121 Hwy. 19 West
Bryson City, NC 28713
Phone: 800-468-7238
        800-GOT-RAFT

Nantahala River family adventures. Smokies. Thrill to the excitement of whitewater rafting on the most popular river in the Southeast! Experience not necessary. Guides and lodging available. 800-468-7238

•021•   *Page #167*
Jim Thorpe River Adventures, Inc.
1 Adventure Lane
Jim Thorpe, PA 18229
Phone: 717-325-2570
            717-325-4960
Reservations only: 800-424-RAFT

Whitewater rafting trips through the Lehigh Gorge State Park. Variety of skill levels. Free cookout after all weekend trips. Group rates available. Fun for everyone.

Entertainment

Comedy Club

•022•   *Page #57*
Laugh In Comedy Club
Metro Mall
2855 Colonial Blvd.
Fort Myers, FL 33912
Phone: 941-275-HITS
Fax: 941-275-0936

Great lunches, great dinners, great music plus the funniest nationally touring comedians. Home to the Notre Dame Alumni, Chicago Bears and Washington Redskins fan clubs.

Old Tyme Photos

•023•   *Page #45*
Doc Holliday's of Leadville
314 Harrison Avenue
Leadville, CO 80461

Phone: 719-486-3020

Photos done, by appointment, in the building where Doc Holliday shot Billy Allen, August 14, 1884! A unique opportunity to relive history.

•024•   *Page #108*
Sun Mountain Old Tyme Photos
30 North B Street
Virginia City, NV 89440
Phone: 702-847-0422

Have your picture taken in the old west costume and studio setting of your choice. Special events and group photos with advance notice. Visa / MC / Disc.

Skating

•025•   *Page #26*
Skateworld
1007 Fayetteville Rd.
Van Buren, AR 72956
Phone: 501-474-3705

Buy one admission get one free with proof of train ticket.

Theatre - Live / Dinner

•026•   *Page #26*
Arts Center of the Ozarks
214 South Main
Springdale, AR 72765
Phone: 501-751-5441

Visit Northwest Arkansas' oldest art institution. Programming in theatre, music, visual arts, and dance. Art galleries and theatre open Monday through Saturday. Call for schedule of events.

•027•   *Page #108*
Molly b'Dam Dinner Theatre
30 North B Street
Virginia City, NV 89440
Phone: 702-847-7319 (Reservations)

The Historic Virginia City Players join Molly b'Dam Restaurant for the only live & authentic 1890's entertainment package in Virginia City. Box office reservations & info: 702-847-7319. Visa / MC / Disc.

Food / Beverage

Afternoon Tea

•028•   *Page #132*
Owego Tea Room
24 Front Street
Owego, NY 13827
Phone: 607-687-3830
            800-434-4TEA

English afternoon tea, sweets and savories. Minimum 2, maximum 10 people. Reservations only. Tuesday, Wednesday, and Thursday; 2 sittings each day. $10.00 plus tax. In private home.

Bakery

•029•   *Page #47*
Manitou Bakery and Cafe
110 Canon Avenue
Manitou Springs, CO 80829
Phone: 719-685-5808

The Manitou Bakery & Cafe prides itself on providing freshly baked goodies made from scratch every morning. Organic breads and great coffee make this stop well worthwhile.

Bar / Night Club

•030•   *Page #57*
Flashbacks Bar & Grill
Metro Mall
2855 Colonial Blvd.
Fort Myers, FL 33912
Phone: 941-275-HITS

Great lunches, great dinners, great music plus the funniest nationally touring comedians. Home to the Notre Dame Alumni, Chicago Bears and Washington Redskins fan clubs.

•031•   *Page #96*
Tecumseh Inn
1445 W. Chicago Blvd.
Tecumseh, MI 49286
Phone: 517-423-7401

61 rooms, lounge, shopping plaza within 100 yards.

Fast Food

•032•   *Page #26*
Sonic Drive-In
5th and Broadway
Van Buren, AR 72956
Phone: 501-474-8218

One of the areas best fast food restaurants. Specializing in good food and fast, friendly service - Just the way you like it.

Ice Cream Parlor

•033•   *Page #143*
Village Ice Cream Parlor
   & Restaurant
22 South Broadway
Lebanon, OH 45036
Phone: 513-932-6918

Serving breakfast, lunch and dinner. Old fashioned soda fountain. Open Monday through Saturday 9:00 a.m. to 8:00 p.m. Sunday 11:00 a.m. to 8:00 p.m.

Restaurant

•034• *Page #26*
Armadillo Grill
1100 South 48th Place
Springdale, AR 72762
Phone: 501-756-0066

Come in and enjoy "A Taste of the West" in our lodge-like setting. BBQ ribs, fajitas, salads, sandwiches and much more. Located just off 71 by-pass & Hwy. 412.

•035• *Page #104*
Bonanza Family Restaurant
830 East 23rd
Fremont, NE 68025
Phone: 402-721-4422

Bonanza - Steak • Chicken • Seafood • Salad • Fresh Bakery Products • Dessert Bar • Open 365 days: Group Rates • Private Party Room • Hours 11:00 a.m. to 10:00 p.m. daily.

•036• *Page #117*
Branding Iron Restaurant & Lounge
1511 Hwy. 17, Box 208
Chama, NM 87520
Phone: 505-756-9195

Big Breakfasts • Excellent Steaks

•037• *Page #29*
Café Luigi Patio Restaurant
91 South Main St.
Eureka Springs, AR 72632
Phone: 501-253-6888

"Relaxed Italian eatery with expansive patio for outdoor dining. Robust red sauces highlight good pasta and homemade dressings blanket signature salads." *National Geographic Traveler*. An Arkansas FAVORITE year after year. Located next to historical museum.

•038• *Page #147*
Columbian House
3 North River Road
Waterville, OH 43566
Phone: 419-878-3006

Dine in a living museum. Northwest Ohio's best preserved example of an 1828 Stage Coach Stop & Inn. Fine food and a wide selection of spirits.

•039• *Page #134*
Dillsboro Smokehouse
267 Haywood Street
Dillsboro, NC 28725
Phone: 704-586-9556

Full service restaurant specializing in hickory-smoked barbecue, pork, chicken, beef, ribs & smoked turkey.

•040• *Page #86*
The Egg & I
521 Main St.
Hyannis, MA 02601
Phone: 508-771-1596
Office: 508-775-6549

The Egg & I is celebrating our 25th year of serving Cape Cod's very best breakfast! Children's menu, all charge cards. Open until 1:00 p.m. every day.

•041• *Page #51*
Exel's Family Restaurant, Inc.
329 Savannah Road
Lewes, DE 19958
Phone: 302-645-7458

Breakfast served all day. Open 7 days a week. "Best prices in town".

•042• *Page #57*
Flashbacks Bar & Grill
Metro Mall
2855 Colonial Blvd.
Fort Myers, FL 33912
Phone: 941-275-HITS

Great lunches, great dinners, great music plus the funniest nationally touring comedians. Home to the Notre Dame Alumni, Chicago Bears and Washington Redskins fan clubs.

•043• *Page #43*
Full Circle Cafe
511 Rose Street
P.O. Box 639
Georgetown, CO 80444
Phone: 303-569-3404

Featured on the TV show "Sightings." Named one of Denver's best in *Westword Magazine*. Breakfast • Burgers • Sandwiches. Homemade hot sauce.

•044• *Page #124*
The Gray Fox Pub
246 Main Street
Arcade, NY 14009
Phone: 716-492-9907

Enjoy simple dining in a relaxed atmosphere. Serving breakfast, lunch, and dinner Monday through Saturday and lunch & dinner on Sunday. Daily specials. Full bar.

•045• *Page #84*
Hunan Palace Chinese Restaurant
82 Baltimore Street
Cumberland, MD 21502
Phone: 301-722-3507

We serve traditional Chinese food: Hunan Szechuan. Cantonese cuisine.

•046• *Page #106*
Jerry's Restaurants
2060 Aultman Street
Ely, NV 89301-1828
Phone: 702-289-3905

•047• *Page #90*
Key Largo Lakeside Restaurant
142 E. Walled Lake Drive
Walled Lake, MI 48390
Phone: 810-669-1441

Before or after your visit to Coe Rail, we invite you to enjoy a beverage or snack on our beautiful lakeside deck.

•048• *Page #51*
Lester's Rose & Crown
   Restaurant & Pub
108 Second Street
Lewes, DE 19958
Phone: 302-645-2373

The Rose & Crown is an authentic English restaurant & pub featuring great seafood, steaks, pasta dishes, English fare and homemade desserts. Voted best beer selection.

•049• *Page #172*
Mamma Luisa Italian Restaurant
673 Thames Street
Newport, RI 02840
Phone: 401-848-5257

Fine dining - not expensive. Romantic atmosphere and authentic Italian food made from all natural ingredients. Serving lunch and dinner. Please call.

•050• *Page #108*
Molly b'Dam Restaurant
30 North B Street
Virginia City, NV 89440
Phone: 702-847-0422

Fine dining with Victorian ambience. Our continental culinary artists are sure to please any appetite. Full hours. Visa / MC / Disc.

•051• *Page #165*
Molly's Mill
221 S. Monroe St.
Titusville, PA 16354
Phone: 814-827-6597

Restaurant and lounge with Agricultural theme.

•052• *Page #192*
Mt. Rainier Railroad Dining Co.
54106 Mtn. Hwy. East
Elbe, WA 98330
Phone: 360-569-2505

Fine dining aboard railroad cars. Serving breakfast, lunch and dinner. Cocktails. Open 365 days a year.

•053• *Page #36*
North Coast Brewing Co.
444 N. Main St.
Fort Bragg, CA 95437
Phone: 707-964-3400

Located close to the Skunk station, the brewery offers award-winning beers served in the tap room & grill with fresh seafood, pasta, and great burgers. Free tours of the brewery.

•054• *Page #20*
Old "66" Coffee House and Deli
246 West Route 66
Williams, AZ 86046
Phone: 520-635-0047

Espresso, shakes, Italian sodas, deli sandwiches, salads, soups, sliced meats and cheeses; Enjoy music from the 50s and 60s in an old fashioned, friendly atmosphere!

•055• *Page #57*
Pepper's
4288 Bonita Beach Rd.
Bonita Springs, FL 33923
Phone: 941-992-1516

A mild Mexican restaurant served by enthusiastic locals. (habala espanol) Buenos Dias.

•056• *Page #36*
Perko's Cafe
898 S. Main St.
Fort Bragg, CA 95437
Phone: 707-964-6420

Daily Specials. "The best in family dining." Breakfast - Lunch - Dinner.

•057• *Page #38*
Sizzler Restaurant
201 West Court St.
Woodland, CA 95696
Phone: 916-661-1530

Great steaks, seafood, and salads. Seniors menu • Childs menu • Full bar. All in a relaxed atmosphere.

•058• *Page #132*
Smokey's BBQ
442 North Ave.

continued

Owego, NY 13827
Phone: 607-687-4755

Award Winning, Authentic Western
Style B-B-Q. Sandwiches or dinners.
Eat in or take-out. Open 7 days a
week. Closed holidays.

•059•   *Page #143*
Village Ice Cream Parlor
& Restaurant
22 South Broadway
Lebanon, OH 45036
Phone: 513-932-6918

Serving breakfast, lunch and dinner.
Old fashioned soda fountain. Open
Monday through Saturday 9:00 a.m.
to 8:00 p.m. Sunday 11:00 a.m. to
8:00 p.m.

•060•   *Page #26*
Western Sizzlin
3492 W. Sunset
Springdale, AR 72762
Phone: 501-750-3663

Flamekist steaks • "Country Fair"
buffet • Bakery • Seniors discounts •
Kids meals • Lunch specials • A
"Must Visit" • Just east of the Ozark
Factory Outlet Mall.

•061•   *Page #66*
The Willows Downtown Restaurant
522 Central Avenue
Connersville, IN 47331
Phone: 317-825-5552

Full service casual restaurant serving lunch and dinner including buffet and menu selections. Complete
bar available. For reservations or
information phone 317-825-5552.

Lodging

Bed & Breakfast / Inns
•062•   *Page #15*
Affordable Bed & Breakfast
5101 Electra Avenue
Fairbanks, AK 99709
Phone: 907-479-6918

Clean, quiet rooms. Close to airport,
Riverboat Discovery, and U.A.F. Full
breakfast or light served.

•063•   *Page #120*
Alexander's Inn
529 East Palace Ave.
Santa Fe, NM 87501
Phone: 505-986-1431

Quiet historic inn near Plaza. Antiques, fireplaces, stenciling, beautiful gardens. Delicious homemade
goodies. Romance & superior service
abound. Phones, TV's, bicycles, hot
tubs.

•064•   *Page #29*
All Tucked Inn
39 Mountain St.
Eureka Springs, AR 72632
Phone: 501-253-4000
Reservations: 800-574-2213

Lovely Victorian decor with queen
beds - private entrance and baths -
whirlpools - beautiful gourmet
breakfast - ½ block from shopping
downtown and trolley. Come and be
All Tucked Inn.

•065•   *Page #40*
Animas Country Inn
3310 Main Avenue
Durango, CO 81301

Phone: 970-247-4895
Reservations: 800-253-3869

Quaint, historic country home is the private residence of your host, the Michaelsen's. A separate two story building has twenty large, quiet rooms with kitchens.

•066• *Page #40*
Apple Orchard Inn
7758 CR 203
Durango, CO 81301
Phone: 800-426-0751
970-247-0751

Beautiful location with train passing property. Spacious rooms and cottages, private baths, featherbeds, fireplaces. Hearty breakfast, homemade goodies included. Dinner available by reservation.

•067• *Page #29*
Beaver Lake Bed & Breakfast
Route 2, Box 318
Eureka Springs, AR 72632
Phone: 501-253-9210

Country lakefront setting with spectacular views. Four rooms. Private baths. Queen beds. Full breakfast. Railroad knowledgeable innkeeper. Swim • Fish • Hike • Relax. Nonsmoking adults only.

•068• *Page #172*
Beech Tree Inn
34 Rhode Island Ave.
Newport, RI 02840
Phone: 401-847-9794
800-748-6565

"Best Breakfast in Town." Jacuzzis, fireplaces, suites, outside decks,

cable TV, A/C, phones, ample parking, walking distance to harbor and shops. MC, Visa, AMEX, Discover cards taken.

•069• *Page #157*
The Brafferton Inn
44 York Street
Gettysburg, PA 17325
Phone: 717-337-3423

Experience historic Gettysburg in this 1786 National Registry home. Antiques, elaborate stenciling and portraits grace the ten guest rooms all with private baths and air-conditioning.

•070• *Page #40*
Country Sunshine B & B
35130 N. Highway 550
Durango, CO 81301
Phone: 800-383-2853
970-247-2853

Rustic ranch home on Animas River, nestled in pines. Tastefully decorated, numerous common areas, hot tub, great for families, informal atmosphere, friendly hosts, fantastic breakfasts.

•071• *Page #29*
Crescent Cottage Inn
211 Spring Street
Eureka Springs, AR 72632
Phone: 501-253-6022

Landmark 1881 Victorian on National Register of Historic Places. All rooms with private baths, some jacuzzis, refrigerators. Beautiful antiques and mountain views. Great breakfasts. AAA ◆◆◆

•072• *Page #169*
The Decoy Bed & Breakfast
958 Elsenberger Road
Strasburg, PA 17579
Phone: 800-726-2287

Situated in Amish farm country, we have a spectacular view; 5 rooms with private baths; full breakfast; children welcome; 2 cats in residence; A/C, no smoking.

•073• *Page #45*
Delaware Hotel
700 Harrison Ave.
Leadville, CO 80461
Phone: 719-486-1418

Stay at the "Award Winning" Delaware Hotel. Listed on the National Register of Historic Places.

•074• *Page #157*
The Doubleday Inn
104 Doubleday Ave.
Gettysburg, PA 17325
Phone: 717-334-9119

A fine country inn located directly on Gettysburg Battlefield. Nine lovely guest rooms with cozy antiques and Civil War accents. Central A/C, full breakfast.

•075• *Page #36*
Grey Whale Inn
615 North Main St.
Fort Bragg, CA 95437
Phone: 800-382-7244

A Mendocino Coast Landmark since 1915. Some ocean views, fireplaces, decks, one private whirlpool. Full buffet breakfast. Smoke-free environment. Walk to Skunk train, beaches, restaurants and shops.

•076• *Page #120*
Guadalupe Inn
604 Agua Fria St.
Santa Fe, NM 87501
Phone: 505-989-7422

A "truly Santa Fe" experience. Queen size beds. Private entrances. Private baths. Telephone. Cable. A/C. Great breakfasts. Traditional Santa Fe family hospitality. Close to railroad yard.

•077• *Page #88*
H.D. Ellis Inn - B & B
415 W. Adrian St.
Blissfield, MI 49228
Phone: 517-486-3155

A beautifully restored red brick Victorian house built in 1883. It has four bedrooms with private baths, TV and phones. All are tastefully appointed in period antiques.

•078• *Page #201*
Hampshire House 1884
165 North Grafton St.
Romney, WV 26757
Phone: 304-822-7171

Hampshire House is a completely renovated 1884 home with private baths, A/C and period furniture offering 4 guest rooms, common areas and a full breakfast.

•079• *Page #43*
Hillside House B & B
1034 Main Street
P.O. Box 266
Georgetown, CO 80444
Phone: 800-490-9012

A Victorian Bed & Breakfast in Historic Georgetown. Beautiful windows and woods adorn this wonderful house. Two rooms with private bath. Complete breakfast.

•080• *Page #167*
The Inn at Jim Thorpe
24 Broadway
Jim Thorpe, PA 18229
Phone: 717-325-2599
 800-329-2599

Restored 1840's Inn. Combines Victorian splendor with 21st century comforts. 22 elegant guestrooms, casual dining, Irish pub, AAA 3 Diamond rated - call 800-329-2599.

•081• *Page #172*
Inn at Old Beach
19 Old Beach Rd.
Newport, RI 02840
Phone: 401-849-3479

Elegant Victorian B & B decorated with touches of romance and whimsy. Comfortable guest rooms - all with private baths, some with fireplaces. Easy walk to most attractions.

•082• *Page #86*
The Inn On Sea Street
358 Sea Street
Hyannis, MA 02601
Phone: 508-775-8030
Fax: 508-771-0878

Antiques, Persian carpets, classical music and gourmet breakfasts make this relaxed, charming Inn the travel writers' choice. Steps from beach. One night stays welcome.

•083• *Page #157*
Keystone Inn
231 Hanover St.
Gettysburg, PA 17325
Phone: 717-337-3888

A great 3 story brick late Victorian with wide porches, leaded glass front entrance, handsome chestnut staircase, floral wallpaper, comfy chairs and wonderful breakfasts.

•084• *Page #43*
KIP on the Creek B & B
1205 Rose Street
Georgetown, CO 80444
Phone: 303-569-2923
 800-821-6545

Located on Clear Creek less than an hour from Denver. Three rooms with private baths, scrumptious hot breakfasts, indoor hot tub, loving Teddy bears galore.

•085• *Page #40*
The Leland House B & B Suites
721 East 2nd Avenue
Durango, CO 81301
Phone: 970-385-1920
 800-664-1920

Walk to railroad station. Durango's history in our rooms. 6 luxury suites with kitchens and living rooms. 4 studios. All have private baths. Full gourmet breakfast.

•086• *Page #205*
Pleasant Lake B & B
2238 - 60th Avenue
Osceola, WI 54020-4509
Phone: 715-294-2545
 800-294-2545

continued

Escape to our secluded lake for a romantic retreat. Enjoy a bonfire under the stars, canoe on the lake and relax in your private whirlpool.

•087•   *Page #106*
Steptoe Valley Inn
220 East 11th St.
P.O. Box 151110
East Ely, NV 89315-1110
Phone: 702-289-8687 (June - Sept.)
        702-435-1196 (Oct. - May)

5 rooms with private baths and balconies, ½ block from Nevada Northern Railway. Rose garden, gazebo, hearts and lace. Smoking restricted. Open June thru September.

•088•   *Page #36*
Todd Farm House B & B
100 Hwy. 20
Fort Bragg, CA 95437
Phone: 707-964-6575

There is a room, a suite and a cabin to suit different needs. We are close to beaches, Noyo Fishing Village and the Skunk Train ride.

•089•   *Page #47*
Two Sisters Inn - a bed
   and breakfast
Ten Otoe Place
Manitou Springs, CO 80829
Phone: 800-2-SIS-INN
        719-685-9684

Gracious, award-winning 5-bedroom Victorian B & B with cozy honeymoon cottage. Fresh flowers, antiques, evening treats, creative delectable breakfasts. Knowledgeable, friendly innkeepers. Close to train ride.

•090•   *Page #94*
The Union House
16104 U.S. Highway 12
Union, MI 49130-9608
Phone: 616-641-7268

A century-old Queen Anne Victorian B & B, 15 minutes from White Pigeon. 4 bedrooms, private baths, air-conditioned. Visa / MasterCard. $65.00 plus tax.

•091•   *Page #70*
Victorian Reflections Bed
   & Breakfast Inn
820 NW Third
Abilene, KS 67410
Phone: 913-263-7774

Revel in an atmosphere of wealth and luxury now associated with times gone by in this historic Victorian home in a classic residential area.

•092•   *Page #172*
Willows of Newport
   Romantic Inn & Garden
8 & 10 Willow St., Historic Point
Newport, RI 02840-1927
Phone: 401-846-5486

Cut flowers, turned-down brass canopy beds, breakfast in bed! 3 blocks to waterfront, Best Garden award in '94 & '95. Private bath & parking, A/C. ✷✷✷ Mobile Award. Award of excellence AB&BA. 'Best Places To Kiss'

•093•   *Page #40*
Wyman Hotel and Inn
1371 Greene Street
Silverton, CO 81433
Phone: 970-387-5372

Reservations: 800-609-7845

Built 1902 • Beautifully decorated • 19 rooms. Antique to modern furniture. All with baths. Continental breakfast included. Telephones, TV's and VCR's with large video library. Some jacuzzis.

Cabin/Cottage/Guest Ranch

•094• *Page #134*
Carolina Vacation Lodging
12121 Hwy. 19 West
Bryson City, NC 28713
Phone: 800-468-7238
         800-GOT-RAFT

Mountain vacation lodging. Great Smokies. Near Great Smoky Mountains Railway and Nantahala rafting. Houses • Chalets • Cottages. Families or groups. Great rates. Furnished, A/C, TV/VCR. Rafting reservations available. 800-468-7238.

•095• *Page #40*
Wilderness Trails Ranch
1766 County Rd. 302
Durango, CO 81301
Phone: 970-247-0722
         800-527-2624

Wilderness Trails Ranch provides a personalized vacation in a secluded valley. Kids programs from age 3. Quality horses and instructions. Pool, cattle round-up, September adult weeks.

Campground / RV Park

•096• *Page #70*
Covered Wagon RV Park
803 S. Buckeye
Abilene, KS 67410
Phone: 800-864-4053

Two blocks south of excursion train. Full hookups, pull-thrus, tent sites, cable TV, swimming pool, clean restrooms and showers, shade trees, laundry, propane. Open year-round.

•097• *Page #159*
Foote Rest Campground
R.D. 1, Box 188C
Kane, PA 16735
Phone: 814-778-5336

Shaded sites, water, electric, some sewer, miniature golf, game room, pool, clean showers and restrooms, planned activities, fire truck or hay wagon rides. Snowmobile trails. Grocery and RV store. Open year-round.

•098• *Page #40*
Hermosa Meadows Camper Park
31420 Hwy. 550
Durango, CO 81301
Phone: 800-748-2853
         970-247-3055

Hermosa Meadows is a full service family campground along the Animas River, eight miles north of Durango on Hwy. 550, only ½ mile from the train tracks!

•099• *Page #36*
Leisure Time RV Park
30801 Hwy. 20
Fort Bragg, CA 95437
Phone: 800-700-8542

2 miles east of Hwy. 1 on Hwy. 20. Full, partial, and day camp sites. Cable TV, modern restrooms, laundry facilities, fish cleaning area, boat and RV storage area.

•100•   *Page #117*
Rio Chama RV Park
P.O. Box 706
182 N. Hwy. 17
Chama, NM 87520
Phone: 505-756-2303 (April - Oct.)
          909-982-3732 (Nov. - Mar.)

Tree shaded 60' drive throughs • 30 amp • Full hookups • Adjacent to C&TS Railroad • Photo opportunities as railroad runs through campground.

•101•   *Page #117*
Twin Rivers Campground
   & Trailer Park
272 US Hwy. 84-64
Chama, NM 87520
Phone: 505-756-2218

Located in the Cool Rockies. Nice Utility Building • Washers & Dryers • Private Showers • Clean Restrooms • Supermarket Nearby • Diesel Available • Phone Booths • Well Lighted Camp Sites • Full Hookups • Drive-Thru Sites • Tenters Welcome • Excellent fishing & big game hunting nearby. Free shuttle to scenic railroad depot.

•102•   *Page #94*
Waffle Farm Campground
779 Union City Rd.
Coldwater, MI 49036
Phone: 517-278-4315

Campsites include full hook-up to primitive, on a chain of seven lakes, with good fishing. Located three miles north of Coldwater.

Hotel / Motel

•103•   *Page #15*
AAA Mexico Hotel
3903 Spenard Road
Anchorage, AK 99517
Phone: 907-248-4848

5 minutes from airport, daily and weekly rates, $45.00 & $175.00 and up. Microwave, refrigerator, TV, laundry facilities, parking, phone, and near shopping centers.

•104•   *Page #36*
Baechtel Creek Inn
101 Gregory Lane
Willits, CA 95490
Phone: 800-459-9911

Rest with us in our luxurious 46 room Inn on a beautiful creekside setting. Pool, spa, and continental breakfast. Ask about our "Skunk Train" packages!

•105•   *Page #57*
Beach House Motel
26106 Hickory Blvd.
Bonita Beach, FL 33923
Phone: 941-992-2644

Beach House on the beach. Come to Beach House and enjoy superb shelling, fishing, swimming, and relaxing on our sprawling, natural, sugar white sand beach.

•106•   *Page #26*
Best Western Heritage Inn
1394 West Sunset (Hwy. 412)
Springdale, AR 72764
Phone: 501-751-3100

10 minutes from railroad station.

Ample parking. Indoor pool. Shiloh Museum, Beaver Lake, and University within 30 minutes.

•**107**• *Page #40*
Budget Inn
3077 Main Ave.
Durango, CO 81301
Phone: 970-247-5222

Amenities include an outdoor pool, hot tub, color TV, phones, and laundry at a reasonable rate. Located near attractions and restaurants. For reservations call 800-257-5222.

•**108**• *Page #165*
Casey's Caboose Stop
221 S. Monroe St.
Titusville, PA 16354
Phone: 814-827-6597

21 renovated caboose cars from America's vintage railroads. Adjacent to the Oil Creek and Titusville Railroad.

•**109**• *Page #117*
Chama Trails Inn Motel
2362 Hwy. 17 (P.O. Box 975)
Chama, NM 87520
Phone: 505-756-2156
        800-289-1421

•**110**• *Page #80*
Comfort Inn
Route 1, Box 35
Belfast, ME 04915
Phone: 207-338-2090
Reservations: 800-221-2222

New, 52 ocean front rooms and suites, indoor pool - hot tub, sauna, meeting rooms, free continental breakfast. AAA - AARP discounts. Opening May, 1996.

•**111**• *Page #66*
Connersville Inn
3626 Western Ave.
Connersville, IN 47331
Phone: 317-825-7531

Welcome Train Riders. Show us the *Riding The Rails* book and receive the corporate rate.

•**112**• *Page #84*
Continental Motor Inn
15001 National Hwy.
Cumberland, MD 21502
Phone: 301-689-8835

51 rooms, live entertainment on weekends, lounge, sports bar.

•**113**• *Page #40*
Country View Lodge
28295 Highway 160 East
Durango, CO 81301
Phone: 970-247-5701

Located 6 miles east of Durango in a country setting. We offer clean and comfortable rooms; ideal for families. Reasonable rates.

•**114**• *Page #40*
Days End
2202 Main Ave.
Durango, CO 81301
Phone: 970-259-3311

Amenities include an outdoor pool, hot tub, kings, queens, ADA rooms, and laundry, at reasonable rates. Located near attractions and restaurants. For reservations call 800-242-3297.

•**115**• *Page #20*
Downtowner Motel
201 E. Bill Williams Ave.
Williams, AZ 86046
Phone: 520-635-4041

All rooms include double / queen /
king size beds, free coffee, HBO, A/C
& Heat. Close to Grand Canyon Railway steam train depot, restaurants,
gift shops. Clean rooms, low rates.

•**116**• *Page #40*
Hampton Inn - Durango
3777 Main Avenue
Durango, CO 81301
Phone: 970-247-2600

Durango's newest hotel! Deluxe
complimentary Continental Breakfast, indoor pool and spa. Located on
Main Avenue in Durango.

•**117**• *Page #192*
Hobo Inn
54100 Mtn. Hwy. East
Elbe, WA 98330
Phone: 360-569-2500

Fully Air-Conditioned Cabooses •
Hot Tubs • Jacuzzi Available. 15
minutes from Mt. Rainier National
Park entrance. Open 365 days a year.

•**118**• *Page #149*
The Hugo Inn
1006 E. Jackson
Hugo, OK 74743
Phone: 405-326-HUGO
        405-326-6437

Your hometown motel. Comfortable
rooms, remote control cable TV, free
local calls, credit cards accepted. Just
ten blocks east of the depot. Oklahoma owned / operated.

•**119**• *Page #174*
Kelly Inn
16A and Cemetery Rd.
Keystone, SD 57751
Phone: 605-666-4483

44 large modern quiet rooms - including queens, king deluxe, family.
Sauna, whirlpool, meeting room.
Near restaurants & centrally located
to all activities.

•**120**• *Page #40*
Landmark Motel, Inc.
3030 Main Avenue
Durango, CO 81301
Phone: 970-259-1333
Reservations: 800-252-8853
Fax: 970-247-3854

One of Durango's finest motels, featuring king and queen beds, complimentary continental breakfast, free
cable TV and HBO, free local calls,
jacuzzi, sauna and heated pool.

•**121**• *Page #157*
Quality Inn - Gettysburg
  Motor Lodge
380 Steinwehr Avenue
Gettysburg, PA 17325
Phone: 717-334-1103

1 mile from Gettysburg Steam Railroad. Walk to Battlefield, museums,
shops, attractions and restaurants.
Indoor or outdoor pool, cocktail
lounge, fitness center, whirlpool and
sauna.

•**122**• *Page #40*
The Rochester Hotel
726 East 2nd Ave.
Durango, CO 81301
Phone: 970-385-1920
        800-664-1920

Walking distance to railroad station, this historic, luxury hotel is newly restored and decorated in a western movie theme. A full gourmet breakfast is included.

•123• *Page #57*
Sea Chest Motel
2571 E. First St. Rt. 80
Fort Myers, FL 33901
Phone: 941-332-1545

30 units overlooking the Caloosahatchee River in downtown Fort Myers. Motel rooms and efficiencies. About 6 miles from Metro Mall station.

•124• *Page #29*
Statue Road Inn Motel
Route 1, Box 965 (on Passion
    Play Road)
Eureka Springs, AR 72632
Phone: 501-253-9163
        800-501-7666

Located next to "The Great Passion Play" and just above the ES&NA Railway. Family operated - our motto "Christ Is Our Leader" - Member listing AAA.

•125• *Page #106*
Sure Rest Motel
1550 High St.
Ely, NV 89301
Phone: 702-289-2512

Clean and comfortable units. Located in the middle of town. Will furnish rides if needed. We appreciate your business.

•126• *Page #96*
Tecumseh Inn
1445 W. Chicago Blvd.

Tecumseh, MI 49286
Phone: 517-423-7401

61 rooms, lounge, shopping plaza within 100 yards.

Resort

•127• *Page #57*
Beach House Motel
26106 Hickory Blvd.
Bonita Beach, FL 33923
Phone: 941-992-2644

Beach House on the beach. Come to Beach House and enjoy superb shelling, fishing, swimming, and relaxing on our sprawling, natural, sugar white sand beach.

•128• *Page #174*
Miner's Resort
Hwy. 16A, #522 (P.O. Box 157)
Keystone, SD 57751
Phone: 605-666-4638
        800-727-2421
Fax: 605-666-4508

Enjoy our heated pool and hot tub all with a great view of Mount Rushmore! Easy walking to attractions, shopping, and family restaurant.

Shopping

Antiques

•129• *Page #80*
Avis Howells Antiques
21 Pearl Street
Belfast, ME 04915
Phone: 207-338-3302

continued

Antiques: Specialties Shaker and Chinese 19th century china called "Canton." American furniture pre-1840, other selective antiques and accessories. By chance or appointment in Victorian home.

•**130**• *Page #132*
The Cracker Barrel
202 Front Street
Owego, NY 13827
Phone: 607-687-0555

A delightful heart-warming mix of antiques, gifts, and nostalgic collectibles. Many uniques and unusuals. "Cat's meow" village including Owego customs, Yankee candles. Hours 10:00 a.m. to 5:30 p.m. Monday thru Saturday. Thursday evening til 8:00 p.m. except January and February.

•**131**• *Page #20*
Eagle's Nest Antiques
124 W. Bill Williams Ave.
Williams, AZ 86046
Phone: 520-635-4203

Full line of antiques, collectibles, gifts, Route 66 items, trains and railroad memorabilia.

•**132**• *Page #115*
Popkorn Antiques
4 Mine St. (Near Main St.)
Flemington, NJ 08822
Phone: 908-782-9631

Stangl Pottery • Glassware

Book Store / Newsstand

•**133**• *Page #51*
Books By The Bay
130 Second St.
Lewes, DE 19958
Phone: 302-645-2304

Books for all ages. Fiction and non-fiction. Special orders welcome.

Crafts

•**134**• *Page #80*
Makin Memories
125 High St., Suite 10
Belfast, ME 04915
Phone: 207-338-1544

Craft, painting and stitching supplies • Girl Scout supplies • Ornaments • Gifts. Located next to the Colonial Theater in the High Street mini-mall.

•**135**• *Page #180*
Oak Street Village Shoppes
120 West Oak Street
Palestine, TX 75801
Phone: 903-729-4099

Over 50 vendors under one roof. Open Monday thru Saturday from 10:00 a.m. to 5:30 p.m. and Sunday from 1:00 p.m. to 5:00 p.m. Owner - Jerry Fort.

•**136**• *Page #80*
Patchwork Plus
Route 3
N. Searsmont, ME 04973
Phone: 207-342-5016

"A great country craft shop with very reasonable prices." Open 10:00 a.m. to 5:00 p.m., 7 days a week May through December. Over 100 Quilts • Baskets • Miniatures • Wreaths • Plus more.

•**137•**   *Page #26*
Vene's Native American Gallery
3041 North Oak Street
Springdale, AR 72764
Phone: 501-751-6489

Paintings, pottery, jewelry, rugs, baskets, dolls, knifes, bows, arrows, beadwork, dream catchers, and fans. Made by the American Indians.

Dollhouses

•**138•**   *Page #51*
Tiny Town / Country Crafts
1145 Savannah Road
Lewes, DE 19958
Phone: 302-644-1557

Dollhouses, kits, shells, finished electrical systems, wallpaper, furniture and furniture kits, flooring, bricks, lumberyard, carpet and window treatments, stables, barns and accessories.

Gift Shop

•**139•**   *Page #20*
Autumn Buffalo
212 West Route 66
Williams, AZ 86046
Phone: 520-635-9191

Quality gift items: Indian • Southwest • Metaphysical • Angels • Candles • Figurines • T-Shirts • Cards • Route 66. Please stop by and enjoy a free cup of tea.

•**140•**   *Page #45*
Bonanza Trading Company
316 Harrison Avenue
Leadville, CO 80461
Phone: 719-486-3020

Drums, baskets, reproductions, fetishes, moccasins, pottery and jewelry by over 45 different Native American tribes. Always some new items - Stop by and see us.

•**141•**   *Page #45*
Dee Hive Gift & T-Shirt Shop
506 Harrison Avenue
Leadville, CO 80461
Phone: 719-486-2339

Family owned and operated since 1970. Your one-stop shop for unique Leadville and Colorado souvenirs, shirts, caps, Indian jewelry, pottery, and more.

•**142•**   *Page #20*
Indian House
238 West Rt. 66
Williams, AZ 86046
Phone: 520-635-2572

Large shop catering to Western, Indian, Grand Canyon and Route 66 shoppers. Indian moccasins, artifacts, pottery and jewelry. Also hats - rocks - minerals.

•**143•**   *Page #62*
The Ivy Wreath
125 East Main
Knightstown, IN 46148
Phone: 317-345-5158

Floral and gift shop. We make our own fudge. Yankee candles.

•144• *Page #106*
Knit Knook & Gift Gamut
1280 Avenue F
East Ely, NV 89315
Phone: 702-289-2116

Home of Creative Crafters - The first and oldest handcrafters' co-op. Copper Pictures • Turquoise Jewelry • China • Floss and Canvas • Gregorian Copper, Magnets, Postcards • Music Boxes • Unique Greeting Cards • Sheet Music & Special Orders • Copper Jewelry • Crystal • Yarns & Accessories • Patterns • Music Lessons • Strings, Reeds, Oils, Metronomes, Harmonicas, Guitars, Cables and Special orders.

•145• *Page #29*
The Mustard Seed
46 Spring Street
Eureka Springs, AR 72632
Phone: 501-253-7484

Live dulcimer music while you shop for mountain or hammered dulcimers, tapes, CDs or a vast assortment of Ozark gifts. Inviting and entertaining!

•146• *Page #80*
Northport Landing
U.S. Route 1
Northport, ME 04849
Phone: 207-338-5555

A unique marketplace in a barn featuring everything from food to furniture. Unique gifts, handcrafts, art, collectibles, nostalgia, country furniture, lamps, etc. Major credit cards accepted. Located on U.S. Route 1 between Lincolnville & Belfast.

•147• *Page #124*
Sign of the Pineapple
285 Main Street
Arcade, NY 14009-1212
Phone: 716-492-1500

A country decorating and gift shop located in a circa 1854 building in the heart of Arcade across from the historic Arcade & Attica Railroad.

•148• *Page #205*
Wildwood Flowers
Hwy. 35 South
Osceola, WI 54020
Phone: 715-755-2040

Gift / Floral Shop combined with antiques, dolls, dried florals - we do things just a little different from the rest.

•149• *Page #26*
Williams Florist & Gifts
1221 East Main
Van Buren, AR 72956
Phone: 501-474-3900
          800-288-5494

Wonderful gift shop with beautiful silks, baskets, and a large line of collectibles.

Kitchen / Gourmet

•150• *Page #43*
Gadgets and Gourmet
509 6th Street (P.O. Box 605)
Georgetown, CO 80444
Phone: 303-569-2714

Shops like this are hard to find anymore. Nothing fancy, just wall to wall gadgets, interesting foods, fun, friendliness, personal service, reasonable prices—and collectibles!

Miniatures

•**151**• *Page #51*
Tiny Town / Country Crafts
1145 Savannah Road
Lewes, DE 19958
Phone: 302-644-1557

Dollhouses, kits, shells, finished electrical systems, wallpaper, furniture and furniture kits, flooring, bricks, lumberyard, carpet and window treatments, stables, barns and accessories.

Specialty Shop

•**152**• *Page #20*
Autumn Buffalo
212 West Route 66
Williams, AZ 86046
Phone: 520-635-9191

Quality gift items: Metaphysical • Angels • Candles • Figurines • Indian • Southwest • T-Shirts • Cards • Route 66. Please stop by and enjoy a free cup of tea.

•**153**• *Page #143*
Turtle Creek Gallery
6 S. Broadway
Lebanon, OH 45036
Phone: 513-932-2296

Featuring American contemporary handcrafts: jewelry, functional and decorative pottery, wood and metal sculptures, original artwork. We ship and provide free gift boxes and wrapping.

Railroad Attractions

This **Railroad Attractions** directory includes listings for museums, displays, scenic and dinner trains, and miscellaneous railroad attractions across the country. The listings are arranged in alphabetical order by state for easy reference. On the left hand side of each directory listing you will find an icon(s) showing the type of attraction. The following is a list of the icons used and their meaning.

Railroad museum or display. You will notice many of the museum listings also offer train rides. In some cases it is a short ride around the museum grounds although some do offer longer excursion runs. The admission fee for most of the museums range from free to $5.00. Those over $5.00 usually include admission to a "theme" type park and/or train ride. Most museums will have a gift shop or book store you can visit free of charge.

Train ride. Most of the train rides identified with this icon operate with a limited and/or irregular schedule. You should contact them in advance for current information.

Dinner trains. These train rides generally include an elegant four or five course dinner served on board for a two to four hour long excursion.

Model and toy train museum or display. The listings identified with this icon represent some of the larger and/or more unique displays. Several are dedicated solely to model railroading. Many of the museums listed in this directory also have model train displays.

Alabama

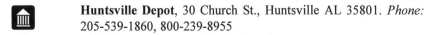 **Huntsville Depot**, 30 Church St., Huntsville AL 35801. *Phone:* 205-539-1860, 800-239-8955

Arizona

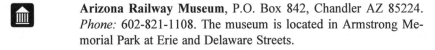 **Arizona Railway Museum**, P.O. Box 842, Chandler AZ 85224. *Phone:* 602-821-1108. The museum is located in Armstrong Memorial Park at Erie and Delaware Streets.

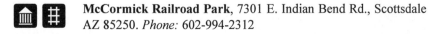 **McCormick Railroad Park**, 7301 E. Indian Bend Rd., Scottsdale AZ 85250. *Phone:* 602-994-2312

Arkansas

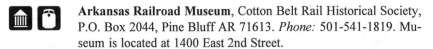 **Arkansas Railroad Museum**, Cotton Belt Rail Historical Society, P.O. Box 2044, Pine Bluff AR 71613. *Phone:* 501-541-1819. Museum is located at 1400 East 2nd Street.

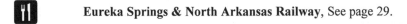 **Eureka Springs & North Arkansas Railway**, See page 29.

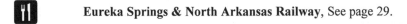 **Reader Railroad**, Reader Industries, P.O. Box 9, Malvern AR 72104. *Phone:* 501-624-6881. Depot is on Highway 368 in Reader.

California

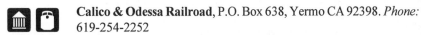 **Calico & Odessa Railroad**, P.O. Box 638, Yermo CA 92398. *Phone:* 619-254-2252

 **California State Railroad Museum**, 111 "I" Street, Old Sacramento CA 95814. *Phone:* 916-445-7387, 916-552-5252 ext. 7245 (recorded information)

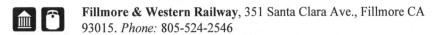 **Fillmore & Western Railway**, 351 Santa Clara Ave., Fillmore CA 93015. *Phone:* 805-524-2546

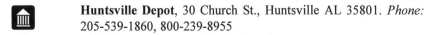 **Laws Railroad Museum & Historical Site**, P.O. Box 363, Bishop CA 93514. *Phone:* 619-873-5950. Located on Silver Canyon Road, 4 miles northeast of Bishop in the old town of Laws.

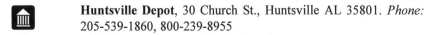 **Lomita Railroad Museum**, 2137 250th St. West, Lomita CA 90717. *Phone:* 213-326-6255

Napa Valley Wine Train, 1275 McKinstry St., Napa CA 94559. *Phone:* 800-427-4124, 707-253-2111

Niles Canyon Railway, Pacific Locomotive Association, P.O. Box 2247, Fremont CA 94536. *Phone:* 510-862-9063. The depot is located at the corner of Main Street and Kilkare Road in Sunol.

Niles Depot Museum, P.O. Box 2716, Fremont CA 94538. *Phone:* 510-797-4449. The museum is located at 36997 Mission Blvd. in the Niles section of Fremont.

Orange Empire Railway Museum, P.O. Box 548, Perris CA 92572. *Phone:* 909-657-2605. Located at 2201 South "A" Street.

Portola Railroad Museum, Feather River Rail Society, P.O. Box 608, Portola CA 96122. *Phone:* 916-832-4131

Railtown 1897 State Historic Park, P.O. Box 1250, Jamestown CA 95327. *Phone:* 209-984-3953. The 26-acre park is located at 5th Avenue and Reservoir Road.

San Diego Model Railroad Museum, 1649 El Prado, San Diego CA 92101. *Phone:* 619-696-0199

San Diego Railroad Museum, 1050 Kettner Blvd., San Diego CA 92101. *Phone:* 619-595-3030, 619-697-7762

South Coast Railroad Museum, P.O. Box 2125, Goleta CA 93118. *Phone:* 805-964-3540. Located at 300 North Los Carneros Road.

Train Town Railroad, P.O. Box 656, Sonoma CA 95476. *Phone:* 707-938-3912. Located on Broadway, one mile south of the Sonoma Town Square.

Western Railway Museum, 5848 State Hwy. 12, Suisun City CA 94585. *Phone:* 707-374-2978

Yosemite Mountain Sugar Pine Railroad, 56001 Yosemite Hwy. 41, Fish Camp CA 93623. *Phone:* 209-683-7273. Four miles south of Yosemite National Park.

Colorado

Colorado Railroad Museum, P.O. Box 10, Golden CO 80402-0010. *Phone:* 800-365-6263, 303-279-4591. Located at 17155 West 44th Avenue.

Cripple Creek & Victor Narrow Gauge Railroad, P.O. Box 459, Cripple Creek CO 80813. *Phone:* 719-689-2640. Train departs from the old Midland Terminal Depot, located at the head of Bennett Avenue.

Forney Historic Transportation Museum, 1416 Platte Street, Denver CO 80202. *Phone:* 303-433-3643

Ski Train - Rio Grande, 555 17th St, Suite 2400, Denver CO 80202. *Phone:* 303-296-4754. Departs from Denver Union Station.

Delaware

Queen Anne's Railroad, See page 51.

Florida

Gold Coast Railroad Museum, 12450 SW 152nd Street, Miami FL 33177-1402. *Phone:* 305-253-0063

High Springs Station Museum, P.O. Box 2008, High Springs FL 32643-2008. *Phone:* 904-454-5377. Located at 20 NW Railroad Avenue.

Seminole Gulf Railway, See page 57.

Georgia

Big Shanty Museum, 2829 Cherokee St., Kennesaw GA 30144. *Phone:* 800-742-6897, 404-427-2117

Southeastern Railway Museum, P.O. Box 1267, Duluth GA 30136. *Phone:* 404-476-2013. Located at 3966 Buford Highway.

Stone Mountain Scenic Railroad, P.O. Box 778, Stone Mountain GA 30086. *Phone:* 404-498-5600. Located on Stone Mountain Freeway east of I-285.

Hawaii

Hawaiian Railway Society, P.O. Box 1208, Ewa Station, Ewa Beach HI 96706. *Phone:* 808-681-5461. The depot is located at 91-1001 Renton Road.

Lahaina Karnapali & Pacific Railroad, P.O. Box 816, Lahaina HI 96761. *Phone:* 808-661-0089, 808-667-6851. Located at the Kaanapali Beach Resort in Maui.

Idaho

Northern Pacific Depot Railroad Museum, P.O. Box 469, Wallace ID 83873. *Phone:* 208-752-0111. Located at the corner of 6th and Pine Streets, at 219 6th Street.

Silverwood Central Railway, North 26225 Hwy. 95, Athol ID 83801. *Phone:* 208-683-3400

Illinois

Illinois Railway Museum, P.O. Box 427, Union IL 60180. *Phone:* 800-244-7245, 815-923-4000 (recorded information). Located at 7000 Olson Road. The Valley View Model Railroad is located 1 mile south, see listing below more information.

Silver Creek & Stephenson Railroad, Stephenson County Antique Engine Club, P.O. Box 255, Freeport IL 61032. *Phone:* 815-232-2306, 815-235-2198. Located ½ mile south of the Stephenson County Fairgrounds at Walnut and Lamm roads.

Valley View Model Railroad, 17108 Highbridge Rd., Union IL 60180. *Phone:* 815-923-4135. The Illinois Railway Museum is located 1 mile north, see above listing for more information.

Indiana

The Children's Museum of Indianapolis, P.O. Box 3000, Indianapolis IN 46206. *Phone:* 317-924-5431. Located at 3000 North Meridian Street.

Corydon Scenic Railroad, P.O. Box 10, Corydon IN 47112. *Phone:* 812-738-8000. Located at Walnut and Water Streets.

Hesston Steam Museum, 2946 Mt. Clair Way - Long Beach, Michigan City IN 46360. *Phone:* 219-872-7405, 219-872-5055

Indiana Transportation Museum, P.O. Box 83, Noblesville IN 46060. *Phone:* 800-234-8724, 317-773-6000. Located on State Route 19 at Forest Park.

Linden Railroad Museum, 514 North Main St., Linden IN 47955

Iowa

Fort Madison, Farmington & Western Railroad, 2208 220th St., Donnellson IA 52625. *Phone:* 319-837-6689

The Iowa Star Clipper Dinner Train, 311 E. Bremer Ave., Waverly IA 50677. *Phone:* 319-352-5467

Railswest Railroad Museum and HO Model Railroad, 72 Bellevue Ave., Council Bluffs IA 51503. *Phone:* 712-323-5182. The museum is located at 1512 South Main Street.

Santa Fe Depot National Historic District, P.O. Box 285, Fort Madison IA 52627. *Phone:* 319-372-7661. Part of Fort Madison's historic district around Ninth Street.

Trainland U.S.A., 3135 N. Highway 117, Colfax IA 50054. *Phone:* 515-674-3813

Kansas

Ellis Railroad Museum, P.O. Box 82, Ellis KS 67637. *Phone:* 913-726-4493. Located at 911 Washington Street.

Kentucky

Hardin Southern Railroad, P.O. Box 20, Hardin KY 42048. *Phone:* 502-437-4555. Depot is located in downtown Hardin.

Kentucky Central Railway, 1749 Bahama Road, Lexington KY 40509. *Phone:* 606-293-0807. Located on U.S. 460 East (North Middletown Road).

My Old Kentucky Dinner Train, P.O. Box 279, Bardstown KY 40004. *Phone:* 502-348-7300. Located at 602 North Third Street.

Nostalgia Station, 279 Depot Street, Versailles KY 40383. *Phone:* 606-873-2497

Railway Exposition Company, P.O. Box 15065, Covington KY 41015. *Phone:* 606-491-7245. Museum is located at 315 West Southern Avenue.

Louisiana

DeQuincy Railroad Museum, P.O. Box 997, DeQuincy LA 70633. *Phone:* 318-786-2823, 318-786-7113. Located on Lake Charles Avenue in downtown DeQuincy.

Louisiana State Railroad Museum, P.O. Box 8412, New Orleans LA 70182. *Phone:* 504-283-8091. Museum is located at 4th and Huey P. Long Avenues in Gretna.

Louisiana Toy Train Museum, 519 Williams Blvd., Kenner LA 70062. *Phone:* 504-468-7223

Maine

Boothbay Railway Village, Route 270 - Box 123, Boothbay ME 04537. *Phone:* 207-633-4727

Fort Fairfield Railroad Museum, P.O. Box 269, Fort Fairfield ME 04742. *Phone:* 207-473-4045. Located on Main Street in downtown Fairfield.

Maine Narrow Gauge Railroad Company and Museum, 58 Fore St., Portland ME 04101. *Phone:* 207-828-0814

Silver Bullet Express, Sunday River Ski Train, P.O. Box 450, Bethel ME 04217. *Phone:* 207-824-7245, 207-824-3000. Boarding areas are located at Presumpscot St. at the Chapman Industrial Park in Portland and on Hotel Road in Auburn.

Maryland

B&O Railroad Museum, 901 W. Pratt St., Baltimore MD 21223-2699. *Phone:* 410-752-2464, 410-752-2490

Brunswick Museum, 40 W. Potomac St., Brunswick MD 21716. *Phone:* 301-834-7100

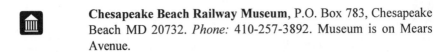

Chesapeake Beach Railway Museum, P.O. Box 783, Chesapeake Beach MD 20732. *Phone:* 410-257-3892. Museum is on Mears Avenue.

Ellicott City B&O Railroad Station Museum, 2711 Maryland Ave., Ellicott City MD 21043. *Phone:* 410-461-1944

EnterTRAINment Line, P.O. Box 478, Union Bridge MD 21791. *Phone:* 800-553-3115, 410-775-8724. Union Bridge Station is located at 41 North Main Street. The Westminster Station is located on Route 27, north of Main Street.

Gaithersburg Railway Museum, Gaithersburg Dept. of Parks & Recreation, 502 S. Frederick Ave., Gaithersburg MD 20877. *Phone:* 301-926-4660. Located at Summit and Diamond Avenues in Olde Towne Gaithersburg.

Massachusetts

Berkshire Scenic Railway Museum, P.O. Box 2195, Lenox MA 01240. *Phone:* 413-637-2210. Located at the intersection of Housatonic Street and Willow Creek Road.

Cape Cod Scenic Railroad, See page 86.

Holyoke Heritage Park Railroad, 221 Appleton St., Holyoke MA 01040. *Phone:* 413-534-1723

Old Colony & Fall River Railroad Museum, P.O. Box 3455, Fall River MA 02722. *Phone:* 508-674-9340. Located at the corner of Water and Central Streets at 1 Water Street.

Providence & Worcester Railroad, P.O. Box 1188, Worcester MA 01601. *Phone:* 508-755-4000 ext. 410. Trains depart from the Providence & Worcester yard at 382 Southbridge Street.

Walker Transportation Collection, Beverly Historical Society and Museum, 117 Cabot St., Beverly MA 01915. *Phone:* 508-922-1186

Michigan

Adrian & Blissfield Railroad, See page 88.

Coe Rail (Michigan Star Clipper Dinner Train), See page 90.

Huckleberry Railroad, Crossroads Village, 5045 Stanley Road, Flint MI 48506. *Phone:* 800-648-7275, 810-736-7100. Located on Bray Road off Stanley Road.

Kalamazoo, Lake Shore & Chicago Railway, P.O. Box 178, Paw Paw MI 49079. *Phone:* 616-657-2423 (recorded information), 616-382-4244 (reservations). Located on Michigan Route 40 off I-94.

Leelanau Scenic Railroad, 9945 Carter Road, Traverse City MI 49684. *Phone:* 616-947-6667

Michigan Transit Museum, P.O. Box 12, Fraser MI 48026. *Phone:* 810-307-5035. Museum is located at Cass and Grand Avenues west of downtown Mt. Clemens.

Minnesota

Depot Museum, P.O. Box 313, Two Harbors MN 55615. *Phone:* 218-834-4898. Located on Waterfront Drive, south of U.S. 61.

End-O-Line Railroad Park and Museum, RR 1 - Box 42, Currie MN 56123. *Phone:* 507-763-3708, 507-763-3113 (off season)

Lake Superior & Mississippi Railroad, Lake Superior Museum of Transportation, 506 W. Michigan Street, Duluth MN 55802. *Phone:* 218-727-8025 (train ride), 218-727-0687 (museum)

Minnesota Zephyr Limited, P.O. Box 573, Stillwater MN 55082. *Phone:* 800-992-6100, 612-430-3000. Located at 601 North Main Street.

North Star Rail, 1418 Rocky Lane, St. Paul MN 55122. *Phone:* 612-858-8859

Old Depot Railroad Museum, 651 West Highway 12, Dassel MN 55325. *Phone:* 612-275-3876

Twin City Model Railroad Club, Box 26 - Bandana Square, 1021 Bandana Blvd. East, St. Paul MN 55108. *Phone:* 612-647-9628

Mississippi

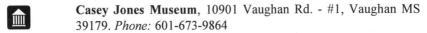

Casey Jones Museum, 10901 Vaughan Rd. - #1, Vaughan MS 39179. *Phone:* 601-673-9864

Missouri

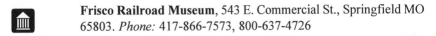

Frisco Railroad Museum, 543 E. Commercial St., Springfield MO 65803. *Phone:* 417-866-7573, 800-637-4726

Museum of Transportation, 3015 Barrett Station Rd., St. Louis MO 63122. *Phone:* 314-965-7998

St. Louis & Chain of Rocks Railroad, 4351 Holly Hills Blvd., St. Louis MO 63116. *Phone:* 314-752-3148. Boarding area is on Riverview Blvd. at Lookaway Drive.

St. Louis, Iron Mountain & Southern Railway, See page 102.

Montana

Alder Gulch Short Line, Bovey Restorations, P.O. Box 338, Virginia City MT 59755. *Phone:* 406-843-5377. Located on SR 287.

Nebraska

Stuhr Museum of the Prairie Pioneer, 3133 West Highway 34, Grand Island NE 68801. *Phone:* 308-385-5316

Union Pacific Historical Museum, 1416 Dodge St., Omaha NE 68179. *Phone:* 402-271-3530

Nevada

Nevada State Railroad Museum, 2180 S. Carson St., Carson City NV 89701. *Phone:* 702-687-6953

New Hampshire

Conway Scenic Railroad, See page 110.

Hartmann Model Railroad and Toy Museum, Main St., North Conway NH 03860. *Phone:* 603-356-9922. Located on Norcross Place on Route 16/302 near the depot for the Conway Scenic Railroad. See page 110 for more information

Hobo Railroad, P.O. Box 9, Lincoln NH 03251. *Phone:* 603-745-2135, 603-745-3500 (dinner train). Located on Kancamagus Highway at Exit 32 of I-93.

Klickety Klack Model Railroad, P.O. Box 205, Wolfeboro Falls NH 03896. *Phone:* 603-569-5384. Located at the junction of Routes 28 and 109A.

White Mountain Central Railroad, P.O. Box 1, Lincoln NH 03251. *Phone:* 603-745-8913. Located at Clark's Trading Post on U.S. Route 3, Exit 33 off I-93.

Winnipesaukee Scenic Railroad, P.O. Box 9, Lincoln NH 03251. *Phone:* 603-745-2135 (year-round), 603-279-5253 (summer). Trains depart from Meredith and Weirs Beach on Route 3.

New Jersey

Pine Creek Railroad, New Jersey Museum of Transportation, P.O. Box 622, Allaire NJ 07727. *Phone:* 908-938-5524. Located in Allaire State Park on Route 524.

Whippany Railway Museum, P.O. Box 16, Whippany NJ 07981. *Phone:* 201-887-8177. Located at 1 Railroad Plaza at the intersection of Route 10 and Whippany Road.

New Mexico

Toy Train Depot, 1991 N. White Sands Blvd., Alamogordo NM 88310. *Phone:* 505-437-2855

New York

Alco-Brooks Railroad Display, Historical Society of Dunkirk, 513 Washington Ave., Dunkirk NY 14048. *Phone:* 716-366-3797. Display located at 1089 Central Avenue (Chautauqua County Fairgrounds).

Batten Kill Railroad, 1 Elbow St., Greenwich NY 12834. *Phone:* 518-692-2160, 518-692-2191

Catskill Mountain Railroad, P.O. Box 46, Shokan NY 12481. *Phone:* 914-688-7400. The depot is on Route 28 in Mt. Pleasant.

City of Rochester Model Train Exhibit, 41 Backus St., Rochester NY 14608. *Phone:* 716-458-5132

Empire State Railway Museum, P.O. Box 455, Phoenicia NY 12464. *Phone:* 914-688-7501. The museum is located off of High Street in Mt. Pleasant.

New York Museum of Transportation, P.O. Box 136, West Henrietta NY 14586. *Phone:* 716-533-1113. Located at 6393 East River Road in Rush. Admission charge also includes admission to the Rochester and Genessee Valley Railroad Museum. See listing below.

New York, Susquehanna & Western Railway, On Track Station, P.O. Box 1245, Syracuse NY 13201. *Phone:* 800-367-8724. Located at 269 West Jefferson Street.

Ontario & Western Railroad Museum, P.O. Box 305, Roscoe NY 12776. *Phone:* 607-498-5500. Located on Railroad Avenue.

Ontario-Midland Rail Excursions, NRHS - Rochester, P.O. Box 1161, Webster NY 14580. *Phone:* 716-224-0581, 716-987-1305. Depot is in Sodus on Maple Street off Route 104.

Rensselaer Model Railroad Exhibit, RPI Student Union, Troy NY 12180-3590. *Phone:* 518-276-2764. Located in the basement of the Davison Hall dormitory.

Rochester and Genessee Valley Railroad Museum, P.O. Box 664, Rochester NY 14603. *Phone:* 716-533-1431. Located at 282 Rush-Scottsville Road. The entrance is at the nearby New York Museum of Transportation. One admission fee covers admission to both museums. See listing above.

Salamanca Rail Museum, 170 Main St., Salamanca NY 14779. *Phone:* 716-945-3133. Located on New York Route 17 in downtown Salamanca.

North Carolina

Floyd McEachern Historical Museum, P.O. Box 180, Dillsboro NC 28725. *Phone:* 704-586-4085. The museum is located at 1 Front Street.

National Railroad Museum and Hall of Fame, Two Main St., Hamlet NC 28345. *Phone:* 919-582-3317

North Carolina Railroad Museum and New Hope Valley Railway, P.O. Box 40, New Hill NC 27562. *Phone:* 919-362-5416. Located in Bonsal on old U.S. 1.

North Carolina Transportation Museum, P.O. Box 165, Spencer NC 28159. *Phone:* 704-636-2889. Museum is located at 411 S. Salisbury Avenue.

Tweetsie Railroad, P.O. Box 388, Blowing Rock NC 28605. *Phone:* 800-526-5740, 704-264-9061. Located on U.S. 321 between Boone and Blowing Rock, just north of the Blue Ridge Parkway (milepost 291, Boone exit).

Wilmington Railroad Museum, 501 Nutt Street, Wilmington NC 28401. *Phone:* 910-763-2634

North Dakota

Bonanzaville U.S.A., P.O. Box 179, West Fargo ND 58078. *Phone:* 701-282-2822. Located on U.S. Hwy. 10 west of Exit 65 on I-29 and east of Exit 343 on I-94.

Ohio

Buckeye Central Scenic Railroad, P.O. Box 242, Newark OH 43055. *Phone:* 614-366-2029. Station is located at 5501 National Road SE in Hebron, Ohio. Phone number is 614-928-6062

Carillon Historical Park, 2001 S. Patterson Blvd., Dayton OH 45409-2023. *Phone:* 513-293-2841

Conneaut Railroad Museum, P.O. Box 643, Conneaut OH 44030. *Phone:* 216-599-7878. Located in the old New York Central station at Depot and Mill Streets.

Dennison Railroad Depot Museum, P.O. Box 11, Dennison OH 44621. *Phone:* 614-922-6776. Located at 400 Center Street.

I & O Scenic Railway, 198 S. Broadway, Lebanon OH 45036. *Phone:* 513-398-8584

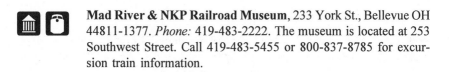

Mad River & NKP Railroad Museum, 233 York St., Bellevue OH 44811-1377. *Phone:* 419-483-2222. The museum is located at 253 Southwest Street. Call 419-483-5455 or 800-837-8785 for excursion train information.

Ohio Railway Museum, P.O. Box 171, Worthington OH 43085. *Phone:* 614-885-7345. Located at 990 Proprietors Road.

Orrville Railroad Heritage Society, P.O. Box 11, Orrville OH 44667. *Phone:* 216-683-2426. Located at 145 Depot Street.

Railways of America, 120 East Mill St., Akron OH 44308. *Phone:* 216-384-1644

Wolcott Museum Complex, Maumee Valley Historical Society, 1031 River Road, Maumee OH 43537. *Phone:* 419-893-9602

Oklahoma

Cimarron Valley Railroad Museum, P.O. Box 844, Cushing OK 74023. *Phone:* 918-225-1657. The museum, open by appointment only, is located on South Kings Highway.

Railroad Museum of Oklahoma, 3805 North Lincoln, Enid OK 73703. *Phone:* 405-233-3051

Watonga Chief, 2936 Bella Vista, Midwest City OK 73110. *Phone:* 405-732-0566. The train boards at the corner of Main Street and Nash Boulevard.

Yukon's Best Railroad Museum, 1020 West Oak St., Yukon OK 73099. *Phone:* 405-354-5079. Museum is located at Third and Main Streets.

Oregon

Samtrak, P.O. Box 22548, Portland OR 97222. *Phone:* 503-659-5452. Boarding areas are located on Southeast Oaks Park Drive at Oaks Amusement Park and 1945 SE Water Avenue at the Oregon Museum of Science & Industry or at Spokane Street, under the east end of Sellwood Bridge.

Spirit of Oregon, 10285 NW Roy Road, Cornelius OR 97113. *Phone:* 503-324-1919

Pennsylvania

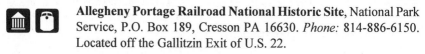 **Allegheny Portage Railroad National Historic Site**, National Park Service, P.O. Box 189, Cresson PA 16630. *Phone:* 814-886-6150. Located off the Gallitzin Exit of U.S. 22.

Altoona Railroaders Memorial Museum, 1300 Ninth Ave., Altoona PA 16602. *Phone:* 814-946-0834. Also see the Horseshoe Curve National Historic Landmark listed below.

Choo-Choo Barn and Strasburg Train Shop, Route 741 East - Box 130, Strasburg PA 17579. *Phone:* 717-687-7911, 717-687-0464

Greenville Area Railroad Museum, 314 Main Street, Greenville PA 16125. *Phone:* 412-588-9479. The museum is located in a park across from Conrail's ex-Erie line.

Horseshoe Curve National Historic Landmark, 1300 Ninth Ave., Altoona PA 16602. *Phone:* 814-946-0834. Located on Kittanning Point Road. Also see the Altoona Railroader Memorial Museum listed above.

Lake Shore Railway Museum, P.O. Box 571, North East PA 16428-0571. *Phone:* 814-825-2724. Located at Robinson and Wall Streets.

Lycoming County Historical Museum, 858 West Fourth St., Williamsport PA 17701-5824. *Phone:* 717-326-3326, 717-326-3673

National Toy Train Museum, P.O. Box 248, Strasburg PA 17579. *Phone:* 717-687-8976. Located at 300 Paradise Lane.

New Hope & Ivyland Rail Road, See page 163.

Railroad Museum of Pennsylvania, P.O. Box 15, Strasburg PA 17579. *Phone:* 717-687-8628. Located on Pennsylvania Route 741 across from the Strasburg Rail Road. See page 169 for more information.

Reading Blue Mountain & Northern Railroad, P.O. Box 215, Port Clinton PA 19549. *Phone:* 610-562-2102. Temple Station is located on Tuckerton Road between Routes 61 and U.S. 222. The Hamburg Station is on Route 61 at Station Road.

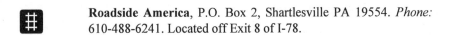

Roadside America, P.O. Box 2, Shartlesville PA 19554. *Phone:* 610-488-6241. Located off Exit 8 of I-78.

Steamtown National Historic Site, National Park Service, 150 S. Washington Ave., Scranton PA 18503. *Phone:* 717-340-5204, 717-340-5200

Stewartstown Railroad, P.O. Box 155, Stewartstown PA 17363. *Phone:* 717-993-2936. Located on Pennsylvania Route 851, four miles east of Exit 1 of I-83.

Stourbridge Rail Excursion, Wayne County Chamber of Commerce, 742 Main St., Honesdale PA 18431. *Phone:* 800-433-9008, 717-253-1960

Tioga Central Railroad, P.O. Box 269, Wellsboro PA 16901. *Phone:* 717-724-0990. Trains depart from Wellsboro Junction, three miles north of Wellsboro on Route 287.

Wanamaker, Kempton & Southern, P.O. Box 24, Kempton PA 19529. *Phone:* 610-756-6469. Located in downtown Kempton, north of I-78.

West Shore Rail Excursions, RR 3 - Box 154 (Route 15 North), Lewisburg PA 17837. *Phone:* 717-524-4337

Rhode Island

Newport Star Clipper Dinner Train, 102 Connell Highway, Newport RI 02840. *Phone:* 800-462-7452, 800-834-1556 (Rhode Island)

South Carolina

South Carolina Railroad Museum, P.O. Box 7246, Columbia SC 29202. *Phone:* 800-968-5909. Located at 230 Industrial Park Road between U.S. 321 and SC 34.

Waccamaw Coast Line Railroad, P.O. Box 2022, Conway SC 29526. *Phone:* 803-347-5301. The station in Conway is located on 4th Avenue North Extension.

South Dakota

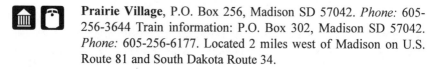

Prairie Village, P.O. Box 256, Madison SD 57042. *Phone:* 605-256-3644 Train information: P.O. Box 302, Madison SD 57042. *Phone:* 605-256-6177. Located 2 miles west of Madison on U.S. Route 81 and South Dakota Route 34.

Whetstone Valley Express, Milbank Area Chamber of Commerce, 401 S. Main Street, Milbank SD 57252. *Phone:* 800-675-6656, 605-432-6656

Tennessee

The Broadway Dinner Train, P.O. Box 25085, Nashville TN 37202-5085. *Phone:* 800-274-8010, 615-254-8000. Located at 108 First Ave. South at Riverfront Park.

Casey Jones Home and Railroad Museum, Casey Jones Village, Jackson TN 38305. *Phone:* 901-668-1222. Located on the northwest side of Jackson at Exit 80A (U.S. 45 Bypass) of I-40.

Chattanooga Choo Choo (Holiday Inn), 1400 Market St., Chattanooga TN 37402. *Phone:* 800-872-2529, 615-266-5000

Cowan Railroad Museum, P.O. Box 53, Cowan TN 37318. *Phone:* 615-967-7365 (recorded information). Located 12 miles west on U.S. 41A and 65 off I-24 (Exit 135).

Texas

Age of Steam Railroad Museum, P.O. Box 153259, Dallas TX 75315-3259. *Phone:* 800-269-4884 (in Texas), 214-428-0101. The museum is located at 1105 Washington Street.

Galveston Railroad Museum, 123 Rosenberg Ave., Galveston TX 77550. *Phone:* 409-765-5700

Gulf Coast Railroad Museum, P.O. Box 457, Houston TX 77001-0457. *Phone:* 713-631-6612. Located at 7390 Mesa Drive.

Jefferson & Cypress Bayou Railroad, P.O. Drawer A, Jefferson TX 75657. *Phone:* 903-665-8400. Located on Austin Street.

Railroad and Pioneer Museum, P.O. Box 5126, Temple TX 76505. *Phone:* 817-778-6873. Located at 710 Jack Baskin Street.

Tarantula Train, 6300 Ridglea Place, Suite 1200, Fort Worth TX 76116. *Phone:* 800-952-5717, 817-625-7245. Train boards at 104 E. Exchange Ave. and at 2318 S. Eighth Ave.

Texas Transportation Museum, 11731 Wetmore Road, San Antonio TX 78247. *Phone:* 210-490-3554

Utah

Golden Spike National Historic Site, P.O. Box 897, Brigham City UT 84032. *Phone:* 801-471-2209. Located 32 miles west of Brigham City.

Ogden Union Station, Utah State Railroad Museum, 2501 Wall Avenue, Ogden UT 84401. *Phone:* 801-629-8444

Tooele County Railroad Museum, 90 North Main St., Tooele UT 84074. *Phone:* 801-882-2836. The museum is located at 35 North Broadway.

Vermont

Shelburne Museum, P.O. Box 10, Shelburne VT 05482. *Phone:* 802-985-3346. The 45-acre village is located on U.S. Route 7, seven miles south of Burlington.

Virginia

Lancaster Train & Old Toy Museum, 5661 Shoulders Hill Rd., Suffolk VA 23435-2362. *Phone:* 804-484-4224

Old Dominion Railway Museum, P.O. Box 8583, Richmond VA 23226. *Phone:* 804-233-6237. Located at 102 Hull Street.

Virginia Museum of Transportation, 303 Norfolk Ave. SW, Roanoke VA 24016. *Phone:* 703-342-5670

Washington

Anacortes Railway, 387 Campbell Lake Rd., Anacortes WA 98221. *Phone:* 206-293-2634

Spirit of Washington Dinner Train, P.O. Box 835, Renton WA 98057-0835. *Phone:* 800-876-7245, 206-227-7245. Located at 625 South 4th Street.

West Virginia

Cass Scenic Railroad, See page 198.

Harpers Ferry Toy Train Museum, Route 3 - Box 315, Harpers Ferry WV 25425. *Phone:* 304-535-2291, 304-535-2521

Wisconsin

Camp Five Museum Foundation, RFD #1, Laona WI 54541. *Phone:* 800-774-3414, 715-674-3414. The "Lumberjack Special" steam-powered train takes visitors from a depot in Laona 2½ miles to the Camp Five Museum.

Kettle Moraine Railway, P.O. Box 247, North Lake WI 53064. *Phone:* 414-782-8074. Located 9 miles north on State Route 83 off I-94.

Mid-Continent Railway, See page 203.

National Railroad Museum, 2285 S. Broadway, Green Bay WI 54304-4832. *Phone:* 414-435-7245, 414-437-7623

Park Lane Model Railroad Museum, S-2083 Heawig Rd., Reedsburg WI 53959. *Phone:* 608-254-8050

INDEX